Traveling Solo

by
Jennifer Cecil

HarperPerennial
A Division of HarperCollins*Publishers*

HarperCollins books may be purchased for educational, business, or sales promotional use. For information, please call or write: Special Markets Department, HarperCollins Publishers, 10 East 53rd Street, New York, NY 10022. Telephone: (212) 207-7528; Fax: (212) 207-7222.

FIRST EDITION

Library of Congress Cataloging-in-Publication Data

Cecil, Jennifer.
   Traveling Solo / by Jennifer Cecil.
    p. cm.
   Includes index.
   ISBN 0-06-273039-8 (pbk.)
    1. Hotels, taverns, etc.—United States—Guide books. 2. Resorts—United States—Guide books. 3. Recreation—United States—Guide books. 4. Single people. 5. United States—Description and Travel—1981—Guide books. I. Title.
   TX907.2.C43 1992
   917.304'928—dc20   91-2452

92 93 94 95 96 SW/MB 10 9 8 7 6 5 4 3 2 1

To Belden Merims
For her unstinting guidance
and friendship

Contents

Introduction

More and more frequently travelers are taking off on their own, or are at least contemplating a trip on their own. *Traveling Solo* has been written to provide information and inspiration, and companionship, too, for the experienced as well as the aspiring solo traveler—who, I should make clear at the outset, is deemed to be an independent man or woman in search of rest, relaxation or revelation, but not necessarily a mate.

About companionship first: lonely days can be productive and rewarding; however, lonely dinners can ruin a trip. Solo travelers should never have to dine at a table by themselves, unless they choose to do so. That is the underlying premise of this book. Communal dining is key to all but a handful of the 350 vacation suggestions contained in *Traveling Solo.*

As far as the information goes, I wanted the book to be a service to as many people as possible. (About the only limits are geographical: *Traveling Solo* covers the United States, Canada, Central America, and the Caribbean almost exclusively.) Thus 24 activities, a range broad enough to appeal to almost every taste, were surveyed in three different ways: from my own perspective, from that of other travelers, and from the experts' point of view.

I did investigate and describe, first for *New York* magazine, where all but one of my write-ups originally appeared, some 40 places and activities that I consider appropriate for solos. Next, more than a hundred "Other Voices" join mine. The experiences of travelers of different ages and backgrounds add depth and variety to the book. The third category under each activity, "Other Choices," contains the suggestions of experts in each field. To round things out, each chapter includes a bibliography at the end.

The text is not the only group aspect of *Traveling Solo*. While I am greatly indebted to the scores of travelers who so willingly described their solo journeys, this book would not have been possible without the assistance of Belden Merims, Laura Mackay and Audre Philippon, the guidance of Carol Cohen and Andrea Sargent and the support of Deborah Harkins. I would also like to commend *New York* magazine's pay-as-you-go incognito policy. The fact that I paid the going rate and was not known to be a travel writer gives my opinions the same freedom from bias as those of the "Other Voices."

One final note: Price categories have been substituted for actual rates. Listings have been judged to be Inexpensive, Moderate, Expensive or Very Expensive on a chapter-by-chapter basis. A key at the end of the introduction to each chapter defines the rate-to-price-category ratio for that particular activity. These categories, into which $45 for two meals a day has been factored if meals were not included in the original rates, are meant only as guidelines. Contact each establishment, agency or outfitter for the definitive cost.

As the reader will discover, the many contributors and I thoroughly enjoyed our solitary sojourns. My hope is that our experiences will be of value to other solo travelers.

Seillans, France

At The Inn

Near at hand and sympathetic, country inns make ideal weekend retreats, yet solos seldom occupy their pretty rooms. The ubiquitous four posters are usually filled with couples. The inns in this chapter are more solo-accessible, however, because dinner is almost always served family-style. Surrounded by congenial tablemates, solitaires flourish.

There's no pigeon-holing these inns and resorts. Small, rustic lodges and elegant Georgian mansions offer communal dining, as do historic summer hotels and 3 of the 20 US members of the prestigious hotel group, Relais & Chateau. Pack a floaty dress or a tuxedo for gala dinners at The Point; a jean skirt or khakis are fine for Saturday night at Moose Mountain Lodge.

Consider also jaunting inn-to-inn. Vermont, which must have more inns per capita than any other state, pioneered the genre. You can ride horseback, canoe, hike, bike, and ski cross country inn-to-inn in the Green Mountain state. Programs have also been implemented in other regions. Canoeists paddle inn-to-inn in Minnesota. Cyclists peddle inn-to-inn all over the world. Check the HIKING, BICYCLING, CROSS COUNTRY SKIING, CANOEING, and HORSE TREKKING chapters for names of outfitters.

Solos should consider themselves lucky if they face a *modest* single occupancy surcharge, say 10% to 20% above the

---

Pricing Categories

Inexpensive	———	Under $75 a day
Moderate	———	$75 to $125 a day
Expensive	———	$126 to $200
Very Expensive	———	Over $200 a day

per person, double occupancy rate. An inn, or any other lodging, spa, cruise ship, or cycling package that charges singles the per person, or half the double, rate represents a bargain.

THE POINT
Saranac Lake, New York

The teak Chris Craft motorboat idled past the rustic Great Camps of turn-of-the-century millionaires before planing across Upper Saranac Lake toward The Point. Our helmsman that exhilarating fall afternoon was David Garret, owner of the exceptional resort at William Rockefeller's former Adirondack camp. As David described evenings when guests cross the frozen lake on a well-stocked sleigh to sip champagne by bonfire light, it became clear that The Point is a resort for all seasons, and all year 'round there is exceptional food.

The Point's kitchen is under the guidance of three-star restauranteur Albert Roux, chef of London's La Gavaroche. This fact recommends The Point to the affluent, cuisine-addicted single. Long, wine-filled lunches and sumptuous dinners create a lively house party atmosphere to be shared by 24 mannerly guests. True, honeymooners and anniversary-celebrants loiter on the granite terraces and in lovely casement-windowed rooms with beeswaxed walls and chunky granite fireplaces, but the solo traveler secure in solitariness, and more interested in conversation than flirtation, will have a vibrant good time.

"Overkill" punned one wit as he surveyed some 20 antlered, big game heads across a sea of goblets. The repartee begun in the casual pub-poolroom grew more spirited during dinner at the two round tables in the lofty lodge. The white wine which accompanied a gratin of backfin crabmeat and diced artichoke hearts was no match for the Cabernet Sauvignon that followed. In the glow of six tapers set in antler's horns, conversation sparkled.

Morning. The faint rattle of cup against saucer outside the door discreetly announces the coffee tray's arrival. At 9:00 a cart set with fresh raspberries and pineapple and a selection of warm breakfast breads coaxes guests from their crisp cotton sheets. Although four rooms share the Main Lodge, Algonquin in Rockefeller's former library and Iroquois being the two rooms most suitable for singles, luxurious silence prevails. Heavy curtains drawn back to reveal the shimmering lake, another soul-satisfying day begins with breakfast in the fireside wingchair.

Great Camp suits the self-indulgent as well as the vigorous. Curl up before the fire in a Point-provided robe and read or throw on slacks and a casual sweater, and fix a Bloody Mary before a post-breakfast walk. The resort is managed in a friendly, informal manner—except on Saturday nights, when black tie at dinner is *de rigeur*. Weather permitting, lunch is served on the terrace at log tables set with pink linen, where sun-warmed guests chat in clunky log chairs overlooking the lake.

Low-key cosseting is the specialty here. A solo traveler may well be the only unattached guest, but will be taken care of exceedingly well. The Point isn't marble-and-silk sumptuous, but it *is* luxurious. Flower arrangements are flown in from Long Island. The help-yourself bar, included in the price, is open around the clock, and there's the elegant Hacker Craft motorboat for spins around the lake.

Saturday night is gala. Men in tuxedos and women in long skirts and cocktail dresses look alluring. Dinner, served on black cloths, is usually a stunner. One evening, after champagne in the Pub (a short remove from the baronial Great Hall), truffles lent their earthiness to a brilliant bouillon. The *piece de resistance*, a sliced and sauteed melange of fresh grouse, partridge, wood pigeon, and hare, fresh from Scotland and served on a potato pancake with brussel sprouts, fresh foie gras and oyster mushrooms, merited the applause it got. Welcome to the backwoods of Upper New York State.

THE POINT, Saranac Lake, NY 12983, (800) 255-3530 or (518) 891-5678. All meals and drinks included. Very Expensive.

CHALFONTE HOTEL
Cape May, New Jersey

August First dawns bright and warm on the southern tip of the New Jersey coast. Other than a couple of cyclists pedding past the century-old Chalfonte Hotel, where early risers sit rocking on the slightly sagging porch, Cape May's Victorian Historic District is still.

The white, three-story Chalfonte, garlanded with gingerbread and arched porticos, is especially homey, and has 72 rooms for rent. Many of the singles are over 50 but there are plenty of children about with their own supervised dining room. Nevertheless, the hotel is suitable for *anyone* who wants to relax. The old-fashioned seashore scene is so wholesome that the atmosphere is almost a vacation in itself. If returning to a gentler era is appealing, visit the Chalfonte and turn back the clock.

"Isn't it wonderful!" exclaimed another solo, on hearing that besides the fried weakfish, baked tomato, bacon, and scrambled eggs she had ordered there would be spoon bread and beaten biscuits too. "The breakfast is super, and I don't have to eat it alone." Just as the group dining had attracted me, sitting at damask-covered tables for 2, 4, 6, and 10 had appealed to others as well. That and the bargain rates. Best of all, the Chalfonte is less than two blocks from the Atlantic Ocean.

The beaches punctuated by Cape May's nine stone jetties are crowded but often remarkably quiet, thanks to the continually pounding breakers that drown out the occasional radio and the cries of grey-headed gulls. Blue mattresses and umbrellas are available for rent at Barefoot Bar, the most popular of Cape May's scalloped beaches. (Less-populated Queen Beach, east of the modest little Convention Hall, is preferable for swimming). Even on this packed swath of flat, greyish sand, the crowd was considerate, the mood peaceful.

Come 5:00 pm, you can hear beer cans popping open on porches all over town, and Cape May's famous painted ladies, the tarted-up Victorian houses so characteristic of what is perhaps the oldest seaside resort in the US, take on a fraternity-house air. Couples and foursomes glide by more peacefully on awning-shaded pedal bikes.

The Chalfonte's small rooms are equally old-time summery, although some accommodation has been made to the 20th century. Paneled doors that lock now back the hotel's louvered swinging doors, and yellow sheets add a contemporary touch. Some of the electric paddle fans, the varnished floors, enamel wash basins, and bent wire hangers look as though they came with the hotel, as do the claw-foot tubs in the baths across the hall. Most of the bedrooms, many just big enough for two, front the street.

Chalfonte's second dinner seating (the first is at 6:30), conflicts with Vintage Film Night, but allows more time to fiddle with the jigsaw puzzle in the game room and for frosty glasses of white wine in the smallish, convivial King Edward bar. When the clock chimes 8:30, neatly dressed adults gather in the ivory anteroom before being seated by smiling hostesses, who lend sparkle to the long, airy dinning area. Mealtimes are special, thanks to the camaraderie and soul-satisfying menus.

Cape May's Helen Dickenson, the Chalfonte's legendary cook, is no longer in the kitchen—her daughters, Dot and Lucille, now do all of the cooking. The dinner menu, like the breakfasts, are comprised of Southern classics. Ingredients are first rate and the preparation is nearly flawless. Tuesday night is crab cake night. Four inches long by two inches wide and filled with nothing but seasoned fresh Maryland crab meat, Helen's deep fried patties are unrivalled.

Guests chat on overstuffed camelback sofas, or flip through *The Guest Book*, a listing of Cape May attractions, activities and shops, in the lobby after dinner. Next morning they set off past the dazzling B&B's and inns to Cape May's pamphlet-laden Welcome Center, where a video details the efforts taken to preserve Cape May's treasury of whimsical, turn-of-the-century houses. Shopping Washington Street's little pedestrian mall and the small boutiques at the Carpenter's Square Mall is amusing enough, but the merchandise is mostly predictable. The chief attraction of Cape May, and the Chalfonte, is the infectious aura of Victorian seemliness on the Atlantic beachfront.

THE CHALFONTE HOTEL, 301 Howard Street, Cape May, NJ 08204, (609) 884-8409. Rooms come with shared bath or private bath; breakfast and dinner are included. Inexpensive to Moderate.

PILGRIM'S INN AND GOOSE COVE LODGE
Deer Isle, Maine

"Greater" Deer Isle is, in fact, a causeway-connected clutch of islands linked to the Penobscot Peninsula by a delicate, arched green bridge. The Pilgrim's Inn and Goose Cove Lodge on *the* Deer Isle provide particularly convivial quarters from which to explore this bucolic habitat of artisans.

Flanked by two huge buckeye trees, the 197-year-old Pilgrim's Inn sits, Maine-plain and three stories tall, atop a grassy knoll at the confluence of a mill pond and the Deer Isle Village harbor. Here, Jean and Dud Hendricks dispense hospitality with a down-easterly forthrightness that is in complete harmony with their ruddy clapboard inn.

At 6:00 pm, I clattered down the pumpkin pine stairs past the 12 country-perfect bedrooms, many with woodstoves and private baths, past the muted formality of the two parlors flanking the entrance hall, to the keeping rooms. There, the spirited pre-dinner gathering, a Deer Isle institution, was well underway.

Late afternoon on a summer day. Flowers, not logs, fill walk-in fireplaces in the two, low-ceilinged rooms where guests chat and help themselves to crab dip, locally smoked salmon and chunks of succulent smoked trout.

Outside, the setting sun etches each blade of grass as it slants across the sweeping lawn to the barbecue, where the chef turns Spanish shrimp and Maine scallops over fiery coals. There are few small inns with kitchens the equal of the Pilgrim's. At 7:00 pm, Jean herds guests into the refurbished goat barn, taking special care to seat and introduce those at the group table. The clarity of the cuisine here is a match for the view—the shimmering pond, the tall blue spruce and the now darkening sky.

Nature unvarnished is Maine's chief allure. Canoes are available to rent, and guests can take the mail boat to Isle au Haut for hiking, or commandeer one of Pilgrim's 10-speed bikes. Deer Isle is special. Here, travelers discover first-rate crafts in addition to the scenery. Thank Haystack (see Painting), the outstanding summer craft school founded in 1950, for these. The Edward Larrabee Barnes-designed complex built on a granite ledge near the hamlet of Sunshine is a point of interest, as is Little Deer Isle where Ron Pearson's gold and silver jewelry, William Mohr's Japanese-inspired pottery, and Kathy Wohl's handwoven dresses and coats are on display. Leave time to search through Belcher's barn there for primitive items and country antiques.

Down Route 15 is Stonington, a forthright fishing village where one can smell the sardine factory and admire the trim lobster boats as they thread the stepping-stone islands beyond the harbor. Up the hill lies the spotless Fisherman's Friend restaurant, where Maine-style shellfish stews and wedges of outrageous Toll House pie can be had.

A spreading log-and-shingle lodge and 11 cabins scattered about 70 acres of hemlock, tamarack and spruce comprise Goose Cove Lodge, the quintessential Maine camp resort on the pink granite shore of Goose Cove. Guests relax around the fieldstone fireplace on a melange of plush Victorian rockers, pine benches, and birch twig furniture fashioned by the Penobscot Indians. An unobtrusive VCR and films of the Black Stallion-Key Largo variety offer rainy day relief next to an extensive library complete with Scrabble, Monopoly, Trival Pursuit and, of course, puzzles.

Goose Cove is rustic, but Outward Bound it's not. Color coded blazes mark pine-needley trails. Instructors teach sailing and rent sailboats plus canoes, kyacks, and sailboards. Guests can play ping-pong in the recreation cabin and buy supplies, including natural sodas and decent wine, at the Roost.

The exceptionally relaxed atmosphere, hearty meals, and the enviable waterside location on Penobscot Bay make Goose Cove Lodge a mecca for oft-returning families, but Periwinkle and Fern, the lodge's single accommodations, house a coterie of nature-loving solos. The traveler unaccustomed to or uncomfortable with children should forget Goose Cove; otherwise, know that from 4:00 pm to 6:30 pm, a bevy of high school girls sweeps in to take over the kids. Dinner at the varnished pine tables for four and six is primarily for adults. This is one of many concepts contributed by owners George and Ellie Pavloff, who created an uncontrived, invigorating resort that even a sophisticate can love.

Flair and lack of artifice marked my knotty-pine suite. Shelves of books and two easy chairs invited reading. A firm mattress and flowered cotton sheets, fluffy towels and a newly tiled shower spelled comfort. Modern oils decked the walls and fragrant wildflowers offered welcome. All the weathered shingled cabins have refrigerators, some have kitchens and most a fireplace or stove.

The lighthouse bell summons guests to hors d'oeuvres and bring-your-own-bottle drinks. One August evening, rain drove the lobster picnic into the enclosed dining porch overlooking the bay but the clams, mussels, corn-in-the-husk, potatoes, and 1 1/2-pounders steamed atop an oil drum outdoors. This lobster feast ended like any last night at camp, by the firelight as a guitarist led a sing-a-long.

THE PILGRIM'S INN, Deer Isle, ME 04683, (207) 348-6615. Rates include full breakfast, hors d'ouevres and dinner. Moderate.

GOOSE COVE LODGE, Sunset, Deer Isle, ME 04863, (207) 348-2508. Rates, which include full breakfast, hors d'oeuvres and dinner, are 10% higher in August. Moderate.

 Other Voices _____

GREYFIELD INN
Cumberland Island, Georgia

"I hate resorts where you're supposed to just lounge around. Who wants to get skin cancer lying by the pool?"

Spunky and adventurous at 65, Jessie is a photographer and writer from Martha's Vineyard who has been traveling alone for years. Her vacations tend to be out-of-the-way and ecologically oriented.

"I've been to Cumberland Island, a National Park off the coast of Georgia several times. There's no village, just a few private houses that pre-date the takeover by the park.

"The Greyfield Inn is the only place to stay on the island, and it's run by younger, rather impoverished members of the Carnegie family. The three-story Georgian house, built in 1903, is small, only nine guest rooms, but it's nicely old-fashioned and very well kept. Some people would be bored with the lack of a TV and all communications, but I find it charming.

"The food at Greyfield is remarkably well-prepared. Of course, it's all candlelit dinners, quite formal, really. The other guests are often Georgians, people connected with legislative things or interested in the National Park.

"I think Cumberland Island is gorgeous, with great hiking trails and heavenly beaches; the most beautiful in the country. You see wild pigs and wild horses, deer, bobcats, and wonderful birds. I hesitate to tell anyone about it because I don't want anyone to go there."

GREYFIELD INN, Cumberland Island, GA (mailing address: Fernandina Beach, FL 32034) (904) 261-6408. All meals are included. Moderate to Expensive.

OCEAN HOUSE, INN AT CASTLE HILL, and STONE HOUSE CLUB
Rhode Island

Daniel, a luxury car salesman in Boston and a yachtsman, age 40, likes to weekend at inns to escape. He describes three of his favorites in Rhode Island.

"Watch Hill, Rhode Island, is a wonderful place right on the sea, and the Ocean House is a great big, old hotel. There aren't many resorts like this left. It's a turn-of-the-century, humungous yellow thing that sits up on a bluff, with rambling halls and funky old furniture in funny old rooms that are ugly but have wonderful ocean views. Ocean House opens fairly late in the season and closes early because there's no heat. A walkway goes right down to the most beautiful, shady beach that just rolls in off the ocean.

"The dining room is fabulous-looking, and I think the food is wonderful; fairly up-to-date cooking, the kind of food you'd find in a slick Greenwich Village restaurant.

"There's not much to do in the little town of Watch Hill except look at big homes. By 9:30 there's nothing to do but go to bed. It's a perfect place when you're really 'wrung out.' After a day or two there, you're ready to fight the dragons again.

"And of course I like to go to Newport. If I want to be a recluse, but a grand recluse, I stay at the Inn At Castle Hill. It's a grand old Victorian house, with about 28 acres of land, and it even has a lighthouse on the property. Great views. Fabulous food, too. When I go away on these weekend sojourns, I'm generally so tired I just want to sit in my room and read. Castle Hill is perfect for that; pleasant, just like a Newport summer home, not like one of those baroque piles would have been in its heyday.

"Another wonderful place is in Compton, Rhode Island. It's the deadest place in the world. The Stonehouse Club is an old fieldstone mansion, rather a stark-looking thing, that overlooks the sea. Again, they have a wonderful restaurant. The rooms, maybe 10 or 15 of them, are elegantly furnished, very English with lots of chintzes and things. Smashing views of the ocean and a little pond that's been full of wild swans for probably a hundred years. There's not even a town there, just estates. Nothing to do except relax."

OCEAN HOUSE, 2 Bluff Avenue, Watch Hill, RI 02891, (401) 348-8161. Breakfast and dinner are included. Expensive.

THE INN AT CASTLE HILL, Ocean Drive, Newport, RI 02840, (401) 849-3800. Continental breakfast is included. Moderate.

THE STONE HOUSE CLUB, 122 Saconnett Point Road, Little Compton, RI 02837, (401) 635-2222. Continental breakfast is included. Moderate to Expensive.

STEAMBOAT INN
Steamboat, Oregon

"It's heaven on earth, sitting up on a bluff overlooking the North Umpqua River, which is one of the most beautiful rivers, and probably the premier steelhead river, in the country." E. J. is a 29-year-old freelance photographer from Brooklyn, unequivocal in his loyalty to the Steamboat Inn in Oregon.

"Some people go just to fish. Some go just because it's beautiful. I could go there just to eat. The food is fabulous, wonderful lamb dishes and excellent wines at this yellow pine, split-log dining table from the original inn. There's lots of history along with the place.

"The main building is log and very rustic. It contains the dining room and a fireplace and a big, accommodating kitchen. You can go in and pour your own coffee, it just has that kind of homey feeling. The fly shop is there too, with any kind of tackle, and a book selection with everything about the area.

"Behind this lodge are the original cabins, eight I think, built on a bluff overlooking the North Umpqua River. You can hear the river roaring. Up a way, on Steamboat Creek, they've built a whole new set of modern cabins, but they're just a short walk to the dining room. There are even a couple of Labrador retrievers running around.

"If you don't fish you can bicycle, you can hike. Crater Lake is close by. You can be alone, and you can have company whenever you want. I love the adventure, the river, the fishing. I just love to go and let whatever happens, happen."

STEAMBOAT INN, Steamboat, OR 97447, (503) 498-2411. No meals are included. Expensive to Very Expensive.

SANDERLING INN RESORT
Duck, North Carolina

"You can just walk out onto the ocean beach from the rooms, and across the road, on the bay side, are docks and all the aquatic life, the birds and ducks." Anne, a scientist in North Carolina, 50-ish, spent a long weekend at a new and gracious Queen Anne-style resort in Duck, North Carolina, on the northern end of the Outer Banks.

"The Sanderling Inn is situated on a narrow sand bar, so you have both bay (Currituck Sound) and ocean opportunities. The dining room is an old Coast Guard rescue station, full of all sorts of wonderful woods, and there's a big porch with rocking chairs. They have an informal wine and cheese get-together every evening for guests.

"The rooms are luxurious, with fruit and wine set out when you arrive, nice robes and lovely views of the ocean. It's excellent for relaxing, but with very little effort you can do plenty, even on a long weekend. You can go wind-surfing, fishing, even hang-gliding. Or you can just lie on the beach or by the pool, which is very nice. They have boats to rent. Another possibility is to drive to Kittyhawk and see the museum or down to the national park, where fancy kite-flying is big. Restaurants are plentiful.

"Meeting people is easy, and during my stay there were many singles, both men and women. But you're on your own for meals [seating is not family style or assigned]. You do have to be careful traveling alone. You'll see people by themselves, and they'll want to latch on to you. That might be okay; it might not. When you're by yourself, you're going at your own pace and you don't have to accommodate anyone else."

SANDERLING INN RESORT, SR Box 319Y, Duck, NC 27949, (919) 261-4111. Rates vary depending on room location and season; Continental breakfast, wine and hors d'oeuvres are included. Moderate to Very Expensive.

 ## Other Inn Choices _____

(All Inns listed below serve dinner at group tables)
Zip off the freeway into rural tranquility at the Brookside Farm in Dulzura, 30 miles east of San Diego and 10 miles north of Tecate, Mexico. Horseshoes or a game of croquet is about as stressful as life gets at the 7-bedroom farmhouse owned by former San Diego restauranteur and chef noted for his hearty farm breakfasts and four-course dinners.

BROOKSIDE FARM, 1373 Marron Valley Road, Dulzura, CA 92017, (619) 468-3043. Breakfast is included. Moderate.

There's no pretense about the overnight lodgings at Hilda Crockett's Chesapeake House or about the copious seafood dinners served boarding-house style to all comers from 11:30 am to 6:00 pm. The isolated fishing community of Tangier Island can be reached by the daily 12:30 pm mail boat.

CHESAPEAKE HOUSE, Tangier Island, VA 23440 (804) 891-2331. Rates include breakfast and dinner. Inexpensive.

The Victorian-style Gatehouse Bed & Breakfast, built in 1986, and the equally new, timber-framed Bee Skep Inn make up the Irish Gap Inns located on 285 acres of mountain-top woodlands minutes from the Blue Ridge Parkway southwest of Charlottesville.

IRISH GAP INNS, Route 1, Box 40, Vesuvius, VA 24483, (804) 922-7701. No meals are included. Moderate.

Porch rocking is one specialty of the sprawling white Mast Farm Inn, which evolved from a log cabin built in 1812 by David Mast; home grown vegetables are another. The farmstead, located not far from the Blue Ridge Parkway in North Carolina, is listed on the National Register of Historic Places and is run by a couple of former Peace Corps volunteers who are proud of its citation as "one of the most complete and best-presented groups of 19th century farm buildings in the western part of the State."

MAST FARM INN, PO Box 704, Valle Crucis, NC 28691, (704) 963-5857. Rates include breakfast and dinner. Inexpensive to Moderate.

Rusticity apparently nurtures group dining. Moose Mountain Lodge, seven miles west of Hanover and contiguous to the Appalachian Trail, is another peeled-log abode featuring crackling fires and home-grown food.

MOOSE MOUNTAIN LODGE, Etna, NH 03750, (603) 643-3529. Breakfast and dinner are included. Moderate.

Informality reigns at the October Country Inn, an archetypically cozy Vermont hostelry between Woodstock and Killington, with a hot tub in the patio and a pool out back.

OCTOBER COUNTRY INN, PO Box 66, Bridgewater Corners, VT 05035, (802) 672-3412. Rooms come with shared or private bath; breakfast and dinner are included. Moderate.

Ninety miles northwest of Minneapolis at the Seven Pines Lodge, a paean to Victorian furnishings and hand-hewn logs built by a wealthy grain broker in 1903, you can dine on *truite au bleu* even if you didn't catch the fish in the rustic inn's private stream.

SEVEN PINES LODGE, Lewis, WI 54851, (715) 653-2323. Continental breakfast is included. Inexpensive.

For 2 years I've been trying to reach Smoke Hole Lodge, the electricityless West Virginia hideaway Ed Stiefel built of pine and stone. It's a 2-hour trip straight up into the Appalachian Mountains for a restorative week of reading, watching the cattle graze, and fishing the swift river that winds through Smoke Hole's green pastures and thick stands of trees.

SMOKE HOLE LODGE, PO Box 953, Petersburg, WV 26847 (no phone). Rates include transportation from Petersburg and all meals and activities. Inexpensive to Moderate.

"We get many single travelers here, and we usually seat them at the head of the large table (after introducing them around during the pre-dinner 'goat cheese hour')" write the owners not only of the 19th-century clapboard Squire Tarbox Inn, but of a small goat cheese plant on the piney grounds that lie on Westport Island just off mid-coastal Maine.

SQUIRE TARBOX INN, Box 620, Wiscasset, ME 04578, (207) 882-7693. Rates include breakfast and dinner. Moderate.

Stonepine, located in a Crocker's former Carmel Valley manse, has been awarded a gold medallion by Relais & Chateau, certification that this equestrian estate is just about as classy as hostelries get. Participate in riding clinics, carriage driving lessons, Western or English saddle trail rides even a hayride picnic before changing into something chic and relaxing on a down sofa for hors d'oeuvres before a gala, "estate style" dinner ($50 a head).

STONEPINE, 150 East Carmel Valley Road, Carmel Valley, CA 93924, (408) 659-2245. Continental breakfast is included. Expensive to Very Expensive.

Traditional fish boils are the specialty of the White Gull Inn located on the Door Peninsula. Whitefish are boiled over a log fire on the white clapboard inn's flagstone patio while diners wait patiently for the feast. The style is country colonial inside the lodge and its various cottages located not far from Sunset Beach Park in the town of Fish Creek (population 100).

WHITE GULL INN, PO Box 159, Fish Creek, WI 54212, (414) 868-3517. No meals are included. Moderate.

Families favor the Wilderness Lodge located on 1200 acres adjoining the Black River in the Ozark foothills, but the country cooking served on trestle tables to guests in the chinked log lodge and abundant sports opportunities, such as volleyball, horseback riding, tennis, frisbee, golf, and swimming also have single appeal.

WILDERNESS LODGE, PO Box 90, Lesterville, MO 63654, (314) 637-2295. Breakfast and dinner are included in the rates. Inexpensive to Moderate.

In October, fall color enthusiasts threading Vermont's red, maple-lined lanes throng Vermont's welcoming inns. One such is the Windham Hill Inn, two-time winner of Uncle Ben's "Best Inn" award presented to ten properties a year. The owners take pride in the renovated, 15-bedroom farmhouse and in making singles feel at home around the mahogany Queen Anne table.

WINDHAM HILL INN, RR1, Box 44, West Townshend, VT 05359, (802) 874-4080. Breakfast and dinner are included. Expensive.

Bibliography

The Discerning Traveler, 504 West Mermaid Lane, Philadelphia, PA 19118, (800) 673-7834 or (215) 247-5578. A newsletter that describes the best sights, inns and restaurants in the Northeast, Middle Atlantic, and the South. A one-year subscription (8 issues) is $50.

The Yellow Brick Road, 2445 Northcreek Lane, Fullerton, CA 92631, (714) 680-3326. An eight-page newsletter covers California's inn scene as well as hostelries and destinations throughout the West. A one-year subscription (12 issues) is $36.

Country Inns and Backroads North America, by Jerry Levitin ($12.95, HarperCollins, New York, NY, 1990) is the 25th edition of this pioneering and reliable guide originated by Norman Simpson.

The Innkeeper's Register, ($7.95, Independent Innkeepers Assn., PO Box 150, Marshall, MI 49068, (616) 781-2494) is a small and handy guide to the 210 inn-members of the Independent Innkeepers Association.

America's Wonderful Little Hotels and Inns USA and Canada, edited by Sandra W. Soule ($18.95, St. Martin's Press, New York, NY, 1991) bases its recommendations on reader descriptions and suggestions as do the series' smaller regional volumes.

The Best Places to Stay in New England, by Christina Tree ($14.95, The Harvard Common Press, Boston, MA, 1990), an authoritative, well-written book; part of a series that also includes the Southwest, California, Florida, and Hawaii.

Bermuda and the Caribbean

It's true. With the exception of various Club Meds and Hedonism II on Jamaica, tourism in the Caribbean isn't geared to singles. Couples flock to soaring Hyatts, ginger-breaded cottage-hotels and deluxe resorts in the 26 island-states, where they are housed two by two. Still, in the course of a dozen trips to this watery playground, I've found a number of convivial places to stay as well as a couple of new ways to get around that might appeal to impecunious and mildly adventurous solos.

The Explorer Pass, sold by the regional airline LIAT (Leeward Islands Air Transport) based in Antigua, encourages hopping around the Caribbean by plane. The pass, which costs $357, is good for 30 consecutive days of travel to any (or all) of the LIAT's 26 destinations, Caracas and Guyana included.

Try the recently inaugurated *Emeraude Express* (011-596-60-12-38 or 011-590-83-12-45), a fast, new 240-passenger ship, for travel between Martinique, Guadaloupe and Dominica, or travel the Grenedines aboard the *M.V. Snapper* or raffish island schooner not for the squeamish or weak of stomach. Schedules available from the St. Vincent & Grenadines Tourist Office, (212) 687-4981.

Still, Caribbean island hopping is in its infancy. Most travelers prefer to thaw out in one place. For them, I can recommend

Pricing Categories

Inexpensive	——	Under $75 a day
Moderate	——	$75 to $125 a day
Expensive	——	$126 to $200
Very Expensive	——	Over $200 a day

17

a number of out-of-the-ordinary hostelries. See also SCUBA and CRUISING UNDER SAIL.

GUANA ISLAND CLUB
British Virgin Islands

The Guana Island Club, an iconoclastic 60-year-old outpost built on the foundations of an 18th-century Quaker settlement in the British Virgin Islands, is now the attentively-run domain of Henry and Gloria Jarecki. The metals magnate and his family bought the 850-acre island in 1974 and became the zealous guardians of Guana's ecological and aesthetic status quo. Only 30 people at a time share this nature preserve with seven beaches, many miles of hiking trails and a waterside tennis court.

The vacation begins minutes away from the Beef Island Airport, where guests are spirited across the channel in the resort's 26-foot motorboat. After greetings all around, everyone piles aboard a convoy of vans for the laborious climb up precipitous Pyramid Peak.

Few Caribbean hideaways boast such a view. The ivory stucco complex with six weathered stone cottages and a more recent sculptural aerie glow like a Greek village perched 200 feet above land. There, shimmering from horizon to horizon, the silver-blue Atlantic, assorted Virgin Islands and the translucent Caribbean bid guests welcome.

Weathered jalousies shade cottages ranged alphabetically, Anageda through Greneda, along the saddle of the hill. During my first visit, I stayed in Dominica, from which I could look down on pale pink flamingos standing on one leg in Salt Pond. Recently, I lodged in Barbados, a dream cottage with a king-sized bed and a queen-sized terrace facing a rare coral tree and Muskmellon Bay. Up two steps was a sculptural bath with bouganvillea blossoms visible through the shower's wooden louvers.

This cottage's simple charms are so alluring, the view so panoramic, that I'd recommend any of Guana's 15 rustic, stone-faced rooms to all but those favoring grand luxe. Certainly, Guana's the perfect getaway if escape to a blissful island with a good book is the objective. Novels and reference works spill from shelves in the cottages, in the library next to the common room, and even in the well-stocked honor bar in the main lodge.

The Club attracts a group as diverse as the titles in the cluttered library. When the gaudy sun sets, guests drift into the bar to check the evening seating chart: the banker, the biology professor and the kindergarten teacher, the fashion trainee and the commodity trader, the Parisienne, the Boston Brahmins. After party chatter around the hors d'oeuvres tray, the batik-and-rattan living room is abandoned for candlelight, Chardonnay, and crayfish at tables for 10 outside on the sheltered terrace.

Lunch is buffet style; dinners are more formal. The atmosphere is lively, especially at night. There is no stigma in being here alone. The only downside is the price. One has to be relatively affluent to afford a week at this island resort begun in the late 30s by a Boston architect and perfected in the 80s by the Jareckis.

Guests don't have to be ecologically-oriented to enjoy the island, but nature appreciation helps. *Guana*, a pamphlet describing the local doves, lizards, frogs, fish, and flora is an invaluable aid. After syrup-drenched banana pancakes for breakfast, hikers often lace up their boots and hit the island's rocky, well-marked trails.

Others walk slowly down the steep road past the croquet and tennis courts to the blush-pink beach rimming White Bay, there to read and converse when not snorkeling, windsurfing or quenching their thirst with beer and soda from the ice chest in the beach house.

Vacationers charter the Club's 28-foot motorboat to lunch at Tortola, explore caves, raffish bars, and Roadtown's shops on neighboring Virgin Gorda. Mostly they head for one of the beaches. Guana discourages yachts—anchors damage coral—and the island's seven sandy coves are also pristine. Serenaded by quail doves, some picnic at sandy Muskmellon Bay, and salve their sunburns later with soothing aloe sap. I followed a blazed trail to Crab Cove to snorkel above waving sea fans and branch coral, pausing to watch as aggressive boobies snatched prey from the beaks of dive-bombing pelicans.

The island is a designated nature preserve, and a satisfying sanctuary for care-worn humans.

GUANA ISLAND CLUB, Timber Tail, Rye, NY 10580, (800) 544-8262 or (914) 967-6050. Rates include all meals and use of the club's windsurfers, sunfish and sailboats. Very Expensive.

KAILUUM
Yucatan, Mexico

Kailuum is an upscale version of the beachcomber's hammock slung between two swaying palms. This thatch-covered tent colony built along a ribbon of cool, limestone beach south of Cancun on the Yucatan Peninsula is also unique in the Caribbean. Few resorts are in closer contact with the elements; fewer still lodge guests immediately on the sand.

Hurricane winds wiped out the imaginative resort in September 1988. A year later, when I drove in past the soaring new palm-roofed bar/dining area to halt in front of the Kailuum's white oval office, leaves sprouted from the tops of the chaca wood fences and new palms grew out of coconut shells. What Hurricane Gilbert obliterated, the fecund tropics and the Herculean effort of the Bilgore family and staff have restored.

Those arriving early in November when Kailuum opens may be alone, but the hammocks slung in front of each of 40 tents don't take long to fill up. Daily, the mood grows more convivial, thanks also to the uncommonly zealous and friendly staff.

Kailuum is a family enterprise and guests are treated more like kinfolk than as paying customers. Arnold Bilgore's children are involved in running Kailuum, while Arnold's ex-wife manages the resort's folk shop, the best place in the region for handwoven clothes and Central American handcrafts.

The Maya-style compound, with its *ovalados* (oval-shaped huts) and *palapas* (thatched shelters) is located between Puerto Morelos and Playa del Carmen on the Yucatan mainland. Guests roll out of hammocks to comb 10 miles of uninterrupted beach and to dive or snorkel the translucent sea above Palancar, the famous underwater reef off shore. This is also Maya territory. Daytrip south to the seaside ruins in Tulum, and inland to magnificent but only partially-restored Coba. Chichenitza, one of the most monumental of the Mayan cities, is a must for an overnight stay. Itineraries and sightseeing trips can be arranged through Kailuum's reservations agency, Turquoise Reef Resorts, or an air-conditioned bus at Playa del Carmen, 10 minutes away by cab, also gives tours. Cars are for the steel nerved; road-hogging buses play "dodge em" with tourists on shoulderless Highway 307.

Lazy Sundays are great for snorkeling fleets of darting fish at Xcaret's *cenote* (limestone spring). Mayan fragments line the shady paths leading to the rocky inlet. Kailuum provides annotated itineraries of other coastal sights as well, among them once-somnolent Playa del Carmen, the now-bustling terminus for ferries to Cozumel. Here, a taco-and-enchilada lunch beneath the banana fronds at El Limon provides a soothing pause from the dusty streets.

Pitch-roofed tents with zippered flaps maximize both fresh air and privacy. The nicest tents, in the first of four staggered ranks, have an unobstructed view of the Caribbean. Glass chimneys sheath the candle lamps on two wooden-box tables beside the *rebozo* (scarf)-covered platform bed. Four orange crates serve as a bureau, towel rack and closet. Effectively sensible by day, the compound, which boasts no electricity, becomes romantic at night when soft yellow flares illuminate the pathways, pricks of light shine from oil lamps and the boomerang-shaped dining and bar pavilion glows with dozens of candles.

A flashlight powerful enough for reading is a must. Candles in the tents glimmer only faintly and kerosene lamps in the bathhouse shed just enough light enough to bathe in the big, black-and-white-tiled stalls.

Special drinks, such as a Cointreau, brandy, rum and lime "Between the Sheets" enliven the evenings. Luckily, hefty appetizers such as Buffalo chicken wings and guacamole help to buffer the alcohol before guests are seated.

Outsiders flock to Kailuum's 100-seat dining room with hypnotic sea views and sandy floors. Both the tasty breakfasts (unlimited refills between 7:00 and 11:00) and dinners are imaginative and carefully prepared. Each night the host describes the menu, often Mexican specialties served on crude, green-glazed pottery by young Mayans in snappy, brimmed caps. Finger bowls and hot hand towels offered between the entree and dessert are a surprising touch.

Kailuum's simplicity gives the elements full play; no stucco walls mute the swoosh of waves on the beach; no bright lights blur the shadows cast by the moon. Still, Bilgore's resort reflects a sophistication that attracts worldly sorts.

Singles don't get much of a price break here. I paid only $10 less than the couples. Solitaries are, however, catered to with an enthusiasm some resorts save for pairs.

KAILUUM, c/o Turquoise Reef Group, PO Box 2664, Evergreen, CO 80439; (800) 538-6802. Rates include breakfast, dinner, tips, and tax. In season, there's a minimum 3-night stay. Inexpensive.

WATERLOO HOUSE
Bermuda

"In Bermuda, vacationers get off the airplanes two by two, like the animals on Noah's ark. That's no place to go alone," advised an island-savvy pal. Still, the narrow, 22-mile-long island's reduced scale make Bermuda a tempting destination. A solo-traveling acquaintance suggested Waterloo House. "I go there at least twice a year and *always* make new friends," he said. I reserved my room the moment the Waterloo clerk told me in a lilting voice, "You'll have plenty of company Mum, as long as you arrive in time for tea."

The Bermuda-pink house with fluted white trim, shining brass railings, and the tamed welter of tropical blooms on Hamilton Harbor is a wonder! Yellow doors open into party-sized rooms off a maze of sunny corridors that lead, inevitably, to more gardens and the water. A dipping pool decorates one cul de sac. In the English-style parlor off the welcoming bar, a fire is laid in the elaborate brass grate.

Chintz-swathed room #10, facing yachts at anchor in the harbor, is a winner. The French door to a small balcony with white iron furniture stands open invitingly. On either side, grassy grounds are shaded by sea grape and palms. Engulfed in lightshot comfort, I felt very much at home.

Waterloo House is intimate, and cozy. A uniformed maid hands around tea in chinoiserie cups at 4:00 pm while guests, settled into parlor chairs, help themselves to warm scones. Come 7:00 pm, cocktails are served and the green and rose parlor and the bar grow more lively.

Singles occupied 16 of the hotel's 25 bedrooms during my visit. In the waterside dining room the solitaries, mostly businessmen, seemed content to sit at the spacious pink-cloaked tables alone, enjoying the intricate, six course dinners. (Waterloo's "Dine Around Plan" covers dining at sister properties: Newstead in Paget, and Horizons nearby).

Waterloo House is situated 3 minutes from Front Street shopping, 5 minutes from the ferry, and 10 minutes from the bus depot. The hostelry's only drawback—the beaches are a bus or cab ride away—is no deterrent off-season, when it's too chilly for swimming anyway. The 65 to 72 degree December weather is ideal for golfing (the nine-hole Horizons course is open to Waterloo patrons) as well as for island tripping and shopping.

Soft carols chime through Hamilton's department stores in December. Friday nights, many of the stores in the winsome harbor-front shopping area stay open late for shopping sessions pre- and post-tea. "Duty-free" shopping usually leaves me cold, but not in Hamilton, Somerset or ever-so-picturesque St. George.

Civilized stores offer refreshingly pleasant service and some real (and not so real) values. When you tire of Shetlands and cashmere, perfume, Wedgewood and Spode, seek out the purely Bermudian. Outerbridge's Sherry Pepper Sauce gives Bloody Marys new zip; Gosling's Black rum is unique. The reddish local cedar is practically extinct, but handmade souvenirs of the fragrant wood are worth finding.

I recommend sightseeing by ferry and the ubiquitous pink-and-navy-blue busses. With a timetable, and lots of bus change, Bermuda is easy-going. Another alternative is the sturdy ship *Deliverance*, which travels to the Dockyard, a fortified complex built for the British Fleet after the American Revolution. The limestone mini-city is an austere contrast to the white-roofed pastel buildings that typify the rest of the island. The Dockyard's Maritime Museum, in particular, is well worth exploring. The #7 bus returns to Hamilton via the shell-pink southside beaches, and a transfer permits exiting and reboarding at will. There's usually a gracious Bermudian to give directions when tourists lose their way.

WATERLOO HOUSE, PO Box HM 333, Hamilton HM BX, Bermuda, (800) 468-4100. Breakfast is included. Moderate.

CLUB MED
Paradise Island, Bahamas

Three days at Club Med on Paradise Island in the Bahamas may leave you as fit and restored as the nicely refurbished and newly mature Club itself. Not only are the gracious British colonial manor houses and stately grounds evocative, but the 30-ish crowd seems pleasingly adult. Although most singles come for not-so-chance encounters, the overall tenor is conversational and friendly. According to the Chef du Village, about half of the Paradise Island guests arrive unpartnered. Beyond the mating game, there's always tennis. This club is tennis-oriented, with 20 courts, 8 lit for night play.

No clapping and chanting, no provocatively swaying hips greeted me upon arrival. Travelers are spared the traditional Club Med hoopla when they opt for a long weekend, rather than the 7-night package, at Paradise Island. The registration procedure is like that of any other resort except that the G.O. (*Gentile Organisateur*) who loads the gear onto a dolly may wear a hibiscus over her ear and a snug sarong.

The thought of an unknown roommate may give pause when contemplating a visit to the Club Med alone. Any effort to wheedle a separate room upon arrival will be futile; guests *can* change roommates, but must share a room or pay a 20% to 50% surcharge. I was apprehensive as the G.O. trundled my bags beneath Royal Palms toward the eight, pale pink Colonial-style dorms. The cool, just-roomy-enough cubicle with a Portuguese marble bath and two of everything else—wide beds, modern chairs, and chests—was reassuring and my roommate turned out to be perfectly agreeable. Better yet, our room was only strides away from the bottle-green Atlantic and the long blue-tiled pool.

Frolicking G.M.'s (*Gentils Membres*) throng the crescent beach with its sailboats and loungers. The more contemplative lie supine in glistening rows around the pool, their shiny new novels unread. Tennis buffs lend motion to the botanical-garden grounds. Here, the sound of the sea lulls guests to sleep a merciful distance from the club's eating-drinking-dancing hub where G.M.'s disco late into the night.

The airy dining pavilion's a honey, and because it's cantilevered over the busy shipping channel, the oval wooden tables overlook bustling Nassau and the huge cruise ships. When it comes to food, quality still takes a back seat to quantity. Bland seasonings and as-much-as-you-want meals washed down by all the wine you can drink are the norm, whether one reserves a French meal at Grayleath or an Italian dinner at the Harborside Restaurant, or opts for a group table in the main dining area.

Still, even the pickiest eater will find palate pleasers. In May the very fit crowd seemed to favor the lavish salad bar over the meat dishes, and there was always a run on fresh tropical fruit.

The club's location across the harbor from Nassau is one of its most pleasing aspects. The *Capricorn*, a goat-like little ferry, crosses the channel hourly. No bus, no fuss when one wants to do a little shopping or sightseeing. The ferry takes about 10 minutes and is free. So is the jitney, which travels from the lushly planted entrance to the Paradise Island casino.

After three fulfilling days, I decided that the club's 22-acre spread, the antiquity of the original, pedigreed buildings, and the "new morality" had much to do with the surprisingly tranquil mood. Prospective Club Med junkies should be assured, however, that a different activity is scheduled every hour between 7:00 am and midnight.

CLUB MEDITERRANEE, 3 East 54th Street, New York, NY 10022, (800) 258-2633 or (212) 750-1687. Rates include all meals, wine and activities. Depending on the season, single occupancy is 20% to 50% more than double. Weekly rates and air and transfer packages are available. Moderate to Expensive.

THE GOLDEN LEMON
St. Kitts, West Indies

A singsong "Good Morning" woke me at 8:00 am exactly. The vision in bright yellow suggested I climb back into my antique white iron bed while she set up breakfast. Melon, fresh nutmeg-sprinkled porridge and brewed decaffeinated were quickly set out on the faux-pewter service. The first course digested, piping hot fish filets and lemoney breakfast cake arrived. Welcome to the stylish and thoughtfully-embellished kingdom of Arthur Leaman.

Leaman is one of the Caribbean's most attentive hosteliers. He greets everyone warmly, makes a point of saying goodbye, and dines with guests at the glistening mahogany table he hosts at least once during their stay. Although the Golden Lemon sports a tennis court, smallish pool and a palmy grey beach, the inn is more remarkable for cosseting a la Arthur than for its resort facilities.

The West Indian-style quarters opening onto the Great House's balcony are the nicest for the solo traveler. The elegant Lemon Court and Lemon Grove duplexes hidden behind stark white walls cost considerably more. Guests sleeping in the original building's canopied beds share an antique-filled drawing room and long, wooden balcony, as well as the convenience of having the bar, the pool patio (where coconut muffins accompany afternoon tea) and the dining room downstairs.

The house party assembles nightly in the cozy, pillowed bar. Couples make up the majority of guests but unaccompanied women are equally at ease.

The luscious Golden Lemon sits, in studied contrast to the ramshackle fishing village of Dieppe Bay, at the end of a narrow street about 40 minutes from the Kittian capital of Bassterre. Climb Mt. Misery, a dormant volcano, shop in Basseteree, and visit one or all of St. Kitt's three plantation inns for lunch or tea. Verdant St. Kitts is an interesting study, the only Leeward Island where sugar cane is still the major crop.

THE GOLDEN LEMON, Dieppe Bay, St. Kitts, West Indies (809) 465-7260. Rates include breakfast, tea and dinner. Very Expensive.

 **Other Voices** _____

HEDONISM II
Negril, Jamaica

Janet, a 30-year-old real estate broker in Maryland, went solo to Hedonism II in Negril, Jamaica.

"I was looking for something relaxing, and the 'all-inclusive' plan made Hedonism affordable for me. They have loads of things to do: kayaking, competitions, volleyball, a gym, horseback riding, tennis, dancing, reggae lessons, biking. When I was there, there were more men than women, but I've heard women complain of the opposite. I felt wonderfully cared for. It was just so personal.

"Hedonism's gotten a bad press due to people's expectations. Because of the name, some think they can do whatever they want. If you go by yourself, they pair you up with a roommate. Mine was about 40, into the nude beach. She was there to meet men. That wasn't why I went.

"The people were wonderful. Sure, plenty of men hit on me, but I let them know I wasn't interested. There were people there like me who were trying to get away, have fun, meet some others and enjoy Jamaica. I met two people from Wall Street, someone in politics in Massachusetts, a man in construction in Wisconsin, and ended up with a band of eight, protective big brothers.

"Without getting involved in the wet t-shirt or the nightgown contests, I thoroughly enjoyed myself, and I met a group of people I really liked and kept in touch with. I'd go back there in a minute."

*HEDONISM II, PO Box 25, Negril, Jamaica, West Indies,
(800) 858-8009 or (516) 868-6924. Rates are all inclusive,
and there is a 3-night minimum stay. Very Expensive.*

HEDONISM II
Negril, Jamaica

"You can wear anything you want, or nothing, to the Pajama Parties at Hedonism II. It's the freedom I like. You eat whatever you
want, whenever you want. You can play tennis, or just lie back
and do nothing." Andrew, 27, is a travel agent in New York.

"The coordinator from the hotel meets you at the airport and offers you a rum punch, Red Stripe beer, or a soda.
You party on the bus all the way to the hotel about an hour
and a half from the Montego Bay airport.

"You're assigned a roommate of the same sex, and
chances are you'll have orientation the first night. The minimum stay is 3 days. Hedonism II holds about 500 guests, so
even if you go alone, you have plenty of people to meet right
away, at orientation.

"The building's two-story, with average-sized rooms and
mirrors on the ceilings. Some of the rooms face the ocean. All
meals are served buffet-style, with snacks served at 5:00 pm
and again at midnight.

"The resort has nude and regular beaches. People come
from all walks of life; doctors, secretaries, plumbers, everybody, and there's a wide cross-section of ages, from 20s to
60s. All the sports facilities are great, but I liked scuba diving
best. They have certified Jamaican instructors, and you rent
equipment. Tennis and squash are also good, and they have
guided, English horseback riding trips.

"Meeting people and having fun is the reason to go."

*HEDONISM II, PO Box 25, Negril, Jamaica, West Indies, (800)
858-8009 or (516) 868-6924. For rates, see "Janet," above.*

CLUB MED
Caravelle, Guadeloupe

"My experience changed my mental image of Club Med. I
didn't find a crowd of desperate singles trying to 'hook up.' I

met professional people who needed a vacation and didn't want to worry about planning it, tipping, finding nice beaches."

Mary Louise, a travel writer from Long Island, describes her non-stereotypical Caribbean Club Med vacation.

"I had a week and I wanted to get away someplace warm, so out of the blue, I called Club Med. The counselor asked me my name and my age. She sent me to Caravelle in Guadeloupe.

"The night I arrived I was jetlagged and tired, but I saw there was classical music on the beach at 5:00 pm, so I went down and ended up meeting four people I adored. From then on I didn't feel obliged to participate in anything.

"I went alone and decided against a roommate. When I travel, I worry about how comfortable the bed is, if there's plenty of hot water in the shower and if the phone works. I don't quibble about the lithograph on the wall. Besides, in a place like Club Med you don't spend much time in your room. They weren't designer interiors, just your basic beach motif and perfectly functional.

"Club Med food is island food. They always have good bread, good cheese, lots of fresh fruit and juices. In a hot place like that you don't really want Steak Diane for dinner. If they grill something and provide lots of salads, I'm happy.

"It's a beach place, and it's fine if you want to get a tan, relax, play your sport, see the shows and dance at night."

CLUB MEDITERRANEE, 3 East 54th Street, New York, New York 10022, (800) 258-2633 or (212) 750-1687. Rates include all meals and activities; air and transfer packages are also available. Moderate to Expensive.

 ## Other Bermuda and Caribbean Choices

Casual and far from chic, La Casa Del Frances has for years been a destination for sophisticated, budget-minded solos who don't mind making their way via ferry or island hopper to the island of Vieques off Puerto Rico. Other attributes of Casa del Frances-lovers; tasteful decor isn't a priority and they don't mind being ribbed by the owners.

LA CASA DEL FRANCES, PO Box 458, Vieques Island, Puerto Rico 00765, (809) 741-3751. Rates include breakfast, dinner, and taxes. Moderate.

Rush Little, whose very personal province is Mary's Boon, doesn't encourage short stays at his 12-room property close by St. Martin's airport. He doesn't have to. The airy housekeeping rooms right on the beach seem always to be filled with happy returnees, singles among them. The one-story Mary's Boon is a pleasant spot for solitaries, especially for those over 50. House guests share a long table and conversation with Little if they wish; otherwise they dine beside the flood-lit green sea.

MARY'S BOON, PO Box 2078, Phillipsburg, St. Maarten, Netherlands Antilles, 011-5995-44235. US representative ITR Travel, (212) 545-8469. Expensive.

The Mark St. Thomas is an inn-lovers dream. A decorator and his partner have transformed a Danish building from the late 1700s into one of the most captivating city-inns in the Caribbean. Not only are guests treated to imaginatively-decorated rooms and imaginatively-prepared dinners but, situated not far from the shops at the top of Charlotte Amalie's 99 steps, they have a marvelous view of St. Thomas' bustling and scenic harbor.

THE MARK ST. THOMAS, Blackbeard's Hill, Charlotte Amalie, St. Thomas, US Virgin Islands, 00802, (800) 343-4085 or (809) 774-5511. Breakfast is included. Moderate to Very Expensive.

Planters built their sugar mills and manor houses of tawny stone blocks during Nevis' 18th century heyday. Today, tourism has supplanted sugar, and inns now occupy the handsome estates. Two of the six, Montpelier Plantation Inn and Hermitage Plantation, feature delicious, family-style dinners, and should appeal to singles. Montpelier, run with high style by Brits, is, with a lovely pool, a tennis court and a private cabana on Pinney's Beach, the most elegant. The Hermitage, which also has a pool but is owned by Americans, is homier, but guests are catered to with the same care and diligence that can be found at Montpelier.

MONTPELIER PLANTATION INN, PO Box 474, Nevis, West Indies. US representative Ray Morrow, (800) 243-9420. Rates include breakfast, dinner and taxes. Very Expensive.

HERMITAGE PLANTATION, Gingerland, Nevis. US representative ITR, (212) 545-8469. Breakfast and dinner are optional. Very Expensive.

Situated in the curve of Long Bay on Antigua's easternmost tip, the all-inclusive Pineapple Beach Club is heavily beach-oriented. Most vacationers wile their days away sailing, windsurfing, snorkeling, eating, plunging in the pool, or enjoying nightly entertainment within sight of the sand and the tranquil cove. The 45-acre resort also sports a tennis court, a gym and airy rooms with either sea or garden views. Pineapple Beach is less hectic than some of the other Caribbean clubs that cover all drinks, meals, sports, taxes and tips in the tariff.

PINEAPPLE BEACH CLUB, c\o ITR, (800) 223-9815 or (212) 545-8469. Rates are all inclusive. Very Expensive.

Bibliography

Birnbaum's Caribbean 1992 ($17.00, HarperCollins, New York, NY), includes Bermuda, the Bahamas and the Mexican Caribbean, is fun to read and perhaps the most useful of the all-purpose Caribbean guides.

Best Places to Stay in the Caribbean, by Bill Jamison and Cheryl Alters Jamison ($13.95, Houghton Mifflin Company, Boston, MA, 1990) contains well-written, astute descriptions of a wide range of accommodations.

Caribbean Choice, by Michele Evans ($13.95, Warner Books, New York, NY, 1989) can't be beat for reliable and detailed information about the deluxe and first class properties in the region.

Fitness and Beauty Spas

Tranquilizing facials are as much a part of a spa sojourn as pulse-racing aerobics. Spas minister to our overall well-being, toning both muscles and psyches. While men may eschew the beauty treatments, they too check into spas for tune-ups and vacations. Attracted by top-notch sports facilities, group classes, shared meals and nurturing environments, singles of both sexes find health, rejuvenation and companionship at spas.

Men who want to work out with other men might take the advice of the late Jeffery Joseph, an experienced spa consultant, who ticked off spas with 25% or more male participants: the Canyon Ranch, in Tucson, Arizona; Rancho La Puerta in northern Mexico; the New Life Spa in Killington, Vermont; and the Sheraton Bonaventure Spa, inland from Fort Lauderdale, Florida.

New Age spas, holistic health centers and retreats are also exceedingly popular. Because they appeal to a different audience, these alternative facilities are listed separately in the next chapter.

Pricing Categories

(Note: Rates for spas listed in this chapter always include meals.)

Inexpensive	Under $75 a day
Moderate	$75 to $125 a day
Expensive	$126 to $200
Very Expensive	Over $200 a day

CANYON RANCH
Lenox, Massachusetts

Three revitalizing days constituted my first Canyon Ranch experience, and while I hadn't visited the 13-year-old Tucson original, the "what-else-can-I-do-for-you" attitude at their Berkshire spa seemed exceptional, considering that the $40 million spread on the 120-acre Bellefontaine mansion's grounds is relatively new.

The Lenox, Massachusetts branch of Canyon Ranch, 2 1/2 hours from Boston and three hours from New York, has more than a staff ratio of nearly 2 employees for each of 200 guests to recommend the facility. The cornucopia of exercise programs, beauty treatments, outdoor sports, and health consultations get raves. "Fantastic," Jill rated the 50-minute reflexology massage of her feet and hands. Adrian found the "Positive Power" workout simultaneously exhausting and invigorating. Bonnie was high on her Body Composition consultation. Gordon lauded the squash facilities.

Oh, there was some complaining. Still, a few gaffs are forgivable when a pedicurist goes out of her way for a pair of flip flops to protect freshly polished nails, when the pool man comes by during laps to offer kickboards or hand paddles, when, unasked, the dining room hostess hikes to the registration area—about three long city blocks—to get a woman the New York Times.

The rectangular Beaux Arts mansion, a brick-and-marble relic of Lenox' Gilded Age modeled on Versailles, adds an historic fillip to the zingy modern 100,000-square-foot spa and the commodious, if motel-like, rooms at the inn. Connected to Bellefontaine by white pillared corridors, the linear new buildings are faced with grey clapboards for a somewhat starchy New England effect. Valets whisk guests' cars away as they arrive and usher spa-goers into the clubby interior washed in shades of green, apricot and peach. The deluxe (the cheapest category) bedrooms, with a pair of quilt-covered double beds, remote-controlled TVs and VCRs, and nice, big tiled baths, are comfortable but not inspired.

Inspiration at Canyon Ranch is saved for the program. A phalanx of uniformed staffers sees participants through the registration process, which begins before arrival with a call to Guest Services to discuss needs and to book personal services appointments. Changes or embellishments to the pre-arranged program can be organized through the Program Coordinator's office after the brief get-acquainted tour.

Tucson's variety of excellent services has been transplanted intact. While fitness buffs pound the treadmills in the Aerobic & Strength Training Room, others lie stretched out in mirrored Gym 6, inhaling deeply during Breathing. When the Canyon Ranch van leaves for cross country skiing, many are taking Aquafit in the shallow, 75-foot pool. After a walk through fresh snowdrifts in winter, hikers can check dry, windburned skin in for a facial.

The 3-night package provides two Personal Services; a 5-night stay provides four. Beauty treatments are offered in the stylish Salon, where a pedicure secures a padded chair that massages the back while allowing one to drink in a Berkshire view. Herbal and aroma wraps and hydrotherapy had their devotees, but I used my freebies for the masseur. The fitness and arthritis consultations cost extra, but classes focusing on nutrition by Canyon Ranch's ultra-slim menu planner are free.

It is possible to nibble, sip and nosh to the heart's content without gaining an ounce, so carefully are the calories plotted. The meals served beneath elaborate faux pewter chandeliers are low-calorie and visually appealing. Fruit is available 24 hours a day, and imaginative snacks staunch pre-dinner hunger pains. Load a small plate with endive and enoki mushrooms to crunch while waiting to be seated at one of the three Captain's Tables reserved for solitaires.

The less complicated entrees seemed the most successful. There were festive salads and hearty soups to choose from, as well as several main course specials every day. Strawberries Romanoff and other desserts were offered, but fluffy yogurt "ice cream" was the favorite, served with herbal teas and rich decaffeinated coffee.

No one seemed particularly happy to leave.

CANYON RANCH, Kemble Street, Lenox, MA 01240, (800) 742-9000 or (413) 637-4100. Weekend and week-long packages are available. Very Expensive.

NORWICH INN AND SPA
Norwich, Connecticut

Glowing with eucalyptus oil and fragrant with mint balm, everyone emerged toned and lighter from the 2-day program at Connecticut's Norwich Inn and Spa. Using up 1,200 (for women) to 1,500 calories (for men) a day, and receiving one evening lecture, four skin treatments, and four fitness courses plus a fitness evaluation ($25 extra) leaves guests feeling splendid. My only caveat about the "48 Hour Revitalizer Program" concerns men; although gents worked out in the neo-Roman spa when I was there, all 30 program participants were women.

During this, my first spa visit, there were few if any gripes. Veterans of La Costa, Guerney's Inn and Canyon Ranch ranked Norwich among the best spas they'd been to and agreed that it was especially suitable for single women. The Norwich Spa, they reported, is more fitness-oriented and more lenient when it comes to calories than its former sibling, the Greenhouse in Dallas. "All you have to do at the Greenhouse is chew" said one former guest.

A massage at 4:30 pm is the perfect antidote to city grime and thruway trauma. Long, supple fingers knead out the kinks; a massage, accompanied by ephemeral New Wave music, can begin 44 hours of highly professional and educational cosseting. An important suggestion here: call the Scheduling Department and arrange a schedule *before* arrival to profit most from a limited stay. Check into the chintz-covered lobby of the country-English Norwich Inn at 4:00 pm and there will still be enough time for orientation and a treatment in the Spa before get-acquainted snacks at 6:30, followed by a calorie-counted dinner.

I also advise getting a fitness evaluation at the start of the first (and only) full day. This can be key to the overall effectiveness of the short program. Besides weight and other appalling statistics, spa personnel calculate body fat and outline a program designed to reduce it to an ideal 22% of the whole.

The post-dinner lectures over herbal tea are also rewarding. A disciple of Covert "Fat or Fit" Bailey may outline the Target Concept of food groups: the closer to the center one eats, the healthier and thinner they'll be. Next evening a nutrition consultant might help to calculate a "slow, sensible weight loss program."

Stick to meals such as those issuing from the Norwich Inn's spa kitchen to lose weight faster. Some dishes look better than they taste, but all are low-calorie and distinguished by beautiful garnishes and stylish service.

Designer exercise outfits and modish sportswear are most popular at dinner. Some participants pass up the celery-colored dining room and opt to dine in the silk moire-swathed Norwich Grill, the inn's full-service restaurant. With just 2 days to shed bad habits, spa-goers may prefer the calorie-controlled meals. The fruit is top-quality and ripe, and there are successful diet sweets.

Breakfast is bolstered by fluffy pillows in a firm bed. The 65-room Norwich Inn, built in 1930 and renovated in 1983 is enviably substantial. Green carpets muffled treads as guests hurried past Mexican doves to the Etruscan-style spa for their 8:30 am "Limber and Tone" class.

Lolling on low turquoise banquets against walls hand-sponged for a marble effect, we tried to look patrician in our chunky terry robes while awaiting summons to the white treatment rooms. Schedules that alternate exercise classes with treatments and free periods are particularly successful. Vigorous exercises called "Bodyworks" should come after the fitness evaluation and before lunch. Save Thalassotherapy for the end of the schedule; being slathered with pureed seaweed, wrapped in mylar and cooked under an heavy electric pad sounds like a recipe for lobster, but in fact the European skin treatment is wonderfully soothing. Now who'd risk turnpike tension after that? Have the cab take the "new you" to the train station, perhaps with a new friend.

NORWICH INN AND SPA, Route 32, Norwich, CN 06360, (800) 892-5692 or (203) 886-2401. Packages include the "48-Hour Revitalizer Program" as well as a 5-night program. Very Expensive.

Other Voices_____

RANCHO LA PUERTA
Mexico

Annie, a TV director in her late 30s who lives in New York City, compares Rancho La Puerta in northern Mexico with Canyon Ranch in Tucson.

"At Canyon Ranch you feel like you've missed some activity, because people are always running by you. I find a calmness and a serenity at the Rancho, and although the treatments are not as hotsy-totsy, pristine-pink marble, state-of-the-art, 70-massages-a-week kind of thing found at some spas, it doesn't matter.

"Rancho La Puerta has a desert atmosphere, but it's beautifully planted and landscaped. The buildings are all adobe style, very southwestern. Cuchima, which the Indians believe is a magic mountain, is mysterious. It's also invigorating when you hike up the mountain in the morning.

"I get up at 5:30 am for the walk, and like returning to find my breakfast ready, and then going on with my day. Basically I work out very hard in the morning and lay out by the pool or take maybe one class in the afternoon, plus 'treatments'—massages, facials, etc. The rooms have no phones or TV, but a movie is shown every night at 8:00, and there are lectures or poetry readings if you're interested.

"Eighteen classes go on at once, all structured so people stretch to their ability. The exercise people are highly professional and very enthusiastic. I did the ballet bar every day, a 4-mile walk and an aerobic walk. Then I'd swim some laps, soak in the whirlpool, sit in the sun and finally, relax.

"The food is fine, and you can eat with others, or by yourself. Lunch is buffet; dinner is served, and you have a couple of choices. It's vegetarian, although you get fish twice a week, and lots of Mexican food. They do a good job.

"If you're looking for a man, this is not the place. You're there to relax and feel good about yourself, they stress that. You bring sweatpants and t-shirts; no one dresses, even for dinner. It's the kind of place that makes you all feel like part of the family."

RANCHO LA PUERTA, 3085 Reynard Way, San Diego, CA (619) 744-4222. Expensive to Very Expensive.

THE GREENHOUSE SPA
Arlington, Texas

"Nobody at The Greenhouse is fat. This is a grooming and taking-care-of-yourself, not a weight loss place, but you do lose weight, at least 5 pounds, and lots of inches. Seven or eight inches is not unusual. You're really working, and you're not eating," recalls Betty, a mother, world-traveler and French linguist from Maine. In her 50s, she has been to The Greenhouse perhaps a dozen times.

"It's a very ritzy place. You arrive at the airport with one or two other women and all their gorgeous luggage and look for a man wearing a pink rose in his lapel. He's the chauffeur. At the Greenhouse, your luggage disappears and a very chic lady shows you to your room. Shortly, dinner appears.

"The rooms, each different, are really elegant; queen-sized beds, with mountains of pillows in the most beautiful linens and lace, a canopy over the bed, and at least two floor-to-ceiling windows looking out onto the golf course, or the pool or the walking trails. In the bathroom there's a sunken tub, a bidet and two sinks in a long, marble counter.

"You *are* catered to. A doctor and nurse check you out the night you arrive. Next morning a uniformed maid opens the drapes and sets out your breakfast: paper-thin toast on fine china, maybe an egg, maybe a half grapefruit. You make up your own menu. With the flower on your tray is your little schedule, which you fill out and pin to the yellow dressing robe you found in your dressing room with several sets of navy tights and leotards and matching headbands. Except at dinner, if you go to dinner, everyone looks the same, which is great. It really neutralizes everybody.

"I organized my schedule so all my exercises were in the morning, followed by my massage. Everyone begins to really look forward to the mid-morning potassium broth. Then a beautifully arranged, low-calorie lunch is served by the pool, and you resume your exercises.

"Dinner is dressy and very formal. First, 'cocktails' in the living room. They give you a bouillon or one celery stick with a shrimp on the end, all very elegant. The maitre d' rings his bell, and some 30 to 36 women charge for the dining room, where you sit at these gorgeous tables for six. The food is minimal, of course, but excellent.

"After dinner, there might be a talk on astrology, a demonstration of floral arrangements or a cooking class. Of course, you *can* stay in your room and lick your plate with no one to see you.

"These women are very serious about their beauty. You learn a lot about cosmetic stuff, like where to go for an eyelid lift, and then there's a whole crowd of working, professional women who come just to get away.

"It's big, big bucks. Still, the programs are wonderful. You come away looking absolutely remarkable."

THE GREENHOUSE SPA, PO Box 1144, Arlington, TX 76010, (817) 640-4000. Very Expensive.

NEW LIFE SPA
Killington, Vermont

"I go to Canyon Ranch in Tucson every year, in February, but I get to the New Life Spa in Vermont whenever I get a chance," reports Carol, an editor in New York.

"Mel Zuckerman, founder of Canyon Ranch, first told me about New Life. That's where Mel goes when he wants to get away. New Life is utterly relaxed and unpretentious. No one wears fancy workout clothes. Mostly, we go around in sweats all day.

"There's a wonderful camaraderie at New Life. You chat with people hiking along Vermont's hard-packed dirt roads and trails. There's lots of hiking. Most people make it up to the top of Stratton Mountain by the end of the week, and you talk a lot around the communal table at meals. Everyone eats together and the vegetarian dishes, which include fish and chicken at night, are excellent. Jimmy LeSage, the founder and owner, was a chef, and while I always lose weight at New Life, I always feel I've had enough to eat.

"Sometimes we'll get together and go discount shopping at the outlet stores in Manchester. Occasionally, we'll go into town for a movie, but Jimmy usually has a speaker at night.

"New Life was housed in a chalet-style lodge at the foot of Stratton Mountain, but recently moved to Killington and I don't know if there have been any major changes in the straightforward and fairly Spartan program." [LeSage reports that New Life spent ten million dollars on their new Killington facility, but that the character of the program hasn't changed—*Editor*] "Yoga and hiking are stressed, which suits a maximum of 40 people, about 50% of whom arrive alone, just fine.

"I don't go to New Life for beauty services; there are none. I go to modify my eating habits and to get a heightened sense of well-being. We stretch, do gentle aerobics, work out in the pools, on the tennis courts and in winter take advantage of the area's cross country and downhill skiing. We are a mixed lot: lawyers, professors, other professionals from all over the Northeast. We get into fairly intense conversations, but that's all part of the fun. New Life is small and cohesive, and as a result of numerous visits, I've made several new friends."

NEW LIFE SPA, PO Box 395, Killington, VT 05751, (802) 422-4302. Expensive.

THE ASHRAM
Calabasas, California

"The Ashram is like a house, with single and double rooms, run by two Swedish women and a very dedicated staff. The owner is really into the spiritual side of Eastern philosophy, but yoga and meditation are optional. Some people get involved, some don't." Donna went to The Ashram for the workout. A 45-year-old world-traveler and linguist, she checked in for the week and left diminished by 8 pounds and 17 inches. "Besides, you come out very poised. Why? 'Work' is the key word.

"You arrive on Sunday; they'll meet you in L.A. and take you to Calabasas, about an hour away in the Santa Monica hills. You relax, weigh in after a light supper, discuss your medical history, get organized. Monday the program begins with a hike and a very light breakfast. There were only 8 people when I was there [11 is the maximum], and we gathered around one table for informal meals; interesting, attractive, well-prepared meals, but light. Off to one side is the living room, with books and windows that overlook the mountains.

"The hikes are fun. You can choose a light hike or you can really challenge yourself. The morning hike is several miles, after which you have a choice of activities. The water volleyball is fun, the water feels great, and it's tremendous exercise.

"You rest awhile after lunch, then someone leads you through calisthenics on the roof. You can lift weights and use the aerobic machines, but it's very structured; nobody's going to let you just go out there and start lifting things. Late afternoon means another hike, maybe along the beach in Malibu, then supper, after which the evening's yours to read, take a hot bath, do yoga, whatever.

"The Ashram is not about pampering and moving your arms and legs up and down a bit. It's work. I mean, this is hiking. Hard. They give you two fresh t-shirts and jogging pants every day; you don't have to bring anything but your toothbrush. It's a great leveler. The Golden Door this isn't. It's very down-home.

"The Ashram is a very caring place. They offer a lot of encouragement, and there's a real contagion there. If you're going to really work hard on yourself, these are the kind of people you need around."

THE ASHRAM, PO Box 8009, Calabasas, CA 91372, (818) 888-6900. Very Expensive.

GREEN MOUNTAIN AT FOX RUN
Ludlow, Vermont

"Green Mountain at Fox Run is not a spa, really. It's more a health and fitness resort for women without much pampering," is the way Evelyn describes this community on 20 wooded acres in Vermont. A legal professional in New York, aged 36, Evelyn was intent on changing her lifestyle as well as her shape."I had a weight problem, and I had already lost 20 pounds, but I wanted to learn about proper nutrition and physical fitness. I had become very sedentary, so I took the basic Green Mountain program, for a month. I lost another 10 pounds there and continued to lose about 15 pounds when I got home. What I got into was an exercise regime, which I have kept to since that first visit 3 years ago.

"Physically, it's a very simple resort on a mountain across from Okemo. The buildings are like small chalets, with forests nearby. At capacity Green Mountain takes about 50 people. The rooms have been refurnished. Not luxurious, but comfortable. It's cheaper once you've been there for a month.

"The day begins with a pleasant walk on a mountain track after breakfast. Those more advanced hike up a giant hill. After that, programs might include a behavior-modification talk to address Green Mountain's approach to making food choices. The schedule alternates active and non-active programs.

"Lunch. Then there might be an exercise modification to deal with your particular physical problems or limitations. You're not exhausted or starved at the end of the day. Green Mountain tries to be realistic. For example, they don't have advanced, sophisticated exercise equipment because they want to give you exercises you can do at home, without becoming dependent on a gym.

"The food is very nice, and vegetarians have special options. They stress eating like a normal person; normal portions of even pizza and ice cream. At some point, they encourage you to have at least one restaurant meal to incorporate what you've learned.

"Women come from all over the country and Latin America, a broad spectrum of ages from 20 to 60. Most are very interesting people who work outside the home. They don't go to Vermont for pampering; these are people with very serious goals.

*GREEN MOUNTAIN AT FOX RUN, PO Box 164, Ludlow,
VT 05149, (800) 448-8106 or (802) 228-8885. Moderate to
Very Expensive.*

 ## *Other Spa Choices*

The 30-year-old Golden Door, a serene, Japanese-inspired
complex that caters to 40 mostly-unaccompanied guests at a
time, will be found at the top of any "Best Spa" list. All
rooms are for one at this stylish 177-acre spread with seclud-
ed meditation gardens run by the Szekely family (creators
also of the 50-year-old Rancho La Puerta) for women only.

*GOLDEN DOOR, PO Box 1567, Escondido, CA 92025, (619)
744-5777. Very Expensive.*

The warmly welcoming and informal Heartland Health
Spa is located in the cornfields of middle America, 80 miles
south of Chicago. Weight loss is a part of the general fitness
program at this homey, mainstream spa-in-a-barn near a lakeside farmhouse where about 50% of the 28 guests are singles,
about 25% of them men.

*HEARTLAND HEALTH SPA RETREAT, RR1, Box 181, Gilman,
Illinois 60938, (815) 683-2182 or (312) 427-6465. Very Expensive.*

Most experts agree that the caliber of beauty treatments
at the top-ranked Palm-Aire Spa Resort is unbeatable. Still,
up to 388 guests at a time also tone up and shape up with
hikes and carefully supervised aerobics and exercises, or get
fit on the 5 golf courses, 37 tennis courts and 3 pools to be
found on the resort's 700-acre grounds.

*PALM-AIRE SPA RESORT, 2501 Palm-Aire Drive North,
Pompano Beach, FL 33069, (800) 272-5624 or (305) 972-3300.
Very Expensive.*

"I don't want anyone to discover Rancho Rio Caliente,"
said Jack, a retired advertising executive. "I spend every May

there in the mountains about an hour from Guadalajara taking yoga, eating wonderful vegetarian meals, soaking in the hot mineral springs, and losing weight, all for $46 a day." Sorry Jack, but bargain-priced Rio Caliente, with its horse-back-riding program and two pools seemed too good a secret to keep although one former guest felt the 80-person spa was too isolated and too Spartan.

RANCHO RIO CALIENTE, c/o Barbara Dane Associates, 480 California Terrace, Pasadena, CA 91105, (818) 796-5577. Inexpensive.

The Wooden Door, located in the pinewoods of Wisconsin beside Lake Geneva, offers its women-only clientele many chances the Golden Door does not. Campers get to carry their own bags, scrape their own dishes, share a cabin with others. They also get a salt-free, 900-calorie diet and a chance to canoe, waterski, sail and in winter, cross country ski, as well as to exercise and pay extra for beauty treatments.

THE WOODEN DOOR, 628 Mulberry Court, Milwaukee, WI 53217,(800) 800-7906 or (414) 228-8980. Moderate.

 Reservations Agencies _____

CUSTOM SPAS WORLDWIDE, 1318 Beacon St., Brookline, MA 02146, (800) 443-7727 or (617) 566-5144. Represents traditional and alternative spas.

SPA FINDERS TRAVEL ARRANGEMENTS LTD, 91 Fifth Avenue, New York, NY 10003, (800) 255-7727 or (212) 475-1000. The largest spa-only agency, also produces *The Spa Finder,* an excellent catalog that describes over 325 spas.

SPA TREK INTERNATIONAL, 470 Park Avenue South, New York, NY 10016, (212) 779-3480. Specializes in traditional spas.

Bibliography

The Best Spas by Theodore B. Van Itallie MD & Leila Hadley, ($21.95 hardcover, Harper & Row Publishers, New York, NY, 1988) dissects 30 US spas and about 30 other spas around the world in 429 pages of clear and careful prose.

The Ultimate Spa Book by Pam Martin Sarnoff, ($24.95 hardcover, Warner Books, New York, NY, 1989). Photographs enhance this slick book which, in 276 colorful pages, discusses the pluses and minuses of 49 American spas and 23 spas overseas.

The Spa Finder, (Spa Finders Travel Arrangements Ltd., 91 Fifth Avenue, New York, NY 10003, (800) 255-7727 or (212) 475-1000, $4.95 softcover). Describes over 300 spas in 8 categories.

New Age Spas and Retreats

Many mainstream spas integrate yoga as well as flotation tanks and other New Age treatments and classes into schedules emphasizing conventional sports, exercise and fitness programs. This chapter describes the reverse: places where yoga, a holistic, mind-body-spirit approach or other conceptual method takes precedence over treadmills, Nautilus equipment and go-for-the-burn aerobics.

Included also are Catholic and Buddhist monasteries and yoga and New Age retreats, which offer sanctuary to paying guests of any religious persuasion. Expect vegetarian meals (all meals are included in spa rates), walks and hiking trails and, occasionally, swimming and boating, but no pampering.

There are plenty of solos at these alternative spots and, as is true of the more traditional spas, most, but not all the guests, are women. Spa Finders Travel Arrangements (see Bibliography for FIT-NESS AND BEAUTY SPAS) points out that "plenty of men attend courses at the Omega Institute for Holistic Studies, the seminars and weekends sponsored by the Himalayan Institute, and places like Sivananda Yoga Camps."

Pricing Categories

Inexpensive	Under $75 a day
Moderate	$75 to $125 a day
Expensive	$126 to $200
Very Expensive	Over $200 a day

DAI BOSATSU ZENDO
Lew Beach, New York

A bald monk on the grassy slope played a recorder while, against a backdrop of trees in full leaf, a canoeist paddled across Lake Beecher. The dull rat-a-tat-tat of a woodpecker was the only other sound. The perfection of that summer afternoon at the Guest House of the Dai Bosatsu Zendo seemed almost artful.

A friend's description sent me to the Dai Bosatsu Zendo. Accommodations are at the Japanese-style Zendo itself, or at the property's original, shingled summer cottage set beside the highest lake in the Catskills. Guests who sleep at the Guest House can meditate and take yoga classes ($6 extra) at the monastery, but are fed and cosseted as at an inn. Those electing a futon room for one or two at the monastery will eat (silently) with the community and participate in whichever ceremonies seem interesting as well as Zendo housekeeping tasks if desired.

At the Guest House, a New Yorker whose sixth visit this was took over as informant for a group of six weekenders. She introduced us to the Japanese soak tub, the impressive vegetable garden, and the *sangha*, or community, meadow dotted about with benign little buddhas and polished granite gravestones. Nearby was a moving, larger-than-life-sized bronze of a shirtless young man in blue jeans, meditating in the lotus pose, which nicely celebrated the American adoption of the ancient Zen Buddhist practice.

Still, one needn't stray far from the inn with its summery, wainscotted bedrooms and flowered spreads. A student of Zen from Poland cooked and served us blueberry pancake breakfasts and lunches of tabouleh and ratatouille-style dishes. The vegetarian fare at dinner was equally inventive and savory. During the day we lounged on the pier, rowed or paddled around Beecher lake, walked or just relaxed.

Students and guests seldom mix company, but one Monday night the Guest House gang was invited to a party to celebrate the completion of the rigorous, 100-day *kessei*, or training session, held twice yearly at the Zendo. Standing in a gauzy white dress at the intersection of the slate passageway and grassy courtyard, the wife of Roshi, the Abbott of the Dai Bosatsu Zendo, clapped two long blocks of wood together. About 25 students, four bald but very American monks, and Roshi, the Japanese Abbot, helped themselves and their guests to a vegetarian feast before pulling round black cushions from under the low tables and sitting down cross-legged to eat.

The attractive multi-national cast around the rectangular table had just ended *sesshin*, a week-long, silent retreat, but a party mood took hold as wine and beer were consumed. The first act ended, the throng returned to the Guest House where music, laughter and singing continued well into the night.

Next morning, there was chanting and *zazen*, or meditation, at the Zendo as usual, beginning at 5:30 am. The gong sounds somberly at 5:00 am, but there are other, shorter sessions later in the day. Even the novice who can barely get past a count of four without a distracting thought finds meditating eminently soothing.

Join a student as he shows visitors through the austere but aesthetically gratifying shrine and meditation room, and the spotless large kitchen, to pick up lore about the Zen Studies Society (223 East 67th Street, New York City) and its affiliate, the Dai Botsatsu Zendo, which belong to the liberal, outward-looking *Rinzai* school of Zen.

Certainly, the American monks are worldly, as well as wry, witty and wise. Yoga under the lithe abbot's militant leadership was rigorous. The Office Manager was instructive, and kind. The religious duties and studies are, of course, serious and exacting, but overall, the mood at the Zendo is relaxed, natural, and when not inappropriate, funny, which makes Zen, as practiced here, appealing.

Arrive at the monastery on overload, and leave centered and focused. And bring warm socks: the slate floors are cold and you must leave your shoes at the door.

DAI BOSATSU ZENDO, HCR 1, Box 171, Livingston Manor, NY 12758, (914) 439-4566. Inexpensive.

Other Voices _____

KRIPALU INSTITUTE
Lenox, Massachusetts

"I originally went to the Kripalu Institute in the Berkshires for the yoga, and I've been dozens of times since," says Diane, a how-to writer from New Jersey.

"The Institute is a beautiful place on 250 acres with a big lake and a bathing beach. The four-story building, a former Jesuit seminary, has everything, even a wonderful sauna. Kripalu gets a wide range of people from all walks; very successful, very targeted people who come to find rest and relaxation. The program addresses the spiritual as much as it does the psychological.

"The *raison d' etre* is to help people be well, in the largest sense of the word. One part is enjoying oneself, another part is spiritual and another is being physically healthy. About 200 people live in the community, but you needn't participate in communal activities unless you want to. Friday and Saturday nights the community holds a *satsang*, which is like a religious service, with incense and bells and music.

"Kripalu is so well run that management consultants go up there to study. They're computerized up to their ears. When I arrive they already know the programs I've taken before. What's more, you're always treated with tremendous friendliness and nurturance, which is really the reason I go. After three visits you feel like you've joined a family.

"The programs used to be more inner-oriented. Kripalu does more yoga-oriented programs, more physically-oriented programs now. But you can go there and not do anything, just use it as a resort. Tanglewood's next door and you walk into Lenox if you don't have a car. There's plenty to see in the Berkshires.

"Out of 300 program participants at Kripalu, there are plenty of men on any given weekend, but I wouldn't go there to meet men.

"Kripalu is very inexpensive, pretty casual and immaculately clean. A few rooms have private baths but most are very simple, with white cinderblock walls, two beds, a sink, and there are dorm rooms, too. You don't need much, because you're almost never in the room."

KRIPALU INSTITUTE, Box 793, Lenox, MA 01240, (413) 637-3280. Dorms, standard rooms and deluxe rooms are available. Inexpensive to Expensive.

OMEGA INSTITUTE MAHO BAY PROGRAM
Maho Bay, St. Thomas

"I've taken two Omega Institute trips, one of them to Maho Bay. Omega has a big, 4-week winter session there every year. Wonderful," recalls Sara, the 65-year-old Long Island business woman with a taste for the new and different. "People with different talents lead workshops and seminars for a week at a time. They had yoga, nutrition, lectures, or demonstrations of, say, the Alexander technique.

"One lecture was held during a sailing trip. Dr. Stephan Rechtschaffen, who was one of the lecturers, talked about nutrition while we were on the boat. Most of the workshops were experiential and amusing. For example, I really liked an empowerer called Gail Straub a lot. She empowers you to do what you want and really gets it across.

"I shared a tent with a girl who I wasn't particularly close to, but as we didn't spend much time in the tent, it didn't matter. We spent time on the beach playing games, instead of lying around like sardines. Omega got you out doing things."

OMEGA INSTITUTE, Lake Drive, RD 2, Box 377, Rhinebeck, NY 12572, (800) 862-8890 or (914) 338-6030 until mid-May; (914) 266-4301 from mid-May to mid-September. Inexpensive.

TASSAJARA
Carmel, California

"I go to the Zendo to totally relax and recommend it highly," said Caroline, a 40-year-old Californian who was in the midst of a career shift from TV production to theater management during her last visit. "Tassajara, tucked into the mountains inland from Carmel, California is just the perfect place to wind down.

"A Sensory Awareness Workshop was in session over Memorial Day weekend but that wasn't why I was there. I took lots of books and when I wasn't reading, I hiked some, did a little yoga and soaked a lot. The hot sulfur baths at Tassajara Hot Springs were well known before the Zen Center of San Francisco began their monastery in 1966. Now there's a bath house beside the creek and segregated plunges. Women bathe nude and alone; the men's baths are co-ed. I find the waters restorative and the food really good.

"The vegetarian meals served family-style are almost gourmet. Are you familiar with the Tassajara cookbook? Many of the recipes in the book, made with vegetables organically grown at the Zendo, are still featured.

"Everything is done for you. Even my room, one of several in a low, redwood building, was cleaned every day. There are all sorts of lodgings on the shady, timbered grounds: women's dorms (three beds each), rooms in redwood cabins with shared baths, rooms with private baths, Japanese-style rooms furnished with futons, as well as pine rooms, stone rooms, and yurts. A series of paths, lit at night by kerosene lamps, connect the rooms and bathhouses with the monastery up on the hill.

"Participants in the Work-Study and Guest Practice Programs help residents operate the Center during the guest season, which runs from late April to September. Workshops and a retreat program that includes daily meditation, lectures, a class on Buddhism, teas, and private meetings with retreat leaders are routine. Tassajara is rustic but it's very natural and very beautiful. I go back as often as I can."

TASSAJARA, 300 Page Street, San Francisco, CA 94102, (415) 431-3771 (summer) or (415) 863-3136. (Mail reservations before mid-April; Phone reservations after April 23.) Inexpensive to Expensive.

HIMALAYAN INSTITUTE
Honesdale, Pennsylvania

"It's a nice place, a retreat which used to be owned by the Trappists. You get room and board, and all the lectures, for about $100 for the weekend, and that's attractive in itself. You think to yourself, 'Well, these guys obviously aren't scam artists.'" Paul is referring to an introductory weekend at the Himalayan Institute in Pennsylvania. He's an economist from Ottawa with an interest in Eastern thought, which he pursued during a subsequent 1-week program on deepening meditation.

"The Institute is affiliated with a university nearby, and they are certified to grant degrees. Courses are offered in yoga and meditation. They also do psychological experiments, biofeedback and stress reduction, which you can participate in. I wasn't as impressed with the master as I thought I'd be, but there was a guest lecturer who was quite charismatic, an amazing presence. Some of the other speakers were also excellent. The lectures weren't theoretical at all, but geared to everyday life.

"You live in dorms, but you have a choice. In fact, they were overloaded during my stay, so some of the 300 people camped out, others stayed in hotels. They served vegetarian meals, and you could take yoga and meditation exercises, but the principal thing was the workshops. I like their attitude. They're not there to convince you of anything, or to make you a follower. One of the basic themes in Eastern philosophy, in fact, is that you control your own self-growth. You follow your own path."

HIMALAYAN INSTITUTE, RR 1, Box 400, Honesdale, PA 18431, (717) 253-5551. Moderate.

VIPASSANA MEDITATION SOCIETY RETREAT
Cedar Edge, Colorado

"The Vipassana Meditation Society holds a 10-day session at an old summer camp in Cedar Edge, Colorado in late July— early August. It's very cool there, and the days are beautiful," Molly says. Her comparisons with an earlier, Insight Meditation Society retreat at Jemez, New Mexico, are especially instructive.

"Vipassana is a little stricter. They don't have a walking meditation. Of course, you're free to walk around, but they try to make you understand that your mission at the retreat is to be as quiet as possible in order to still your mind. The Vipassana Society doesn't feel that's possible if you're distracted by nature.

"The accommodations are rough; little rooms with four cots per room. Basic, but not uncomfortable. I'm kind of a rough-it type anyway, but I don't think most people minded. The hard part is the withdrawal from the world. You share a great deal with these roommates, and yet you never speak to them. At the end, it's like a waterfall, everyone talks at once.

"Vipassana has a leader named Goenka, an incredibly charismatic Indian man. Every evening you watch a video of one of his talks, which are very enlightening. If you are hypersensitive to this sort of thing, you might call it proselytizing, but you aren't expected to join the Society and I thought this retreat was excellent. There are counselors available to help if you have any questions.

"In the Buddhist tradition, you give what you can afford for the course. So you're not bothered by thoughts about money: 'My God, I paid $800 for this course! Am I getting enough out of it?'

"The experience isn't for everyone, but unless you're really fighting it, only the first couple of days are difficult. Last time, on the ninth day, I was thinking to myself, 'It would be wonderful to do a 30-day course.'"

VIPASSANA MEDITATION SOCIETY, PO BOX 24, Shelburne Falls, MA 01370, (413) 625-2160 or the California Vipassana Center, PO Box 1167, Norfolk, CA 93643, (209) 877-4386. Pay what you can afford.

OMEGA INSTITUTE
Rhinebeck, New York

"During this fabulous tap dancing class I took last year, the African drumming workshop was going on nearby. We would hear them while we rehearsed. The drums were drumming, the tappers were tapping—it was just one of those peak experiences in life. Next year I'm taking the drumming." That will make eight consecutive summers at the Omega Institute for Aline, 34, a college admissions officer in New England.

"Omega's had the site for nearly 10 years, before that it was a Yiddish culture camp. It's still set up like a camp, with tents, bunks and cabins. Tenting is the least expensive. The bunks accommodate about 10 people with partitions and common bathrooms. There are private cabins and some to share.

"Omega can handle up to 250 people at a time. It attracts a wide range of types and ages, different economic and educational backgrounds, as well as single, divorced, married, straight, gay. There's a very accepting environment. As a single person, you don't feel outnumbered by couples. The emphasis is on group activity and on being alone.

"Evening activities and eating are communal. The food is vegetarian and absolutely wonderful. I'm not vegetarian, and I look forward to the food every year. It's wonderful, just being exposed to the learning, the people, playing bocci in the morning, swimming in the afternoon. They have a lake and canoes, woods to hike in. Omega's very reasonably priced, and they have a scholarship fund called the Robin Hood Fund, which enables people to come who couldn't otherwise.

"I took a workshop on 'Transforming the Workplace,' run by an organizational development company, which attracted people from all over the world. The leaders and groups are very well selected. In 7 years, I've just had one or two courses that disappointed me. My favorite was African Dance.

"Don't go to meet someone, but if you want a place to feel completely comfortable and not feel alone, this is it. It's an ideal mesh between being with other people and having time alone. I like the challenge. You're really free to do what you want."

OMEGA INSTITUTE, RD 2, Box 377, Rhinebeck, NY 12572, (800) 862-8890 or (914) 266-4301 (May 15 to Sept 15) (914) 338-6030 (Sept 15 to May 15). Participants choose either a private cabin with bath or a shared tent. Inexpensive to Moderate.

SIVANANDA ASHRAM YOGA RETREAT
Paradise Island, Bahamas

"Right after finishing law school and the bar exam, I just couldn't bear the thought of going to work and planning my vacation. I wanted to go somewhere and just *be*. So I went to this yoga camp. It certainly fit my budget." "It" was the Sivananda Ashram Yoga Retreat, right next to Club Med on Paradise Island in the Bahamas. Kathleen, a 27-year-old attorney in Boston, was comfortable with the relative asceticism of the camp, but she had mixed feelings about the quasi-Eastern religiosity there.

"The emphasis is on self-denial, self-effacement. They tell people to be subservient, suppress feelings of anger and always be at someone else's service. I think that's good to a certain degree, but it's not for me. They didn't try to push it, so I didn't feel dishonest being there.

"After the 6:00 am meditation and a discussion session afterwards, you do a yoga class from 8:00 until about 9:45 on a beautiful dock. You look into the ocean, the gentle waves. The weather isn't too hot, even in summer, and you're shaded by overhanging trees. Lunch, of course, is vegetarian. After that, you're free until more yoga at 4:00 pm, followed by dinner and evening meditation. Then you could go for a walk on the beach if you wanted.

"You weren't supposed to go over to the mainland at night because they had no evening boat back, but during the day you just had to let them know you wanted to go over to Nassau. The boat went several times a day.

"They don't allow any alcohol, cigarettes, radio, or TV on the premises. When I was there they were short on staff and had only a handful of guests. I liked it that size. You really got to know the other people. One guy had started out at one of the flashy hotels, then decided he'd rather do this.

"It was a pretty close-knit group: a fellow who teaches massage in North Carolina, a philanthropist from New Jersey, and a New Jersey school teacher with a guy from New York City. I'm still friends with an interesting artist I met there, and I have some very good memories."

SIVANANDA ASHRAM YOGA RETREAT, PO Box N-7500, Paradise Island, Nassau, Bahamas, (809) 363-2902; or contact the Sivananda Yoga Vedanta Center, 243 West 24th Street, New York, NY 10011, (212) 255-4560. Inexpensive.

◪ Other New Age Spa and Retreat Choices

Body, mind and spirit are given equal time at the Bluegrass Spa, where mostly 30- to 45-year-old career women take yoga, tai chi, body movement, and aqua-aerobic classes, as well as experiential workshops in the evening. Innovative massages and beauty treatments are also part of the 7-day program offered at an 1831 mansion in Central Kentucky's thoroughbred country.

BLUEGRASS SPA, 901 Galloway Road, Stamping Ground, KY 40379, (502) 535-6261. Expensive.

A 33-year-old pioneer in vegetarianism, the Hippocrates Health Institute in West Palm Beach, Florida stresses a "living foods" diet composed of organically grown fruits and vegetables and their juices, along with gentle exercises, health lectures, rubs, and facials. A heightened awareness is achieved as 25 participants at a time detoxify from processed foods and meats under a certified health consultant's supervision.

HIPPOCRATES HEALTH INSTITUTE, 1443 Palmdale, West Palm Beach, FL 33411, (407) 471-8876. Moderate to Expensive.

A meditation retreat that also incorporates traditional Indian rejuvenation therapies is the Maharisi Ayuyveda Health Center, housed in an elegantly-appointed brick mansion outside Boston. Sound and aroma therapy, a Neuromuscular Integration Program, as well as a natural weight loss strategy, please a celebrity-laden clientele very much at home in this swank, suburban setting.

MAHARISI AYUYVEDA HEALTH CENTER, 679 George Hill Road, Lancaster, MA 01523, (508) 365-4549. Very Expensive.

Forty minutes from Portland in Maine's Sebago Lake Region, Northern Pines is a serene, rustic retreat with a gentle schedule that begins with meditation at 6:30 am and includes a stretching class and morning walk before breakfast at 8:45. In winter, up to 30 guests can ski cross country; in summer, up to 50 people swim and take part in special 3-day myth making, stress management and other workshops.

NORTHERN PINES, RR 1, Route 85, Box 279, Raymond, ME 04071, (207) 655-7624. Moderate to Expensive.

The White Lotus Foundation, a small, yoga-intensive retreat within sight of the Pacific in the mountains high above Santa Barbara, is as exotic as it sounds. Guests who elect a personal retreat live in round, Mongolian-style yurts erected on the foundation's grounds, while those in the spa's regular program can sleep outside in tents or inside simple rooms. "Unless you are spiritually balanced, you can't have the deeper relaxation and health," says yoga master and co-director, Ganga White.

WHITE LOTUS FOUNDATION, 2500 San Marcos Pass, Santa Barbara, CA 93105, (805) 964-1944. Inexpensive.

 ## *New Age Spa Reservations*

SPA FINDERS TRAVEL ARRANGEMENTS LTD., 91 Fifth Avenue, New York, NY 10003, (800) 255-7727 or (212) 457-1000. Represents over 25 "New Age Retreats," which are described in the $4.95 *Spa Finder* catalog (see BIBLIOGRAPHY FITNESS AND BEAUTY SPAS).

CUSTOM SPAS WORLDWIDE, 1318 Beacon Street, Brookline, MA 02146, (800) 443-7727 or (617) 566-5144. Represents a few alternative spas.

Bibliography

Contact your local Archdiocese for the names of Catholic retreats. For names of Buddhist monasteries, and yoga and New Age workshops, check the ads in the *Yoga Journal* and *East West Magazine*.

For more descriptive information, consult one (or all) of three thorough, carefully researched and annotated guides to holistic health centers, Catholic retreats and Buddhist monasteries published by John Muir Publications, PO Box 613, Santa Fe, NM 87508, (800) 888-7504.

The Traveler's Guide to Healing Centers and Retreats in North America by Martine Rudee and Jonathan Blease ($11, John Muir Publications, PO Box 613, Santa Fe, NM 87508, (800) 888-7504, 1989).

Catholic America:Self-Renewal Centers and Retreats by Patricia Christian ($13.95, John Muir Publications, PO Box 613, Santa Fe, NM 87508, (800) 888-7504,1989).

Buddhist America, Centers, Retreats and Practices, edited by Don Monreale ($12.95, John Muir Publications, PO Box 613, Santa Fe, NM 87508, (800) 888-7504, 1988).

Affordable Spas and Fitness Resorts ($12.95, Ventana Press, PO Box 2468, Chapel Hill, NC 27515, 1988) contains more general, New Age spa information.

Cruising on Ocean Liners and Motor Yachts

Cruise ships ply the rivers, lakes and oceans of the world in ever-increasing numbers and configurations. Motor vessels range from jumbo liners, like the Royal Caribbean Cruise Line's 2,350-passenger *Monarch of the Seas*, to an 83-foot Maine packetboat refitted and christened *Pauline*.

The cruising fleet of sailing ships is equally diverse. Passage is available on Majorie Merriweather Post's *Sea Cloud*, one of the largest private sailing ships ever built, or on a sturdy, 41-foot ketch bound for Tahiti. Newly fashionable are the sail-assisted motor yachts. The *Club Med I*, at 612-feet, is currently the longest of a breed that includes the 148-passenger *Windstar*. To impose some order on this burgeoning field, "Cruising" has been divided into two chapters: motor-driven ships, including the motor-sailing hybrids; and sail-powered craft.

A single cabin is the ideal way to cruise alone. Who would turn down a nicely-located berth for the approximate per person price of a double? Sixteen of the 25 fleets affiliated with the Cruise Lines International Association (CLIA), an industry group, have ships with single staterooms, but not in quantity and not on their newer ships. The posh *Sea Goddess*, *Club Med I*, the suites-only 212-passenger Seabourn ships, and the eight Renaissance yachts offer no concessions to solos. Two-person cabins are now the norm on the new megaliners, too. This trend confounds another trend: the annual, 10% increase in single cruise ship travel over the past several years. So what's the solo to do?

Many solitaries opt to pay the single supplement charged for a double cabin; generally, 150% to 200% of the per person price. Others, unfazed by an unknown roomate, arrange for a "single share." Again, 16 of the 25 CLIA member-lines will try to find solos same-sex, smoking or non-smoking cabin mates (and if they don't, solos may luck out and get a double stateroom for the price of one). During the off-season, look for the "guaranteed single-occupancy fare," which assures passengers a roomateless double cabin for less than the single supplement. To pay even less than the per-person double rate, consider a triple or quad, but only if dorm-style cruising agrees with you.

Pricing Categories

Inexpensive	Under $75 a day
Moderate	$75 to $125 a day
Expensive	$126 to $200
Very Expensive	Over $200 a day

QUEEN ELIZABETH II
"Cruise to Nowhere"

The last night at sea a tablemate in the Queen's Grill ordered Russian vodka to accompany caviar aboard the *Queen Elizabeth II*. Three gentlemen supplied white Pouilly Fumé to drink with the lobster. A woman ordered two bottles of a 1976 Paulliac to go with the prime rib. The sommelier poured my contribution, Moet & Chandon, as the Cherries Jubilee were flamed and we raised a toast to an unforgettable 3-day cruise.

Passengers should stop by the glamorous first-class dining room, glittering with crystal sconces and chandeliers, soon after boarding to check their table assignments even if, as suggested by the Cunard Line, they've told the booking agent that they're traveling alone and would like to be seated with other solitaries. "Oh, you don't want to sit with two couples," said the Queen's Grill manager, erasing my name from the seating chart when I investigated. "I'll put you at Table 67." Fortunately, I had double checked.

Aboard the *Queen Elizabeth II* the choice of cabin determines the dining location. Those who book the muted, wood panelled staterooms on the uppermost decks will eat in either the Queen's Grill or the intimate Princess Grill. Queen's Grill passengers can feast outrageously well (at no extra cost) on lobster tails, escargot, baked Alaska, and caviar for breakfast throughout the trip.

If the brightly painted, cheerful quarters below are elected, the larger, less expensive Mauritania or Columbia restaurants—which may well be the best choice for solos—will be alotted. There, the Captain, ship's officers, and cruise directors host tables for 8 to 12, with an eye to making unattached passengers comfortable. Still, group dining wasn't the only reason I elected the *Queen Elizabeth II*. One hundred eleven single cabins (at little more than the price of a double), and the fact that the multitudinous facilities on the one-class cruises are equally available to all passengers, commend the stately Queen to the solo traveler.

A full compliment of 1,850 passengers arrived at Cunard's cavernous New York pier for a "Cruise to Nowhere" over Labor Day Weekend, many of them in t-shirts and rumpled shorts. Once aboard, everyone quickly changed. The celebrants tossed streamers and confetti, and looked as trim as the recently refitted ship. Tugs nosed the *Queen Elizabeth II* into the Hudson River where it headed for Long Island Sound and Cape Cod. That the shoreline was familiar didn't matter. The 67,139-ton liner itself was reason enough for the trip.

The black-hulled *Queen Elizabeth II*, with its tangerine stack towering above the white superstructure, overwhelms by mere presence, let alone by the facilities within. A passenger can navigate the indirectly-lit corridors for days and still discover a new bar here, an entertainment area or shop there. A quick reconnaissance before sailing turned up handball on screened courts, Irish folk singers, ballroom dancers in the Grand Lounge, and a queue waiting patiently for tea and sawdusty cakes. There are boutiques enough to rival St. Thomas.

The ship lists imperceptibly as it gets underway and the casino opens up. Even during the lifeboat drill intrepid gamblers in orange life jackets pump quarters into the slots. Surprisingly, the quiet, clubby library next door seems almost as popular as the casino. Across the veranda, jigsaw devotees gather around a 3,000 piece puzzle. Meanwhile, at Steiner's of London, passengers reserve manicures and facials. Those not arriving early at the Health Club early may be disappointed to find the masseuses completely booked.

First class passengers have two luxurious, full service retreats when activities prove too daunting: their tranquil cabins and the cream-and-aubergine Queen's Grill Lounge. Polished waiters are on hand to pass *petits fours* or *hors d'oeuvres* or fetch drinks in the lounge with its oblong windows facing the sea. Down below, the smiling steward appears at the touch of the buzzer or ring of the phone. The pampering, first class service is exemplary.

The bustle of the Buffet Breakfast might seem a bit much after a strident floor show and a night of strenuous disco dancing. If so, eat a British breakfast of kippers, English bacon and scrambled eggs from the velvet slipper chair in your steamship-modern stateroom. The TV-equipped staterooms are tastefully decorated in blue, brown and taupe with picture windows.

While sunshine might have been preferable on the 3-day cruise, an atypically cold drizzle didn't seem to dampen spirits. "Who cares what the weather was like," said one passenger descending the gangplank. "This is the first time I've been outside since I came aboard the ship."

THE QUEEN ELIZABETH II, Cunard Line, 555 Fifth Avenue, New York, NY 10017, (800) 247-4400 or (800) 221-4770. The Queen Elizabeth II's schedule changes annually. Very Expensive.

EMITA II
Erie Canal Cruise

The slightly swaybacked *Emita II* looks disarming moored at the low creek bank. Inside, patterned throw rugs cover the dark red metal planking and fringed canopies shade sling chairs on the upper deck. The 67-foot double-decked packet-boat, which plied Maine's Casco Bay before Captain Peter Wiles Sr. bought the beamy craft in 1975, looks as comforting as the crumbly brown sugar cake set out with coffee on the varnished center table. At the sound of three low toots, the crew casts off at 9:20 am.

Voyage with visionaries. A fervent and articulate advocate of the beauty and continuing value of the Erie Canal, Captain Wiles was as iconoclastic as his plucky little cruise boat. The Skipper, a commanding figure with trim beard, sky-blue eyes and flowing white hair, used to navigate passengers through the 525-mile New York State Canal system from June to October; his son, Captain Daniel Wiles, now pilots the ship. My cruise covered the westernmost, Syracuse-Buffalo portion of the Erie Canal. Other 3-day cruises include the Albany-Syracuse journey and the "Revolutionary War" trip along the Champlain Canal. Cruising with Wiles, with his son Dan or one of Mid-Navigation's other captains, is a unique opportunity for history buffs, canal fanatics and collectors of the arcane.

These voyages will appeal to sedentary singles more than the actively inclined. Most of the passengers (capacity, 50) on an early June trip were card-carrying members of the American Association of Retired Persons, happy to snap photos and knit as the grassy banks slipped by the open upper deck or the windowed salon below, but there were also a handful of under-40-year-olds, and 13 of the passengers had come alone. One, a yachtsman from Boston, was so captivated by the dramatic locks and prosperous farms on the Albany-Syracuse run that he had rebooked for the western leg.

Consider the *Emita* for an informative, low-key tour of Upstate New York. Passengers are advised to choose the route that best suits their interests; for example, if waves of green seem more restorative than tedious, elect the Syracuse-Buffalo section which winds through the fertile terrain and somnolent canal villages lying between the Finger Lakes and Lake Ontario.

We moseyed past suburban backyards at 7 miles an hour to Lock #24, the first of 12 locks that would lift us 201 feet during the 3-day voyage. Passengers could follow the 125-mile route and each lock's vital statistics on detailed Department of Transportation maps stocked in the saloon for ready reference.

Huge steel doors clanged open to admit *Emita* to a deep chamber. Once she was tied fast, the powerful portals closed and, as the water poured through the flood gates, the craft began its imperceptible rise to the next level. These transitions were revelatory; what appeared on top was always a surprise. A lockkeeper's cottage with hanging petunias, an ancient flour mill and a how-the-locks-work tour greeted passengers locking through.

The 16 lift bridges situated in spire-crowned Fairport, Spencerport, Middleport, and other picturesque Canal villages were another diversion. Warning bells stopped traffic soon after the *Emita* tooted. Then bridge tenders in two-story towers slowly raised the lacy green bridges, allowing the vessel to continue.

The *Emita II*, despite its small size, is an admirable vehicle, and the traditional crusing niceties aren't slighted. There's a ship's paper. Menus and passenger lists are posted. Elevenses (ice water and lemonade) are passed by members of the nautically-dressed six-person crew as are *hors d'oeuvres* to go with self-serve drinks before dinner. Passengers help themselves to bountiful breakfasts and lunches. Dinners, accompanied the first night by a sweetish champagne, are served at wooden tables made by the Skipper himself.

Luggage is tagged and hauled by the van that trails the *Emita*. The Skipper's hospitality never falters. Forget your film? Need some aspirin? The van driver will fetch it. Passengers overnight in name-brand motels where air-conditioning, privacy and space is available. After dinner beside a grassy embankment, one mannerly group strolled across the street to the Newark Sheraton Inn. In Brockport the next night, everyone filed into a Trailways bus for the half hour trip to a Holiday Inn near Rochester. The motels provided a relaxing respite from hours spent in the open air with new acquaintances. This voyage confirmed the yachtman's observation, "When I travel with a friend, I don't meet anyone. I *do* meet people when I go off alone on these trips."

MID-LAKES NAVIGATION COMPANY, PO Box 61, Skaneateles, NY 13152, (315) 685-5244. Return transporta-

tion to the point of embarcation is included in the rates. Two-day cruises are also available. Moderate.

CLUB MED I

Four mainsails unfurled in unison as the booms swung out from the towering masts and *Club Med I*, choreographed by computers from its Star Wars bridge, headed downwind to Guadaloupe. At such moments Club Mediterranee's new, $100 million hybrid, a 617-foot yacht with 2,990 square yards of sail and two, 2,500 h.p. engines, comes into her own.

I sailed on an early voyage of the 425-passenger *Club Med I*, and while the service and the passengers, even the itinerary, have changed since that cruise, I can recommend the elegantly equipped ship, the excellent water sports program, and the Club Med's esprit. The sensible luxury of the *Club Med I* is further evidence of a maturer, more upscale club. The traditional after-dinner lipsync show, more pre-War Berlin caberet than tasteless carnival, is further evidence of the new style, as is the bijou casino located midship and the sleek disco buried out of earshot on the lowest of eight decks.

The room steward set the breakfast tray down on the king-sized bed before pulling open curtains trimmed in French blue. Equipped with TVs and phones for direct calls overseas, the 197 white staterooms with varnished wooden drawers and trim are undeniabley handsome, as are the private, rounded baths featuring hair dryers, pulsating shower heads and modern chrome fixtures.

Sea views wrapped Odyessey, the less formal of *Club Med I*'s two restaurants, during hot and cold buffet lunches. Some dishes are downright refined. At night, Europeans in silks and double-breasted jackets, as well as G.O.s (*Gentle Organizers*) in one of the nine separate uniforms they're issued, established a somewhat dressy tone. Nouvellish and nicely-garnished dinners in the subdued, somewhat formal La Louisiane restaurant one deck below erased memories of feeding frenzies at Club Meds past. A wine list starring French varietals supplemented the adequate ship wines served gratis.

Club Med hasn't built just another floating hotel. Waterskiers, sailors, windsurfers, and scuba divers enter the water directly from the sports platform that folds open from *Club Med I*'s stern into the sea. The ship's shallow, 16.5 foot draft allows access to seldom-frequented cays and coves. Launches ferry passengers into town; silvery motorboats run them to island beaches.

The majesty of the ship under full sail is sheer delight. The sails cut fuel costs appreciably and add value to the yacht-like nature of the cruise.

CLUB MED Cruise Desk, 3 East 54th Street, New York,, NY 10022, (800) 258-2633 or (212) 750-1687. Very Expensive.

 Other Voices _____

SINGLEWORLD
Carnival Cruise

"He was just one more person I was friendly with in the group. He called me long distance shortly afterwards and invited me to dinner. I said, 'Your place or mine?' and that was that." And so they were wed. Janet, a real estate broker in Maryland, now 35, obviously enjoyed her 7-day Carnival cruise, which she booked through Singleworld.

"I was taking a vacation for myself, by myself. I was anxious to go somewhere with a French accent. This *Festival* cruise started in Puerto Rico and proceeded to St. Thomas, St. Martin, Barbados, and then Martinique. You got a sense of what each of the European countries brought to the Caribbean, and I could decide what I might enjoy for future travel.

"No glitches whatsoever dealing with Singleworld or making arrangements. None. We had a group of about 25 people ranging from 20 to 75 spread all over the ship, a few more women than men, but not badly skewed. Singleworld also has under-35 trips, but I chose to go with the 'all ages' group because I wanted to meet more diverse people.

"There was an introduction of sorts about two hours before sailing, so you could see who was in the group. If need be, Singleworld assigns you a roommate, and tries to match you with someone your age. My roommate, a psychologist and a divorcee, reminded me of one of my best friends from home; we're still in touch.

"Our stateroom was in the second lowest category. You could get a higher category room, or even a private, if you wanted to pay more. We had preferred seating at lunch and dinner, eating as a group at five tables, but you can also move from table to table to eat with different people.

"It was great. We were always having cocktail parties or doing other things together. At Singleworld, if you want to be involved in their activities, fine; if you don't, fine. They offer different excursions from the ones already offered by the boat, so you have a choice.

"My husband and I went on another Carnival cruise to celebrate the anniversary of our meeting, and I actually enjoyed the Singleworld tour and excursions better than [those organized by] Carnival. The *Holiday* was a nicer boat, but with Singleworld we had a host for 25 people. We were better taken care of."

SINGLEWORLD, 401 Theodore Fremd Avenue, Rye, NY 10580, (800) 223-6490. Expensive.

CARNIVAL CRUISE

"I usually meet a few single men on vacation, but not on this trip." Nevertheless, Lynn, the manager of a computer dating service in San Diego, says "I got my money's worth." At 25 she is a fairly seasoned single traveler, relaxed and resourceful to boot.

"I boarded the *Tropicale*, a Carnival liner, on Sunday morning, I think, for a 7-day cruise. Three other women shared this very plain cabin that was smaller than a double; two beds, two bunks, two closets, one bathroom. I called it 'The Cabin from Hell.' One woman was prone to seasickness. Another, 65 to 70 years old, did nothing but complain. It was a smoking room, but only two of us were smokers. The one turbulent night, *everybody* got sick, and that little cabin was awful.

"What I did was make friends with two Long Island girls across the hall. Our table was great because we were all singles; us, two guys from Canada, two senior citizen ladies traveling together, and one girl from my cabin. (Single women outnumbered the men, and there were a lot of senior citizen groups). That was the seating for breakfast, lunch and dinner. The ship has only one main dining room, but there's food all over the ship. Breakfast was a huge buffet, and you could always order room service, 24 hours a day.

"One day was a game day, a sort of mixer, when we played silly pool games. We tried the disco one night, but decided the gambling was better and so we closed the casino every night.

"The first day we landed anywhere was in Puerto Vallarta. I didn't like the time factor; you know, oh my God, we've got to get back to the ship or it's gonna leave without us! At Cabo San Lucas, my favorite port, we didn't have enough time, just 4 hours. A cruise is great, but if you mind time pressure, don't go. On the other hand, there were plenty of things to do on board the ship. I went to Bingo, to the Knobby Knees Contest. Every afternoon, I'd bring my book and have afternoon tea. A cocktail hour preceeded dinner at night, and one night they had a terrible show; this woman could not sing if her life depended on it.

"I felt very comfortable doing things on my own. Of course, I wished I had somebody along, but it was okay not to."

CARNIVAL, 3655 NW 87th Avenue, Miami, FL 33178-2428, (800) 327-9501 or (305) 599-2200. The 1,896-passenger Jubilee has since replaced the Tropicale on the Los Angeles to Puerto Vallarta run. Expensive.

MISSISSIPPI QUEEN

"The *Delta Queen* is an authentic steamboat listed on the National Register of Historic Places. I was a little worried about getting claustrophobic in such small quarters, so I took the *Mississippi Queen*, which is a replica of the *Delta Queen*, but new, more like a regular cruise ship inside." A magazine editor, 35, Laura described her stern wheeler cruise between St. Louis and Minneapolis/St. Paul.

"On the *Mississippi Queen* I went north because I wasn't in the mood for hoop skirts and plantations. The *Mississippi Queen*, even though a recreation vessel, is still a paddle wheeler that runs on real steam. We had enough power, or steam, to light up a small city, I think.

"There were about 300 people aboard, and I was the only New Yorker in the bunch. It was more middle-American than I'd expected. Never saw so many people coming in twos. The crew working the boat were very cordial. If you were interested in the history of the area, you could certainly find out about it. In the theater they had movies on the history of the river, and they put out little informative documents every day.

"I was enchanted by the Mississippi; it's absolutely wonderful and wild. Bald eagles soar around great huge cliffs. The towns where the boat stops are small potatoes: Hannibal, Missouri, which is sort of touristy; Red Wing, Minnesota; Prairie du Chien, Wisconsin. Sometimes the river gets so wide that you don't even know what's river any more. You feel like you're in a huge rice paddy with little islands dotting it."

MISSISSIPPI QUEEN, Robin Street Wharf, New Orleans, LA 70130-1890, (800) 543-1949. Expensive to Very Expensive.

SPECIAL EXPEDITIONS
Seabird Cruise to Alaska

"I celebrated my birthday drinking champagne on a glacier with a bunch of people I'd met on the *Sea Bird*," recalls Mary Louise, a travel writer, 35, from Long Island.

"These are fascinating trips. They have resident scientists, so on every cruise there are at least four experts on the cultural history, the natural history, geography, and the like. You can go to lectures and on field trips if you want. They even have a show-and-tell gathering before cocktails to talk about some interesting flower or some rock someone has picked up....

"The ships are small, maybe a max of 65 to 70 people, and because they are small, you get to know people better. Also, the size makes it possible to get within 10 feet of shore, so the passengers include lots of bird watchers and photographers.

"Dinner is at big tables in one seating. They have a piano bar, and every once in a while a passenger will play, too. It's more intimate than on the larger ships. These are people with curiosity, adventurous and well-traveled, upscale people who want to learn something while they're traveling. It's a nice combination of younger and older. You're never alone unless you want to be."

SPECIAL EXPEDITIONS, INC., 720 Fifth Avenue, NY 10019, (800) 762-0003 or (212) 765-7740. Very Expensive.

 ## Other Cruising Choices ⎯⎯⎯⎯⎯⎯⎯⎯

Abercrombie & Kent and Continental Waterways combine to offer top-of-the-line hotel barge cruises that ply canals and rivers in the Netherlands and England as well as France, Egypt, the coast of Turkey, and Indonesia.

ABERCROMBIE & KENT and CONTINENTAL WATER-WAYS, 1520 Kensington Road, Suite 111, Oak Brook, IL 60521, (800) 323-7308 or (708) 954-2944. The 17-passenger Rembrant goes on a 6-day Bruges to Haarlem cruise. Very Expensive. There are two single staterooms available on the 12-passenger Actif for a 3-night Thames River cruise. Very Expensive. In France, the Layfette has a single cabin available for a 6-night cruise on the Upper Loire. Very Expensive.

The *Caribbean Prince* and *New Shoreham II*, the two 80- and 72-passenger shallow draft ships owned by the American Canadian Caribbean Line, are beloved by their mostly-older passengers, who pay 175% to 200% extra to occupy a double cabin alone on a 12-day cruise.

AMERICAN CANADIAN CARIBBEAN LINE, PO Box 368, Warren, RI 02885, (800) 556-7450 or (401) 245-8303. Moderate to Very Expensive.

Popular is a cruise that loops from Boston via Camden, Bar Harbor and other coastal ports in Maine back to Boston. This 14-day itinerary is offered by the 102-passenger *Nantucket Clipper* owned by the Clipper Cruise Line, which specializes in US trips.

CLIPPER CRUISE LINE, 7711 Bonhomme Avenue, St. Louis, MO 63105-1965, (800) 325-0010 or (314) 727-2929. Very Expensive.

The *Delta Queen*, a 176-passenger paddlewheel steamer launched in 1926 (and now listed on the National Register of Historic Places) still navigates the Mississippi, Ohio, Tennesee, and Cumberland Rivers between New Orleans and Pittsburgh. Management, which levies a singles supplement of 175%, says the line "facilitates" cabin shares.

DELTA QUEEN, Robin Street Wharf, New Orleans, LA 70130-1890, (800) 458-6789 or (505) 586-0631. Expensive to Very Expensive.

The *Pauline*, a perky 6-stateroom vessel, cruises the island-strewn Maine Coast for 3 to 6 days with 12-passengers, all in double bunk cabins.

PAULINE, Windjammer Wharf, POBox 1050, Rockland, ME 04841, (800)999-7352 or (207) 236-3520. Moderate.

"The Society Expeditions cruises are *really* good for curious singles," suggests a Pasadena travel agent. One such is the 17-day cruise to the Hudson Bay. Not only do the accompanying lecturers hold degrees, but tables aboard the 96-passenger *Society Explorer* and 139-passenger *World Discoverer* are set for five or seven people, so solos automatically fit in. Share accommodations can be arranged, and "Because more single passengers want to travel alone, the line is reducing the single supplement to 140% in 1991" says a representative who noted that Society Expeditions inaugurated two new ships this year.

SOCIETY EXPEDITIONS, 3131 Elliott Avenue, Seattle, WA 98121, (800) 548-8669 or (206) 285-9400. Very Expensive.

 ## Singles Policies of Major Cruise Lines ___

CARNIVAL LINE, (800) 327-9501 or (305) 599-2200. Three older liners, the *Carnival*, the *Mardi Gras* and the *Festival* each have 14 single rooms. Fleetwide, a single pays 150% to 200% to occupy a double cabin alone. The Carnival Line also has a "Singles Plan" that guarantees a same-sex share in "quads" or four bunk rooms. (For a first-hand account of cruising quad, see "Lynn" above).

CUNARD LINE, (800) 221-4770. The *Queen Elizabeth II* (see above) has 111 single cabins. The singles supplement for a double stateroom ranges from 175% to 200% on the Cunard fleet as a whole; a singles share program is in effect on some, but not all Cunard liners. The *Princess* and *Countess*, two informal, 800-passenger liners, offer an innovative plan for passengers willing to travel at the last minute: "You may have single occupancy of a double room subject to confirmation 30 days or less prior to departure," according to the catalog. "Earlier confirmation requires payment of 150% of the published fare (grades C through G only)."

PRINCESS CRUISES, (213) 553-1770, is overjoyed with the state-of-the-art *Crown Princess*, their sleek, dolphin-domed "Love Boat." The singles supplement on this newly launched, 1,590 passenger liner is identical to that levied on all the Princess ships: 200% in the four top price categories; 125% below that. The *Sea Princess*, which cruises Alaska and the South Pacific in season, is the only Princess liner with a few single cabins.

THE NORWEGIAN CRUISE LINE, (800) 327-9020 or (305) 447-9660, is geared to warm-weather climes. The L.A.-berthed *Southward* sails to Baja California and Mexico, while the line's other five ships cruise the Caribbean; all are outfitted for snorkeling. There's a single share program in effect on certain of the fleet's ships. Supplements run 150% to 200%, but the young crowd that frequents the line saves money by booking into triples and quads.

ROYAL CARIBBEAN CRUISE LINE, (800) 327-6700 or (305) 379-2601, has recently inaugurated the sleek *Nordic Empress*, featuring 3- and 4-day Bahamas cruises and a large percentage of single passengers. Royal Caribbean's fleet of highly reputable Caribbean-based ships offers, in addition to singles shares and a single supplement of 150%, the "guaranteed single occupancy fare." For about 122% of the full rate, singles are guaranteed an inside double stateroom, but the exact cabin isn't assigned until the ship is boarded.

ROYAL VIKING LINE, (800) 422-8000 or (305) 445-0515, boasts 1 ship with 39 single cabins, the *Sky*. The single supplement is 140% for outside cabins in Categories D through FI on this ship and 160% for staterooms in category Bl through Jl on the new, 125 million Royal Viking *Sun*. Otherwise, the supplement is 200% across the board.

RENAISSANCE CRUISES, (800) 525-2450 or (305) 463-0982, which cruises with naturalists and lecturers, and the SEABOURN CRUISE LINE, (800) 351-9595 or (415) 391-7444, whose *Seabourn Pride* and *Spirit* are the height of luxury, specialize in luxurious craft carrying 100 or 212 passengers and outfitted more like yachts than liners. Neither these ships, nor Cunard's *Sea Goddess I* and *II*, (800) 221-4770, have single cabins, nor do they arrange singles shares, but affluent singles aren't discouraged. They simply pay the 173%, 150%, or 50% to 200% supplement (respectively) and sail off.

WINDSTAR SAIL CRUISES, (800) 258-SAIL, three, 440-foot ships the 148-passenger *Wind Song*, *Wind Spirit* and *Wind Song* to Tahiti, the Mediterranean and the Caribbean. No single shares are arranged and the supplement is 150% on the four-masted, sail-assisted ships.

 ## Cruise Reservations for Solos _____

SINGLEWORLD, (800) 223-6490 or (914) 967-3334. Specializes in cruises (but offers escorted European tours as well) and buys blocks of staterooms on Carnival, Royal Caribbean, Norwegian Cruise Line, and other lines. The organization, with group departures for "under 35 year olds" as well as "all ages," arranges cabin shares, but not single cabins. The group is mostly used by 20- to 40-year-old members who pay an annual $25 fee.

SAGA TOURS, (800) 343-0273. Too old for Singleworld? Anyone 60 or over (whose companion must be 55 or older) can cruise with Saga, which arranges compatible shares for solos who pay only the per person rate if the line fails to arrange for a roommate. The company has an astute selection of "Undiscovered Voyages" that should appeal to the sophisticated older traveler.

WORLD WIDE CRUISES, (800) 882-9000 or (305) 720-9000, has a "Singles Mean Business" division that mans a "Hotline for Singles" to arrange share accommodations.

 ## Cruise Reservation Services _____

Discounting is part of all but the smallest cruise lines' marketing strategy. Look for bargains in the early 1990s. The three dozen new cruise ships coming on line could well cause a stateroom glut, but seldom will passengers find the lines themselves offering less-than-published rates. For the best deals contact a cruise specialist: the cruise manager at your travel agency, or specialized cruise-only agencies, some of them retailers, others, known as "consolidators," who buy space in blocks and pass discounts in the 20% range along to individuals.

BATON ROUGE VACATIONS AT SEA, (800) 999-2493 or (504) 928-3944. A well-regarded cruise retailer.

CRUISE ADVISORS, (800) 235-2118 or (206) 784-7852. Specializes in cruises to Alaska.

THE CRUISE LINE, (800) 777-0707 or (305) 372-2830. Consolidator and cruise specialist.

CRUISES OF DISTINCTION, (800) 634-3445 or (201) 744-1331. Consolidator and cruise specialist.

HARTFORD HOLIDAY, (800) 828-4814 or (516) 466-0335. Specializes in cruise discounts.

SPUR OF THE MOMENT CRUISES, (800) 343-1991 or (213) 839-2418. Specializes in last minute, discounted bookings.

WHITE'S TRAVEL SERVICES, (800) 547-4790 or (203) 233-2648. Cruise specialist and consolidator.

 ## Exploration Cruises

Exploration Cruises on small passenger ships are often interest-oriented and tend to attract older clientele. Bargain-priced these cruises are not, but they are, in the main, first-class. Passengers find naturalists and regional specialists on most of these intimate, 100-or-so passenger cruises. Several organizations offer a variety of exploration cruises.

THE AMERICAN MUSEUM OF NATURAL HISTORY, (800) 462-8687 or (212) 769-5700. Offers 15 to 18 Discovery Cruises annually using Renaissance Cruises and Special Expeditions, among other lines.

THE SMITHSONIAN INSTITUTION, (202) 357-4700. Offers 20 or so cruises on Society Expeditions, Expeditions Cruises or the Clipper Cruise Line ships.

 Freighters _____

Six to twelve passengers, people with flexible schedules and plenty of time, girdle the globe in cargo ships, many of which boast single cabins.

FREIGHTER WORLD CRUISES, (818) 449-3106. North American passenger representative for 17 different cargo lines.

PEARL'S TRAVEL TIPS, (212) 734-6327. Freighter travel specialists in New York for over 25 years.

SEA THE DIFFERENCE, (800) 666-9333. Passenger representative for the 30 cargo vessels of the Mediterranean Ship Company, most of which make trans-Atlantic crossings.

TRAVLTRIPS, 163-07 Depot Road, Flushing, New York, 11358, (718) 939-2400. A 25-year old freighter travel membership group; publishes a bi-monthly newsletter called *Travltips* ($30 per year). One issue listed freighters with single rates that were either less, on a par with, or only 5% to 25% more than double occupancy rates, vessels of the Ivaran Lines, Cast Shipping, Lykes Lines, Bergen Line, Bank Line, and Egon Oldendorff Lines among them.

Bibliography

Travel Companions, a bi-monthly newsletter published by the reputable, 15-year-old Travel Companion Exchange, Box 833, Amityville, New York 11701, (516) 454-0880, devotes a fair share of its space to cruise news, bargains and cruising tips for singles. A six-issue, annual subscription costs $48. (See also Solo Travel Specialists).

Berlitz Complete Handbook to Cruising, by Douglas Ward ($13.95, Berlitz Guides, a division of Macmillan Publishing, New York, NY 1989). Rates and evaluates the international cruise fleet.

Ford's Freighter Travel Guide and Waterways of the World, by Judith Howard ($8.95, 19448 Londeling Street, Northridge, CA 91324, (818) 701-7414). Lists and describes freighters by port of sail and contains an index to expedition cruise ships as well as smaller and more singular craft.

Caribbean Ports of Call by Kay A. Showker ($16.95, Globe Pequot Press, Box Q, Chester, CT 06412, 1990) includes an excellent 16-page comparison "Chart of Cruise Ships."

Cruising Under Sail

Sailboats and windjammers by any name—tall ships, schooners, square-riggers, sloops—hold a powerful allure for those who prefer the tang of salt-spray to the purr of stabilized engines. Aficionados discover historic relevance and timeless beauty as the canvas sails fill and the evocative ships head downwind.

Schooners are especially attractive to singles; so attractive, in fact, that Windjammer Barefoot Cruises now offers "Singles Only" Caribbean cruises on the *Polynesia*. The Maine Windjammer Association estimates that 50% of the passengers aboard its 11 ships are solos. Sailing, it would seem, is solo-friendly, not the least because single supplements (and single cabins) are seldom found below the planked decks where accommodations tend to consist of two, four or six bunks in small utilitarian cabins.

The tall ships are concentrated in, but not limited to, the Caribbean and the Down East Coast of Maine. All tend to have the same, first-come, first-served reservations policy: the early bookers get the choicest berths, and if there are any, the first crack at the single cabins. Sailing clubs, especially those geared to solos, arrange yacht cruises for their members. A New York group,

Pricing Categories

(Note: Cruise fares always include meals)

Inexpensive	Under $75 a day
Moderate	$75 to $125 a day
Expensive	$126 to $200
Very Expensive	Over $200 a day

Singles for Sailing, offers fairly-priced, 16-day trips in Greece and along the Yugoslavian coast. See LEARNING TO SAIL for more information.

OCEAN VOYAGES
Grenadines Cruise

With a Swedish captain at the 5-foot chrome wheel, the *Scherzo* pitched and tossed through deep inky troughs for most of the 25-mile trip from Beguia to Mayreau. This 3 1/2-hour sail in the Grenadines ended when the First Mate threw the anchor onto the sandy bottom of horseshoe-shaped Saltwhistle Bay and it held. The other passengers may not have found the rough crossing thrilling, but there was agreement about the horseshoe-shaped anchorage. The tranquil, sandy crescent we confronted was paradisiacal.

Individuals wishing to cruise aboard the 40- to 60-foot sailing yachts that comprise most of the world's small-boat charter fleet are, it seems, out of luck. Most brokers book by the ship, not by the passenger. An exception is Ocean Voyages, a charter operation that puts singles aboard "head boats," as those few yawls, ketches and sloops are called when they book by the head. Ocean Voyages booked me and a another couple aboard the graceful *Swan 48*, which rode the bucketing seas like a champion.

Few cruises could be more restful and visually satisfying than sailing the Grenadines aboard a Swan, the Rolls Royce of cruising/racing sloops. Bequia, Mayreau, the Tobago Cays, and Union Island; each anchorage we visited proved to be an archetypically Caribbean delight.

On Monday, Bequia's capitol, Port Elizabeth, throbbed with carnival's last spasms. Blaring speakers amplified a local combo to the furthest reaches of Admiralty Bay where the first night of our voyage was celebrated with Blanc de Blanc from Martinique and getting-to-know-you chatter.

A calypso lullaby rocked us to sleep. Droning motor boats buzzed us awake. Morning found everyone on deck with coffee and frothy banana drinks. Soon an inflatable dinghy whisked us to the jumble of clapboard shops screened from the water by ancient fig and almond trees in Port Elizabeth. Chris Doyle's *The Sailor's Guide to the Windward Islands*, discovered at the Bequia Bookstore, informed us about the rest of the cruise.

The second night's anchorage, at Saltwhistle Bay, was idyllic, and Mayreau was fascinating to explore. The island's hamlet, an assortment of varicolored houses with multi-island views and no electricity topped by a weathered stone Catholic Church, can be reached after a 20-minute climb. The hillside graveyard, lily-strewn and filled with grave-stones of 103- and 113-year-olds "carved" in black paint and marked R.I.P., was also memorable. Back on the beach, we inspected t-shirts sold by Mayreau ladies before swimming off to the *Scherzo* for wine and quiche Lorraine, then left for Tobago Cays, an easy, half-hour sail from Mayreau.

By Wednesday night we'd been cruising for 3 days and the atmosphere was upbeat. Lime daiquiris revived snorkelers back from touring reefs rich beyond belief with squirrel and spotted trunk fish, Christmas worms and, among the undulating soft corals, several prehistoric-looking skates. Sails furled, the score of charter boats anchored at Tobago Cays faced into the wind, like gulls. Popcorn and a reggae beat accompanied talk. Below deck, in the glowing teak and beige corduroy saloon, dinner began with tuna marinated Swedish-style, and ended on a high note with fresh mango torte.

Though the *Swan 48* is fairly narrow, the *Scherzo* quartered five handily with two heads (shipboard bathroom facilities), two cabins, and day beds with berths in the saloon. The joys of discovering the secret Grenadines by small boat are myriad. Fresh air and blue water washed away cares, and with an experienced captain at the helm, everyone felt secure. Even stormy weather didn't dampen our pleasure.

Thursday, the wind tore through the rigging, and when the howling ceased, fat drops of rain splashed the boat, now securely anchored off Union Island, a yacht haven that yielded a couple of surprises. Walk 45 minutes to Ashton Village to admire a fine old wooden church. In Clifton, don't miss the waterfront Lambi Bar and Restaurant, walled floor to ceiling with a zillion pink conch, or lambi, shells and a true Caribbean find.

OCEAN VOYAGES, 1709 Bridgeway, Sausalito, CA 94965, (415) 332-4681. Berths are available for people traveling alone on a world-wide assortment of yachts. Moderate to Expensive.

 Other Voices _____

BAREFOOT WINDJAMMER CRUISES

"I really like the windjammer cruises in the Caribbean. They're relaxing, and you get to meet different kinds of people." Ed ought to know. At 45, this Long Island insurance broker is something of a Barefoot Windjammer cruise maven.

"I've been on about 20 cruises, usually on the *Polynesia*. The *Mandalay* is considered the showpiece of the fleet, and probably attracts more couples. The *Polynesia* is better for single people. She's about 250 feet long, a four-masted schooner with 126 passengers, two or six to a room. You can get a single cabin, but they'll charge you 150%. The cabins vary, but most have two built-in bunks and each cabin has its own small but functional bathroom; you can take a shower sitting down.

"A cruise lasts a week, but I usually go for two. *Polynesia* has a 30-man crew and is under sail most of the time. The passengers sometimes help raise the sails, but I don't know whether we help or get in the way. When *Polynesia* takes on water at St. Kitts, a steel band called Coronet, one of the best in the Caribbean, sometimes comes on board. Daytimes, people lounge around the top deck. When you get to an island, the captain will fill you in on things to do, but he doesn't make recommendations. Launches run about every hour from ship to dock.

"There's a little restaurant off Anguilla, on Prickly Pear Cay. It's fantastic. Best lobster I've ever had. You go there when you get to the beach, maybe 10:00 am, and tell them you want lobster for lunch, and about an hour later you'll see a kid walking down the beach with your lobsters. Ah, man.

"I wouldn't call the food on board gourmet, but it's okay. When you see what they have to work with, it's unbelievable. The cooks feed 126 passengers out of a galley, maybe 12 by 12 feet. They do lots of baking. Sit down breakfast is from about 7:00 to 8:30 am. Lunch is usually buffet style, sometimes on shore, sometimes on ship. Dinner is sit down again, with no designated seating. Wine is free with dinner; cocktails you pay for at the bar, which is open from about 10:00 am to 2:00 am.

"By this time next year I will have been on all of the six Barefoot boats except the *Yankee Clipper*. Not many phonies on these cruises. I always meet good people."

BAREFOOT WINDJAMMER CRUISES, PO Box 120, Miami Beach, FL 33119-9983, (800) 327-2601 or (305) 534-7447. Expensive.

BAREFOOT WINDJAMMER CRUISES

"We were 125 aboard the windjammer *Polynesia* out of St. Martin, and this was my first experience going off on a trip alone," recalls Nan, 32, a printing sales representative in San Francisco.

"I had a good time eventually, but the first couple of days I just wanted to die. Of course, on a trip like this, it's luck-of-the-draw who's on board. The group was very couple oriented. Let's say there were 15 single women and 15 single men. Some of the guys were pretty old, over 70.

"The staterooms were just horrible, the pits. The lower deck had no windows, so you couldn't spend any time in your room. And then if you have a roommate with whom you have nothing in common, what do you do?

"I went to meals by myself. No assigned seating. I would usually join an existing group. There was a cocktail hour every night, so you would normally eat with the people you'd been talking with.

"After breakfast, you have story hour with the Captain, who gives you a history of the island and what there is to do, how to pay for taxis and stuff. You can take launches ashore, and the last one back is at midnight. I'm there by myself. What am I going to do until midnight?

"One thing about windjammers. Give me a book, the sun, the beach, and I'm fine. But these sailing ships don't have deck furniture, that's where the sails are. So you lie on deck, which is not conducive to reading. It hurts your back after a while. You can sunbathe for a while, but you can't lose yourself indefinitely in the sun on the deck.

"I wouldn't do it again, not on that kind of boat, without having a buddy with me."

BAREFOOT WINDJAMMER CRUISES, PO Box 120, Miami Beach, FL 33119-0120, (800) 327-2601 or (305) 534-7447. Expensive.

MAINE WINDJAMMER ASSOCIATION

"They really look like sailing antiques; beautiful, and they're Coast Guard-inspected." Conrad, 56, is a retired engineer from Connecticut, and a Maine Windjammer Association enthusiast. "I've sailed on four boats out of Rockland. The captains own their own boats and they take pride in them, always touching up the paint.

"The *Heritage* takes 33 passengers in double cabins, there's one single cabin. Many people come alone, and they try to pair you with another single. It's a mixed group. Every so often somebody comes aboard in high heels, and realizes this isn't for them. Sailing on a windjammer's glorified camping. These aren't luxury cruises; the cabins are small, just a place to sleep.

"The *Heritage* is a schooner. She takes lots of manpower—all the passengers—to hoist the mainsail in the morning. I like helping out. Washing down the deck and whatnot is a lot of fun, but nobody forces you. You can do as much or as little as you want.

"You have no idea where the ships are going when you sign up. You board about 6:00 pm Sunday night and sail until about 7:00 am Monday. The windjammers go the way the wind blows. All you know is that by Saturday noon you'll be back in Rockland.

"The fleet drops anchor every night about 6:00 pm, so you can go ashore, see the sights, maybe picnic on the rocks.

Each harbor is different. Sailing along, you just enjoy the beautiful scenery, look for birds and whales. Sometimes you can almost reach out and touch them.

"Meals? Good schooner food, and more than you should be eating. Out there in the fresh air and salt water, somehow you get a massive appetite. The *Heritage* does most of its own cooking and baking, even bread, on a wood stove. One night we have fresh fish, the next roast beef, the next chicken. Plenty of soups and chowders. You can help make the ice cream with an old fashioned hand crank.

"End of September and October, you never know what you're going to get for weather. You bring winter clothes and long underwear to be safe. Last year it was blowing like crazy. We had strong winds every day of the trip.

"I try to go four times a year if I can. I just enjoy getting away from the work, the news. It's a lovely vacation. Half their business, I'd guess, is from repeaters, or friends of satisfied customers."

MAINE WINDJAMMER ASSOCIATION, PO Box 317, Rockport, ME 04856, (800) 624-6380 or (207) 374-5400. Inexpensive.

CLUB VOYAGES
Cruise to Turkey

"I went to Turkey with Club Voyages. It may have been the best vacation I've ever taken, and I've done a lot of traveling in my life." Dot, 53, is a skier and a pilot, and she sails regularly, often with a large group from New Jersey, where she is an engineer.

"Just about everything was taken care of for us. The trip included transportation, travel in Turkey, touring with local guides, chartering and sailing four boats. There were about 21 of us from all over; some didn't even know how to sail. We had several get-togethers prior to the trip, so we at least knew each other's names before we left.

"We flew to Istanbul, where we stayed in a small hotel in a nice section of the city. We spent several days there sightseeing before traveling to Marmaris where we got our boats: a 36- and a 45-foot Beneteau. I was on the smaller boat with a group of five. We sailed east quite a distance and ended up back in Marmaris. There's so much ancient history in Turkey; Roman ruins along the coast, tombs carved out of sheer cliffs that look like cathedrals, an island with walks covered with flowers and vines.

"We dined out more than we ate on the boats. The definition of "restaurants" was pretty broad along the remote coasts, where the refrigerators are outside, and goats and sheep wander around where you're sitting. The Turkish co-owner of Club Voyages was with us for the whole trip. Of course, he speaks the language, which was so helpful, and he had lots of contacts, so he knew where to moor, whom to call, what to do.

"We all took turns at the helm, but the most skilled person, the one who can fix the engine if something goes wrong, had final say if there was any dissension. In September, the weather was absolutely perfect, about 75 to 85 degrees every day with bright sun and no rain. This was a stunning trip."

CLUB VOYAGES, PO Box 7648, Shrewsbury, NJ 07702, (908) 842-4946. Expensive.

 ## Other Cruising Choices _____

The Danish Brigantine, *Soren Larsen*, carries 30 hardworking passengers, 6,750 square feet of sail, and windsurfing boards on her voyages from New Zealand to Tahiti, the Cook Islands, Somoa, Tonga, Fiji, and Australia. These are hands-on cruises with all passengers standing watch, hauling sails and cooking.

ADVENTURE CENTER, 1311 63rd Street, Emeryville, CA 94608, (415) 654-1879. Moderate.

The *Stephanie Anne*, a 65-foot sailing yacht with five double cabins and some single spaces available, takes a leisurely Saturday-to-Friday cruise between Ketchikan and Juneau, during which grizzlies, whales and glaciers can be observed at close range.

BENDIXEN YACHT CRUISES, c/o Adventure Guides, Inc,
36 East 57th Street, New York, NY 10022, (800) 252-7899 or
(212) 355-6334. Very Expensive.

The 360-foot bark *Sea Cloud* is a very tall ship indeed
and an elegant exception to the no-single-stateroom-on-sail-
ing-ships rule. The size and position of the staterooms, which
include six singles, determines the price aboard one of the
largest and most luxurious private sailing yachts ever built.

THE CRUISE COMPANY, 33 Lewis Street, Greenwich, CT
06830, (800) 825-0826 or (203) 622-0203. Very Expensive.

The 30-passenger *Sir Francis Drake* offers 3-night US
Virgin Island voyages as well as longer cruises through the
British Virgin Islands. They do have a share program. A number of singles are attracted to the poshly-refitted three-masted
schooner because of the short length of its trips.

TALL SHIP ADVENTURES, 1010 South Joliet Street, Aurora,
CO 80012, (800) 662-0090 or (303) 341-0335. Expensive to
Very Expensive.

Old-fashioned but brand new, two 180-passenger Star Clippers have recently taken to the seas. Touted as the tallest clipper
ships ever, the four-masted *Star Clipper* and her sister ship, the
Star Flyer, each 360 feet long and 226 feet tall, will winter in the
Caribbean and cruise the Mediterranean in summer.

STAR CLIPPERS, 2833 Bird Avenue, Miami, FL 33133, (800)
442-0551. Moderate to Expensive.

The 105-foot *Cuan Law* and 95-foot *Lammer Law*,
owned by the Trimarine Boat Co., are billed as the "World's
largest and most luxurious Trimarans." The astonishing, 42-
foot-wide upper decks look like city plazas. Both ships are
outfitted for snorkeling and for diving with air compressors,
tanks, and weight belts. The *Cuan Law* cruises the Virgin
Islands (see SCUBA DIVING) while the *Lammer Law* heads to
the Galapagos with two naturalists from the Darwin Station
on board from its new home port of San Cristobal, Ecuador.

TRIMARINE BOAT CO., PO Box 4065, St. Thomas, US Virgin Islands 00803, (809) 494-2490. Expensive.

 ## Sailing Cruise Reservations _____

DIRIGO CRUISES, 39 Waterside Lane, Clinton, CT 96413, (203) 669-7068. Represents windjammers that sail out of various East Coast harbors as well as out of ports around the globe.

THE MAINE WINDJAMMER ASSOCIATION, PO Box 317, Rockport, ME 04856, (800) 624-6380 or (207) 374-5400. Represents 12 tall ships that depart from the mid-coast towns of Rockland, Rockport and Camden, Maine.

WINDJAMMER BAREFOOT CRUISES, PO Box 120, Miami Beach, FL 33119-0120, (800) 327-2601 or (305) 534-7447. Sails six, refitted private yachts and the supply ship *Amazing Grace* throughout the Bahamas and the Caribbean.

Bibliography

Sailing's big three, *Yachting*, *Sail* and *Cruising World*, carry yacht charter and sailing school ads in the back of the book. The uniform and detailed listings published in the August (winter destinations) and March (summer destinations) issues of *Cruising World* are especially easy to use.

Riding the
Rails

 Take a train when tired of life in the fast lane, or when a change of scenery is needed. Clacking through the shifting landscape is soothing and restorative, the other passengers endlessly diverse.

Solos traveling to Florida, Chicago or Atlanta on Amtrak can book "Single Slumbers," small roomettes with a chair that converts into a berth. Otherwise, overnighting solitaries who don't travel coach pay the two-person rate for an Economy, Family or Deluxe Bedroom in addition to the basic Amtrak fare.

Amtrak berths are in short supply. Book sleeping accommodations well in advance.

The "All Aboard America" plan (800-872-7245), our domestic equivalent to the "Eurail" pass, offers the cheapest rates. Amtrak divides the US into Eastern, Central and Western regions and issues tickets good for one, two or all three regions that allow three stops, unlimited travel, and are good for 45 days.

VIA Rail Canada (800-361-3677 from the US) issues two types of 30-day passes: an Eastern Pass and a system-wide Canrailpass.

Pricing: *The nature of the trips in this chapter makes it impossible to compare prices accurately. Contact the information and reservations services listed for up-to-date train fares.*

AMERICAN-EUROPEAN EXPRESS and SOUTHWESTERN CHIEF

"Oh, you won't need anything to read on board this trip," advised a vivacious hostess as a passenger pondered buying a magazine before the American-European Express left New York. She was right. When you're not gourmandizing in the Zurich, the Wagon-Lits-style dining car, you're socializing in the cushy Bay Club car, a rolling Algonquin Bar.

For me, a trip to Santa Fe is cause for celebration. Hence the train. The jaunt would be one part historic, along the Santa Fe Trail between Chicago and Lamy, New Mexico on the Southwestern Chief, and one part grand luxe, on the American-European Express between New York and Chicago.

The Orient Express-inspired American-European Express —four rehabilitated 1920s coaches appended to Amtrak's Broadway Limited—pulled out of New York's Penn Station about 2:25 pm with 14 passengers on board. (Three American-European Express locomotives have since begun service and, following the route of Amtrak's Cardinal, the enlarged 10-car train now takes 25, instead of 16, hours between New York and Chicago.) The luxurious art deco interior of the club car banished any tentative quibbles I might have had about my packing crate of a sleeping compartment with its tiny powder room and blue upholstered chair in Istanbul. In the Bay Club car, surrounded by leather walls, faux marble, ebony and brass, barmen served champagne in crystal flutes to nattily-dressed passengers.

A Haydn concerto and the house champagne blurred industrial New Jersey. We passed through Philadelphia in a haze of Earl Grey tea and warm blueberry scones. A cocktail party atmosphere prevailed as we glided through fertile Lancaster County. By 7:15 pm we were seated at tables for two or leather banquettes for four in Zurich, the most luxurious train car of all.

Oil paintings, designer floral arrangements, and lots of silver plate accessorized "one of the ten best restaurants in America." The food is good, but this was not Lutece. Of seven courses, only the tenderly-grilled tuna on angel hair pasta and the pate au choux-encased custard and fresh fruit dessert were outstanding.

Darkness fell during the tenderloin of beef; the somber Alleghenies gave way to the bright lights of industrial Pennsylvania as we returned to the club car to sing. Rolling through Pittsburgh at midnight the Kansas City patriarch and his writer son, several Philadelphia couples, a New Yorker and a pair of beaming honeymooners chorused "Bye Bye Blackbird."

Twenty-four hours after a deferential Express waiter served a breakfast of baked-on-board croissants, baby lamb chops, buttery spinach, and a chocolate mousse-filled ganache, a harried gent in a brown apron slapped down three microwaved pancakes on a formica table aboard the Southwest Chief.

My "Economy Bedroom" on the top level of the silvery Chief made the small American-European Express compartment seem like a suite. Once the two orangey chairs had been converted into a bed, there were two choices: dress in the aisle under cover of a door curtain, or wriggle into night clothes on top of the bunk. A trip to the bathroom meant descending a curved staircase to the lower deck. To be sure, comparing the utilitarian Southwest Chief with the elegant American-European Express is grossly unfair. My bedroom and three meals cost $298 for the 22-hour trip between Chicago and Lamy, New Mexico, while the 16-hour New York to Chicago party was a hefty $625.

However, what is lost in luxe aboard the Southwestern Chief, is gained in scenery. Sometime after breakfast, the flat Colorado scrublands give way to the pine-crested hills rising to 7,500-foot Raton Pass. The big moveable chairs in the Sightseer Lounge Car, jammed with movie-watching teenagers the night before, fill up again as the 12-car Chief slows to a 25-mph crawl. Over the intercom, the conductor exhorts passengers to look sharp for beavers and black bears.

To travel slowly across flat-topped mesas beneath assertive Western skies is reason enough to take the train. The super-stylish American-European Express and the all-american Chief with its three sit-up cars packed, in August, with families and kids, is each, in its own way, satisfying. Connecting with other passengers on either leg of the trip was easy. The leisurely transition from lush Eastern seaboard to the red earth, pinon and sage of New Mexico is the engrossing focus of the restful cross-Continental journey.

AMERICAN-EUROPEAN EXPRESS, 329 West 18th Street, Suite 402, Chicago, IL 60616, (800) 677-4233 or (312) 226-5633.

AMTRAK, (800) 872-7245. For Canadian trains, (800) 361-3677.

 *Other Voices* _____

RAILFLITE

"I've taken many trains in my time, but it's just incredible to ride in a private car, nothing like it," exclaims Tim, 59, a school principal in Salt Lake City, UT who, fulfilling a fantasy, took Railflite's two leased private cars that run between Denver and Salt Lake twice weekly in winter. Hooked onto Amtrak, Tim rolled along three times.

"First trip, I took Amtrak to Denver, spent the night, and came back in the Kansas, the private car of the owner of the Rio Grande & Southern Pacific. This is a typical corporate car from the fifties, with a rear platform and dining facilities. It sleeps about eight. We had a meal, served in the grand manner in the dining car, that lasted about 200 miles. I could barely get off in Salt Lake. It was absolutely stupendous.

"I also rode the Caritas from Salt Lake to Denver. It's kind of art deco and sleeps eight to ten. Wonderful meals. I spent every minute of that ride on the rear platform taking pictures. It's just you and the scenery; extraordinary mountain drop-offs and foliage. The trip takes about 14 hours, starting out about 7:00 am after spending the night in a hotel in Salt Lake, and arriving about 9:00 pm in Denver.

"The third time, I flew to Denver and was met by a chauffeur driving a stretch limo. I spent the night in the restored Alexis hotel. Next morning I got on the private car. This time the pictures were even better because in the early morning hours the Front Range of the Rockies looks especially good.

"Step on the rear platform of a private car and it does wonders for your self-esteem. Makes you feel like a Vanderbilt."

RAILFLITE, 2144 South 1100 East, Suite 150, Salt Lake City, UT 84106, (801) 583-4544. The 14-hour trip between Salt Lake City and Denver includes a night in a Salt Lake City hotel, breakfast, lunch, dinner, and drinks aboard the train, and a night in Denver at the Oxford Alexis Hotel. Because of the length of the ride, Railflite recommends a one-way trip, but round trips can also be arranged for slightly less than double the one-way fare.

MONTREALER

"I raised the shade at about 6:00 am, and there before me were the mountains of Vermont. The sun was barely starting to come through the mist brewing around the edges of the mountains. I lay there half asleep feeling like a princess going up the Nile." A New Yorker, 38, who administers a non-profit foundation, Rosamund says she's afraid to fly, so she's always looking for "a way to go someplace interesting, something a little different.

"You board the train in Penn Station for an 8:15 pm departure. A porter shows you how everything works in your roomette. You have your own toilet with a pull-down sink, individually controlled air-conditioning and heat control, a mirror with lights around it for makeup, and a full-length mirror behind the door. If you want to hear what's going on, you can leave the door open but zip up the heavy curtain for privacy. Otherwise, it was quite silent but for the soothing sound of the tracks.

"Dinner is served from boarding until about 9:30 pm on trays at pre-set tables in the dining car. It was airline style, but better, and the car was well maintained. Since I was alone, I had others at my table. There was also a smokey Pub Car, where you can listen to the piano player until about 1:00 am.

"I went back to the very comfortable seat in my roomette and experimented with the furnishings there. When you pull down your bed, the lounge chair collapses, and the bathroom is no longer accessible. There are bathrooms in the hall, however. The bed was firm and very comfortable. I'm not sure about how it would suit a 6-foot man.

"A porter wakes you in the morning, if you want, and brings you coffee. At 8:15 am the Canadian customs officials come aboard, and they want you sitting upright in your chair. After that you can dawdle over breakfast in the dining car. Arrival is at about 10:45.

"I spent the day in the Montreal Botanical Gardens and took an afternoon train to Quebec, about a 3 1/2 hour trip. A very pleasant ride but awful food. After two days in Quebec, I returned to Montreal for the train to New York, leaving at 5:15 pm and arriving rested, at Penn Station, at 7:00 am."

MONTREALER Reservations and Information:call Amtrak, (800) 872-7245. A roomette (sleeps one person) costs extra, and includes all meals. There are no Economy or Deluxe Bedrooms on the New York-to-Montreal run.

CALIFORNIA ZEPHYR

"Trains are a wonderful way to travel alone. People are very congenial. You don't ever have to be alone if you don't want to be. You're always seated with other people in the dining car. It's not cheap travel, so you meet some very interesting people in those roomettes and dining cars." Bobbi, 40, writes a newsletter in California. She's clearly a train travel maven.

"The best train trip I ever took was on Amtrak from Sacramento to Denver, the California Zephyr. Beautiful. You climb out of Sacramento from an old railroad station. The track snakes through the Sierras on the route of the old Central Pacific; you know, where they went to drive the golden spike. You can see Donner Lake and Donner Pass.

"The train stops in Reno, and I stayed overnight at the Union Hotel, and reboarded another Zephyr the next day. The rest of Nevada is pretty grim, but just outside Salt Lake, you start climbing into the Rockies. The track follows the Colorado River and comes out at Winter Park, which is the top of the Rockies at that point. Then you snake into Denver. It's an overnight ride. Going west, you'd leave Denver mid-morning and see the Rockies in the morning sun. Either way, you see the best scenery during the day.

"I like the Economy Bedrooms. They've got two big lounge chairs, with a table in between, that turn into a two-berth sleeping area. You have to leave the room to go the john. The Deluxe Bedrooms are harder to get and much more expensive, but they have johns and showers. For just one night, a roomette is fine.

"Meals are included in your sleeping-car ticket and you eat primarily with other first-class passengers. Even in the observation car, people are congenial. I've been on trains that were hours late arriving, and it was amazing how good-humored people were, as long as the booze holds out. You go for the scenery, and if you go slower, you see more."

CALIFORNIA ZEPHYR Reservations and Information: call Amtrak, (800) 872-7245. This train offers seats for the Basic Rail Fare; Economy and Deluxe bedrooms are available.

PIONEER, COAST STARLIGHT, and DESERT WIND

"I've ridden thousands of miles on Amtrak, and the Denver-to-Salt Lake City-run takes the cake," says Tim, the rail travel buff from Salt Lake, who described the Railflite train above. Asked about his other favorites, Tim described a rail trip from Denver to the Pacific coast and back to Salt Lake.

"Coming in second for scenery is the Pioneer from Salt Lake to Seattle. You leave about midnight and have all the next day to admire the Blue Mountains and a 160-mile stretch along the Columbia River before getting in about 8:00 or 9:00 pm. It's a gorgeous trip.

"From Seattle, take the Coast Starlight to Los Angeles, through the Cascade Mountains, past Oregon's rivers, the forests in northern California and, best of all, the Pacific stretch between San Luis Obispo and Oxnard. Then from Los Angeles, take the Desert Wind back to Salt Lake. That's really a nice trip, and you can jump off the train in Las Vegas and gamble if you want. There's spectacular scenery on this trip too.

"Get an Economy Bedroom; they're not expensive. They give you a little hospitality kit, and the fare includes all your meals, served in the dining car. The trick is to reserve early, because Amtrak's awfully short of sleepers. You almost have to plan a year ahead.

"Trains out west have a sightseeing lounge. If you want privacy you can look out the window in your bedroom, but if you want to meet people and socialize at the bar, you go to the lounge. On Amtrak, you pay according to the number of regions you pass through, so you can just pay one flat rate for your ticket and all your meals at the beginning. West of Denver is all one zone, making this trip a definite bargain."

PIONEER, COAST STARLIGHT, DESERT WIND Reservations and Information: call Amtrak, (800) 872-7245. Call for current fares and information.

 ## Other Rails Choices

The Alaska Railroad is state-owned, and meticulously maintained. The 8-hour Fairbanks to Anchorage journey is a day run, as are most of the journeys mentioned below. Usually, passengers disembark at Denali National Park, to sightsee and spend the night, before completing their trip.. For a posher ride, book a seat in one of the four dome cars the Gray Line attaches to the Alaska Railroad train.

THE ALASKA RAILROAD, PO Box 10750, Anchorage, AK 99510, (800) 544-0552 or (907) 265-2494. Tour packages also available. Reservations are required for the Fairbanks-Anchorage leg.

GRAY LINE ALASKA, 300 Eliot Avenue, Seattle, WA, 98119, (800) 544-2206. The train trip includes a one night stopover in Denali National Park, a 6- to 8-hour wilderness tour, and lunch.

While the popular Canadian, Canada's trans-continental express, no longer crosses the country on Canadian Pacific tracks, you can still journey from Toronto to Vancouver three times a week. The complete, 2,800-mile run takes 5 days and leaves the Great Lakes to cross the wheatlands west of Winnipeg before traversing the glorious Canadian Rockies. *VIA RAIL, (800) 361-3677.*

The Chihuahua al Pacifio railroad traverses the Sierra Madre Mountains in northern Mexico at altitudes averaging 6,500 feet. The 12-hour Copper Canyon trip between Los Mochis and Chihuahua is considered one of the world's great train rides. To better savor the scenery, most passengers break up the trip, overnighting in local lodges.

MEXICO BY RAIL, PO Box 3508, Laredo, TX, 78044-3508, (800) 228-3225.

COLUMBUS TRAVEL, 6017 Callaghan Road, San Antonio, TX 78228, (800) 225-2829 or (512) 523-1400.

 ## Reservations Services _____

AMTRAK sells hotel packages, tour packages and combination trips as well as train tickets. To request *Amtrak's America*, a clearly-written and useful catalog of Amtrak's trains, routes and packages, call (800) 872-7245.

VIA RAIL (800) 361-3677, and BREWSTER TRANSPORTATION AND TOURS, (800) 661-1152, offer train tours in Canada.

Bibliography

Rail Ventures ($12.95, Wayfinder Press, Ouray, CO, 1990) logs the routes of North American trains, hour by hour, mile by mile.

Learning a Foreign Language

The administrators of language schools, and the reservations services that book them, are unanimous: most students attending foreign language programs go by themselves. This isn't to say that language schools are fertile hunting grounds for singles. I'd estimate that 60% to 70% of the students at the Institut de Francais session I attended were married, but out of 72 students, only a dozen enrolled in pairs.

US colleges and universities sponsor about two-thirds of the summer language programs, both here and abroad. Several have campuses overseas, others have ties with a specific foreign university. Most people attending these programs, even in summer, do so for credit. The avocational rest of us life-long learners are more likely to congregate in the private language schools.

Students probably learn more but see less of their peers when boarding with a family. Comfy apartments and gourmet meals generally appeal more to older adults (who can afford them) than the gregarious life on university campuses where meals are in cafeterias and bedrooms are in dorms.

Seldom is a surcharge levied for a single dorm room or a room with a family. Count on paying extra however, for single accommodations arranged by most of the private schools.

Pricing: *The nature of the programs listed in this chapter makes it impossible to compare prices accurately. Contact the schools and organizations directly for up-to-date tuition and accommodation information.*

INSTITUT DE FRANCAIS
Villefranche-sur-Mer, France

"Guun-taire" enunciated Jean Pierre, leaning forward and interrupting a German in mid-conjugation. *"Répétez le verb être, s'il vous plaît."* On the second of 20 days spent at the Institut de Francais on the Cote d'Azur, the industrialist ran through *"etre"* again. One by one, the nine other rank beginners in Debuntante I took their turn. Outside the beige stucco walls a *merle* (blackbird) sang, and through half-closed shutters, we caught a splash of *Dufy* (blue).

The Institut de Francais, located on a lush Mediterranean hillside in Villefranche-sur-Mer, has been teaching French to foreigners since 1969. I was delighted, at the month-long June session, by the ambiance as well as the teaching method, and by my 72 fellow students, a mix of diplomats, college freshmen, CEOs, secretaries, and the idle rich from 20 nations. While learning French was the prime objective, at least among the over-30 set, socializing on trips, at banquets, and at parties was part of the experience.

The institute is a find for the linguistically inclined. It is also well worth a detour for solos with the time, interest and fortitude to immerse themselves in French. To quote a New York stage director and fellow student, "The Institut is far and away the best of the five language schools I've attended in Europe."

Certainly, there was no disputing the school's physical charms. The exuberant, terraced gardens and the five-star Mediterranean view, encountered at first arrival, are striking. It's also impossible not to notice the creamy, arched and tiled villa, which retains its fifties elegance despite the classrooms tucked into terra cotta-roofed cottages about the grounds. But it is on the teaching method and uniformly excellent instructors that the institute's renown rests.

"We have the best teachers and the best program in France" Mme. Pignon, the *Directrice*, had said in her opening remarks. By graduation, few had reason to question her statement. Little is left to chance. One or two more men than women are admitted to each session. Enrollment can be no more than 20% American or 20% German. There's a limit on under-25-year-olds, and over-65-year-olds, and in summer, a limit on teachers. The institute is, in fact, run with almost military precision, against which most of the (highly sophisticated) 17- to 70-year-old students occasionally chaffed. Ultimately, however, the rigid structure proved to be effective and efficient. Take the school's orientation procedure as an example.

We arrived at the manorial wooden doors Monday at 8:30 am. *Et voilà*, at 1:30 pm, lessons began. In the intervening 5 hours we had taken written and oral placement tests, registered and paid the balance of our tuition, and been driven to our various apartments and back to receive our class placements during a filling, three-course lunch. Having dispatched *soupe au Pistou* and *chicken a l'Orange*, the *specialités du jour*, we straggled out onto the gravel terrace. Sleek motor yachts lay anchored in the harbor far below the olive trees and the villas trickling down the hillside. No dawdling. Students are allotted an hour's worth of "pauses" per day, but none after lunch.

Debutante I filed down stone steps to the neat, tiled classroom that would be the center of its universe for the next 4 weeks. There in the *Petit Salon*, behind the slide projector, sat the kind, diligent and talented teacher. Eight professors rotate between the institute's eight classes, Debutante I through Advance II, from May through October. (November through April there are only six classes).

We knew little about each other until a couple of weeks into the session. For many beginners, conversation was pretty much limited to sign language and grunts; students are required to speak French on the school grounds. How we envied the ease with which only those in the more advanced groups stood around making friends and conversing in French!

Monday through Friday, from 9:00 am to 4:45 pm, we struggled. Some of the older students had to learn how to learn all over again. Finally, by the third week of incessant, audio-visual drills, language lab and homework, as well as guessing games under the garden arbors and teacher-led lunch conversations, the French started seeping in.

Most students had apartment mates. The school controls some 35 rooms and apartments in Villefranche and takes great pride in match-making. Anne, a museum curator from Norway, and I shared a plain but roomy and immaculate two bedroom apartment with a balcony facing across the harbor to Cap Ferrat and, exceptionally, a television. We honed our French on the French Open Tennis Championships, on movies and, over croissants and morning cafe au lait, and the daily news.

Breezy, 80- to 85-degree June days eased the 10-minute perpendicular climb to the school and encouraged sightseeing. The institute, following a standard, 4-week session script, hosted a welcome sangria bash, a bistro dinner and a Saturday outing to Antibes, Vence and Tourette sur Loup. For many, the intense, 8-hour school day precluded more ambitious trips. Weekends, students tanned at Cap Ferrat and on local Villefranche beaches.

Nice, with its colorful Cours Salaya markets and vibrant Old Town webbed with dark, narrow streets, was only 10 minutes away. A car was an asset, but not a necessity. Students hopped the yellow Nice-Menton bus to Monaco and Nice. After hours, they used the ubiquitous Mercedes taxis.

Genteel, sun-washed Villefranche, with its own small but inviting Vieille Ville, was a pretty place to live—as long as you kept a hand on your wallet and the shutters locked. Petty thievery is commonplace.

Exhausted after a good-bye gala, several of us spent our last warm and enveloping night in a harborside pizzeria. As the clock in the 17th century bell tower struck 11:00, we wondered if we would be among the 10% who returned to the Institut de Francais. *Absolutment*, said three of the group before saying goodnight and walking back up the Old Town's stone steps to pack.

INSTITUT DE FRANCAIS, 23 Avenue General Leclerc, 06230 Villefranche-sur-Mer, France, 011-33-93-01-88-44.

Other Voices _____

LANGUAGE OUTREACH
Dartmouth College, Hanover, New Hampshire

"I'm your basic language-learner freak. I don't take classes just to brush up before going overseas." Donna is, in fact, a linguist *and* a world traveler. She studied Italian at two, 10-day summer sessions at Language Outreach run by John Rassias, a Dartmouth professor, on the Dartmouth College campus.

"Rassias is effective and affectionate. His method of teaching is non-traditional and encouraging. Naturally, you have to learn vocabulary and verbs and drills, but you do it through games and skits. He has several Dartmouth students who have studied abroad working as assistants in the courses, and his spirit is contagious.

"They teach six languages, including English as a second language.... On arrival you take a placement exam. Eight of us were assigned to advanced Italian, 12 to 15 were in the beginning Italian class. Each language group eats meals together, speaking only their language. You have about an hour after lunch to do as you wish. Then, after dinner at night we played games and had talent shows.

"We lived in the Dartmouth dorms where each language had it's own floor, and we tried to speak our language all the time. The first year I was assigned a roommate, blind. We became friends quickly and we're still friends. The dorms are organized in suites with bedrooms off a common study area and bath. They were very comfortable, but the second year I got a room of my own.

"These are very intense courses. You're immersed in the language, which is really the only way to learn, and it's frustrating. My roommate and I *made* ourselves speak Italian the whole time, which is tiring, and there are always people who speak better than you. So at meals, where seating is up to you, you can either really reach to keep up, or find someone less skilled than you to speak with. I really enjoyed it."

LANGUAGE OUTREACH, Wentworth Hall, Dartmouth College, Hanover, NH 03755, (603) 646-2922. The 10-day intensive courses in French, Japanese, Italian, Chinese, German, Modern Greek, Russian, Spanish, and American Sign are held during June and July.

NATIONAL REGISTRATION CENTER FOR STUDIES ABROAD
Quito, Ecuador Program

"I've had good experiences at all the schools I've attended through NRCSA. The Cemanahuac School in Mexico was fine, but the one I went to in Ecuador is probably the best," says Paul. He's a Spanish teacher, age 46, in Danville, Illinois, who hones his skills by taking courses in Latin America through the National Registration Center for Studies Abroad. Paul describes a school in Quito, Ecuador, where he took two, 2-week sessions.

"Lots of Europeans, especially Swiss, study at the Academia de Espanol in Quito. Out of 25 to 30 students, very few were Americans, either time. Every student has his own Ecuadorian instructor, but you have two program choices: you can take the concentrated, 7-hour-a-day *Intensiva* program or the *Activa* program courses in the morning and cultural outings in the afternoon. Classes are held one-on-one in little cubicles in the Academia's new building.

"There's a break for lunch, when you can eat at the school if you want. That's your opportunity to meet the other students. The Academia arranges your family stay, but my family lived too far away for lunch. They do a wonderful job with the families. You can do whatever you want, be as active socially as you like.

"I'd classify the teachers as serious, although you could joke around with a few of them. The school made arrangements for you to attend festivals and craft fairs and the like. The teachers organized an event for the whole school once a week: a party, a dance, a soccer game with teachers and administrators against the students.

"There's nothing I would have changed about the experience."

NATIONAL REGISTRATION CENTER FOR STUDIES ABROAD, PO Box 1393, Milwaukee, WI 53201, (414) 278-0631. The 1-week Activa program is held at the Academia de Espanol; the 4-week Intensiva program fee includes tuition and room and board with a Quito family.

LA FERME
Bordeaux, France

"I really solidified my subjunctive. The only trouble was that I spent the third week traveling around France, and I froze, couldn't speak a word. I think that's classic. Had I stayed a third week at the school, and traveled the fourth week, I would have been fine," recalls 51-year-old Betty, a French teacher from Maine. She attended La Ferme, an intimate French language school 2 hours north of Bordeaux.

"Mireille, who's French, and her husband, Farrar Richardson, an American, run this program. Farrar's the cook, the accountant, the guy who holds it together. Mireille runs the school, and she's extremely competent.

"Five to 14 students arrive on a Sunday night. The Richardsons show you to your white stucco room with a simple bedstead, nightstand and wonderful ceiling beams in the farmhouse. Below us was the large classroom.

"After drinks and hors d'oeuvres, you have dinner with your classmates. Of course, you're speaking French.

"You're up around 8:00 am for breakfast, in French again. You discuss the day's news, world events, whatever. I was in a group with two other students, but sometimes you get to work one-on-one. The professor talks to you, asks you questions. Then you get into grammar and the skills. The excellent workbooks Mireille wrote are the best composite grammars I've seen. Everyone meets in the kitchen for coffee at 11:00. Again you're speaking French. Then it's back to work till lunch at 1:00. By the time lunch is over at 2:30, you're too exhausted from working so hard to communicate.

"Dinner is from 8:00 to about 10:00 pm. The food was simple but very good. Farrar accommodated my vegetarianism very nicely. You get to know the Richardsons and your fellow students quite well.

"Weekends are very quiet. The closest town is a 20-minute walk, and there's nothing to see or do there. La Ferme is in the country, a tranquil, very nice place to be. I liked the other students; Americans mostly, a German, a Swede, an Indian, most of them working in France. We had a computer expert, and a wine importer from California. Fascinating people."

LA FERME, c/o H. Robertson, 73-450 Country Club Drive, #291, Palm Desert, CA 92260, (619) 568-6773. In addition to the standard 2-week course, more costly, "Super-Intensive" courses are also offered.

THE FRENCH SCHOOL
Middlebury College, Middlebury, Vermont

"It's hysterical watching all these Americans running around the soccer field, speaking Arabic, Russian, Chinese." This polyglot soccer game was part of the otherwise *tres serieux* (very serious) French School held each summer on Middlebury College's Vermont campus. The participant was 26-year-old Susan, an American publicist for French hotels.

"Soccer is a big deal. Each language has its own team; when you play another country, which you do once a week, you're not allowed to speak any language but the one you're studying. In fact, the only time you are allowed to speak English during the entire 7 weeks is on the first day. The year I was there three people were kicked out for speaking English. It's very strict.

"But it's wonderful. You're in a dorm with just your language group, 130 in the French dorm my year, and the dorms are broken down by ability levels, so everyone on your floor speaks at about the same level. It's difficult, but you're all in it together. You eat with your professors, who are mostly French. They come to Middlebury with their families as a sort of vacation.

"The coursework is fairly regimented. Placement exams are written and oral. I enrolled as an intermediate student and after a week realized it was too easy. I approached the Dean about getting into the master's program, and he said, 'By all means, take the test.' So I skipped a year. They really do pay attention to your needs.

"I've never seen such formidable language labs and facilities. Middlebury offers foreign films frequently, and they have theater and choir singing. You can attend as many events in your own language, or others, as you want. I took a fabulous theater course: I was forced to speak spontaneously, to recite in French, to memorize. The deans and the instructors are excellent. In fact, everything about this program is tops.

"Students must be college graduates. One woman in my class was 78. You'll see Japanese teachers there learning French or a German student learning Russian, but the students are mostly Americans studying French or Spanish, and almost all of them are teachers. You develop friends based on your language ability...."

THE FRENCH SCHOOL, Middlebury College, Middlebury, VT (802) 388-3711. Fees for a 7-week, total immersion program in any one of eight different languages include room and board.

 ## Other Language Choices _____

The American Institute for Foreign Study (AIFS) specializes in academic programs for US college students abroad, but adults also enroll in their programs, especially the language classes offered in the summer. This year AIFS celebrates *glasnost* with intensive, 4-week Russian language courses at Leningrad Polytechnic, and the fall of the wall with 4 weeks of German classes at Karl Marx's alma mater, Humboldt University in East Berlin.

AMERICAN INSTITUTE FOR FOREIGN STUDY, 102 Greenwich Avenue, Greenwich, CT 06830, (203) 869-9090.

Students at the Centro Di Cultura Italiana Casentino benefit from the school's location in the little Tuscan hill town of Poppi. From April through October, the school's an integral part of the medieval hamlet's life. Five nights a week, school members dine communally at the Ristorante

Casentino. During the day, 30 students maximum—the majority of them German speakers (the rest mainly American and Brits)—take Elementary, Intermediate and Advanced Italian classes at the Centro, often enrolling in two, 2-week sessions, back-to-back.

CENTRO DI CULTURA ITALIANA CASENTINO, c/o Stephen Casale, One University Place, Apartment 17-R, New York, NY 10003, (212) 228-9273. The fee for the 4-week session includes tuition, meals and sightseeing.

High school and college students work, study and travel abroad under the aegis of the Council on International Education, a non-profit organization with 32 offices in the United States and 8 locations (6 of them in France) abroad. Adults also take advantage of the 45-year-old Council's services, especially their charter flights and their Eurocentre reservations service. Eurocentre offers classes at 22 locations in Spain, France, Italy, and Switzerland. There is a choice of "holiday" (morning only) or "intensive" (morning and afternoon) courses, and homestays are arranged for students at all but the Paris Eurocentre school.

COUNCIL ON INTERNATIONAL EDUCATION, Eurocentre Department, 205 East 42nd Street, New York, NY 10017, (212) 661-1414. Tuition, room and board are included in the fees for a 4-week course.

The luxuriant gardens and arched, ivory stucco walls of Mexico's Instituto Allende are characteristic of the town of San Miguel de Allende itself. This Spanish Colonial landmark is also a famous arts colony, and the Instituto is known for its roster of painting and crafts classes as well as for its Spanish classes. A maximum of 8 students are allowed in each of the 5 4-hour, intensive classes. Also offered are 2-hour semi-intensive classes. Lodgings are available in apartments, hotel rooms or quarters with Mexican families.

INSTITUTO ALLENDE, San Miguel de Allende, Gto., 37700 Mexico, 011-52-465-20190.

Since 1982, the United States-China People's Friendship Association, a US organization devoted to the study of Chinese, has run an 8-week summer trip to China incorporating 2 weeks of travel with 6 weeks of language study at the Beijing Language Institute. The course is recommended for students with a smattering of Chinese; not rank beginners. This is an intensely personal program, with a large "people-to-people" component. Spring and Fall courses are also offered.

UNITED STATES-CHINA PEOPLE'S FRIENDSHIP ASSOCIATION, 50 Oak Street, Room 502, San Francisco CA 94102, (415) 863-0537. The 8-week program includes tuition, all travel, housing, and a stipend for meals.

If French, German, Italian, or Spanish is your goal, you have four highly reputable but bargain-priced institutions to choose from.

The French government helps subsidize the Alliance Francaise, France's cultural presence abroad, as well as the Alliance's language schools in Nice, Cannes, Toulouse, Marseilles, Montpelier, Rouen, and Paris, France. Minimum enrollment is 4 weeks. The Alliance helps to arrange room and board with families in the provinces; in Paris, students eat in the school's cafeteria and stay at Left Bank hotels.

ALLIANCE FRANCAISE, 101 Boulevard Raspail, 75270 Paris, France. 011-33-1-44-38-28.

The Goethe Institute is Germany's answer to the Alliance Francaise. This government-supported cultural network underwrites language schools for foreigners. The 8-week compact program is *pro forma*, but 4-week refresher courses are currently offered at 3 of the Institute's 13 locations in Germany's western half.

GOETHE INSTITUTE, 666 Third Avenue, New York, NY 10028, (212) 972-3960.

Many, many American students interested in learning Italian have studied at the Universita Italiana Per Stranieri in Perugia where courses last a minimum of one month.

UNIVERSITA ITALIANA PER STRANIERI, Palazzo Gallenga, 4 piazza, Fortebraccio, 06100, Perugia, Italy, 011-39-75-64344. Room and board, which can be arranged at the University's housing office, is separate from tuition.

Salamanca, home of Spain's oldest university and the small, distinctive private school called Salminter, for Escuela Salmantina de Estudios Internacionales, attracts hordes of foreign students year round.

SALMINTER, 34-35 Calle Tono, 37002 Salamanca, Spain, 023-211-8089. Program fees include tuition and room and board with a family for the 4-hour-a-day course. (The University of Rhode Island's month-long Summer Program at Salamanca, (401) 792-4717, includes a room, 3 meals, 3 excursions, cultural activities, and 6 hours of classes a day).

 ## Language School Reservations Services

THE NATIONAL REGISTRATION CENTER FOR STUDY ABROAD, PO Box 1393, Milwaukee, WI 53201, (414) 278-0631. In 1990 some 35,000 students enrolled in over 800 programs offered by the center.

FOREIGN LANGUAGE/STUDY ABROAD PROGRAMS, Box 5409, Grand Central Station, New York, NY 10163, (212) 662-1090. Represents a "Foreign Home Stay" program as well as traditional language schools abroad.

LANGUAGE STUDIES ENROLLMENT CENTER, PO Box 5095, Anaheim, CA 92814, (714) 527-2918. Concentrates on schools in Central America.

Contact the CULTURAL AFFAIRS section of a foreign embassy or consulate for information about a specific country's language schools, the Cultural Office of the Spanish Embassy, 2600 Virginia Avenue, Washington, DC 20037; the Italian Cultural Institute, 686 Park Avenue, New York, NY 10021; the French Cultural Service, 972 Fifth Avenue, New York, NY 10021. *Work, Study, Travel Abroad*, $10.95, published annually by the Council on International Educational Exchange, 205 East 42nd Street, New York, NY 10017, contains the names and addresses of all the appropriate cultural offices, plus other information of interest to young adults.

Bibliography

Vacation Study Abroad ($26.95 plus $3 postage, Institute of International Education, 809 United Nations Plaza, New York, NY 10017, 1991) describes some 1,400 summer programs, few of which are given for credit.

Cooking

A woman's place may no longer be in the home, but women are more prevalent than men in cooking classes—at least in the more avocationally-oriented schools. Professional, degree-granting institutions are choc-a-block with men. But no matter who attends, cooking classes can be the foundation for a three-star vacation. Burgundy, Tuscany, the Napa Valley, and similar cooking school venues are great for sightseeing, too. Many schools plan excursions, festive parties, and forays to top flight restaurants in addition to classes.

Pricing: *The nature of the programs listed in this chapter make it impossible to compare prices accurately. Contact the schools and organizations directly for up-to-date fee information.*

THE GREAT CHEFS AT THE ROBERT MONDAVI WINERY
Oakville, California

A floral map of the Napa Valley blanketed the massive table, and Easter egg-colored balloons bearing tiny gondolas fashioned entirely of minute plants and blossoms floated above the miniature vineyards. The hostess raised a glass of Mondavi Vineyard's 1986 Chardonnay as the participants in the Great Chefs Long Weekend took their seats in the skylit dining room. "Welcome," said Robert Mondavi's articulate and vivacious Swiss wife Margrit Biever, "you are about to experience 3 days of complete fantasy."

The chatelaine of Mondavi's adobe-style headquarters in Oakville, California was good to her word. Daily cooking demonstrations by 35-year-old Jacques Chibois, one of France's culinary stars, produced extraordinary banquets which were served in dream-like settings. With every meal, the dramatic decor had, as if by magic, entirely changed.

These indulgent weekends, a more or less quarterly event at the Mondavi Vineyards since 1976, are, according to Great Chef Paula Wolfert, the "creme de la creme" of US cooking classes. Alice Walters, Wolfgang Puck, Paul Bocuse, and the Troisgros have been among the featured chef-teachers.

Making his first appearance in the stainless steel Mondavi teaching kitchen, Jacques Chibois was an inspired and charismatic teacher. With translator Biever at his side, the cherubic, 38-year-old Chibois, Chef of the two-star Royal Grey Albion Hotel in Cannes and a former chef-apprentice of Michele Girard's, chopped, sauteed and baked his way through each of three, 2-hour demonstrations.

We sat in deck chairs facing Chibois and the tilted mirror reflecting the ingredients, pots and his hands, learning technique as each dish progressed. The chef's method of adding seasonings at every step of a recipe created profoundly flavored dishes of great complexity. As produced by the team of four Great Chefs under Chibois' supervision, the creations were the *raison d'être* for the Lucullan repasts that followed.

Chef Chibois, who joined the students at meals, and the astonishing floral decorations, were the stars of this long weekend masterminded by Margrit Biever. Madame took charge with wit and high style the moment we arrived from San Francisco by white Lincoln Continental. The chauffeur for the weekend furnished details about the cooking series during the drive. "Yes" he replied to a question, "singles attend regularly, 99% of them women." After a tour of the winery, participants chatted as they sipped Mondavi's Reserve Chardonnay 1986, a 1986 Puligny Montrachet, and three 1984 wines made mostly from Cabernet Sauvigon, including a $50 Opus One, the product of a joint Mondavi-Rothschild venture. Thus launched, we entered the dining room with its sweeping vineyard view for a welcome lunch prepared by the Vineyard's own talented Great Chefs. On the Steinway, a pianist played *La Vie en Rose*.

Gracious attention to each student's needs has been a Great Chefs hallmark since the program began. Axel Fabre, the program's Director and her crew of Great Chef regulars merit high praise for their implementation of this program, a subtle marketing strategy designed to link Mondavi wines with great food. Students are kept hopping. Even with two limos at our disposal, there was scant time to sightsee or shop. The chauffeurs did little more than shuttle participants between Yountville's Vintage Inn, where we slept, and the Mondavi Vineyard. There, in the Spring-scented California evening, waiters in trim waistcoats waited in front of Buffano's looming statue of St. Francis to escort us into the Saturday night black tie gala.

We were thoroughly familiar with the menu, having watched Chibois prepare each dish during the earlier demonstration. There, he flourished a tray of steamed lobsters, baby string beans, zucchini, greens, and cherry tomatoes for the first course, *Papillon de Homard a la Chiffonade de Mesclun*, then prepared orange, lemon, basil leaves, Adonio olive oil, coriander, and tomatoes for the sauce. A recreated lobster with chive tendrils was greeted with applause. After preparing the fish course, *Le Loup aux Aubergine Douces a la Cannoise d'Olives Noires*, a sunny Mediterranean eggplant and sea bass conceit, Chibois proceeded to the main course, *Filet d'Agneau avec Ses Baluchons et son Gratin*, a lamb, chard and potato composition redolent of Provence. We annotated our folder of printed recipes, sipping water between sauce tastings. This second of three cooking classes featured an intricate dessert, *Le Palmier de Pamplemousse*, or Honey Grapefruit Palm Trees with Coconut Sorbet.

Palmiers, created by Great Chefs' talented floral designers, reached skyward in tribute to Cannes, Chef Chibois' home base. A soprano in mauve taffeta sang as guests circulated in cocktail finery drinking Perrier-Jouet. Our sparse student ranks were complemented by the Mondavi's friends and associates. Saturday night, journalists, wine buyers, Valley restauranteurs, and Mondavi officials took their places at card-designated seats with participants from Sudbury, Ontario; San Francisco; Toronto; Alaska; and New York, as eight waiters marched in bearing Chibois' lobster creation on warm, white plates.

Participants were housed in fireplace rooms at the Vintage Inn, 5 minutes from the winery. A basket of red tulips and a bottle of Mondavi Pinot Noir '86 welcomed me to expansive taupe quarters. Exercise classes were a Saturday morning option. A large pool decorated the grounds, and a series of fountains helped obscure traffic noise from nearby Highway 101.

Passion and excellence in equal measure marked the 2 1/2-day course last April. Oh, not every table decoration matched the inventiveness of that first, balloon-theme luncheon. Not all the wines measured up to Mondavi's 1986 Reserve Chardonnay, nor was every Côte d'Azure-accented Chibois creation on a par with his melting Tuna Tart with Vinaigrette. Still, that gala weekend transcended the mundane. Shorter, less expensive Great Chefs demonstrations are also offered. While the price doesn't include lodging or transportation, you can sample the indulgent Mondavi version of *La Bonne Bouffe*, a truly Lucullan feast.

THE GREAT CHEFS AT THE ROBERT MONDAVI WINERY, PO Box 106, Oakville, CA 94662 (707) 944-2866.

 Other Voices _____

LA VARENNE
Joigny, France

"The chef critiques your work, you have aperitifs and eat your dinner. Then they roll you back up the hill to your room. It's like that for 6 days. You eat and drink, drink and eat." An innkeeper from Wilmington, North Carolina, Kate is describing a hands-on cooking course, one of three she has attended, at the summer school operated by La Varenne, the *Ecole de la Cuisine* Simone Beck and Julia Child made famous.

"The classes, for 12 people, are held in the Chateau de Fey, an 18th-century chateau overlooking the Rhone valley. Anne Willan and her husband have turned one wing into a kitchen, and they also have a swimming pool, tennis courts, beautiful grounds. The last class I took there was 'Bistro Cooking.'

"La Varenne picks you up in Paris and buses you 90 miles to the chateau. That first evening everyone gathers for a tour of the grounds, the moat, the old kitchen house. Then you share aperitifs and dinner on the terrace overlooking the gardens. That night you get your packet of recipes and sign up for the meals you'd like to work on. School starts after breakfast, with morning classes and preparation until 12:30 pm.

"After critiquing and eating that meal, you have a couple hours off to do whatever you'd like. By about 3:00 pm, it's back to the kitchen until 6:00. Everyone there loves food— the taste, the methodology. After dinner we have a demonstration geared to our coursework. Early mornings we go to the markets for special ingredients. Friday night, there's a wine tasting at a local vineyard, followed by dinner at a three-star restaurant. Saturday, you're driven back to Paris.

"There aren't many couples in the classes, though there are men as well as women, mostly American, Japanese and Canadian. It's very elegant, but you still learn a lot, and everyone works hard. The best part is you don't have to do your own dishes."

LA VARENNE, US Office: PO Box 25574, Washington, DC 20007, (800) 537-6486 or (202) 337-0073. Tuition for the 6-day, 6-night course includes all wines, meals, activities, and excursions.

GIULIANO BUGIALLI'S SOHO KITCHEN
New York City, New York

"His recipes are pretty complex. I mean, he has you boning rabbits, making your own vinegars and baking stone breads and pasta all the time." "He" is Giuliano Bugialli, in whose Soho kitchen in New York David and a group of like-minded friends have taken some 30 classes. They are taught in clusters of 4, usually within a group of 12. More fun however, are probably the sumptuous 1-week classes the Tuscan Chef offers in Florence. For his part, David, a psychiatrist, remains a devoted follower in New York.

"Bugialli's a potter, an art historian, a man of the world from Tuscany. The teaching kitchen in his home has granite counters and four Garland stoves. This is as good as it gets.

"Our class shows up at 6:00 pm and gets printed menus, including a pasta course, a vegetable, a main course, a dessert, and often an antipasto as well. We all make everything, and we all eat everything. We do many interesting, difficult pastas. We even cooked quail on a spit.

"By 9:00 pm, we've had good white wines during class, and when we sit down to eat our meal, we talk over the red wine Giuliano has selected. We eat in classic Italian style, dish by dish, until about 10.00. If it gets interesting, we'll have some *grappa* [Italian brandy].

"With Giuliano, you don't just learn how to prepare a few recipes. You get a real feel for the food. The best meals I've ever had have been at his classes. I mean, you can't buy food like this anywhere in the world. You just can't."

GIULIANO BUGIALLI'S SOHO KITCHEN, PO BOX 1650, Canal Street Station, New York, NY 10013, (212) 966-5325. The fee for a week in Florence includes classes, room, meals, and excursions.

TANTE MARIE'S COOKING SCHOOL
San Francisco, California

"The course was 'Cooking from the Wine Cellar.' We'd discuss the menus and why the teacher chose each wine. He was very good." Coming from a family of chefs, Gail, a 26-year-old editor, is in a position to judge. She describes a 3-day course she took at Tante Marie's Cooking School in San Francisco.

"The kitchens are new and huge, stocked with only topline equipment. We'd start at about 10:00 am, preparing four courses per meal in groups of three or four. You could pick your course. I already bake well, so I wanted to learn how to bone fish and leg of lamb. The instructor taught us lots of techniques, short cuts and tricks. Each group was responsible for cooking, plating and presenting its course.

"We were usually done by 1:30 or so. Then we'd eat for about 2 hours: leg of lamb one day, veal with caper sauce, our own fettucini another. God, it was good. As you ate, the teacher graded your preparations, sort of, and suggested how you could improve your dish. The results were so professional. We'd be out by about 4:00 pm. Then, before returning to Campton Place, my hotel, I'd explore the city. Being in San Francisco was a treat. Besides, it was kind of nice to have the time alone.

"There was only one man in my class. Two women were housewives, one actress, another young woman and me. Tante Marie also runs a degree program, and places its graduates in restaurants all over the States. Mary Risley, the owner, is very well-respected."

TANTE MARIE'S COOKING SCHOOL, 271 Francisco, Street, San Francisco, CA 94133, (415) 788-6699.

 ## Other Cooking Choices ─────────

Victor, the wine expert, and famed Italian cooking authority Marcella Hazan, have switched the venue of the Marcella Hazan School of Classic Italian Cooking from Bologna to their apartment in a 16th-century *palazzo* in Venice, where six students participate in six morning sessions followed by wine discussions and a leisurely meal. The tuition for the Hazan Master Class doesn't cover transportation or accommodations. Marcella Hazan also sponsors four Bread Baking Workshops In Bologna taught by Margherita Simili, an associate from Hazan's Bologna days.

HAZAN CLASSICS, PO Box 285, Circleville, NY 10919, (914) 692-7104.

Traipse through the gastronomic haunts of Europe and go deluxe with Annemarie Victory, a life-long traveler and Austrian by birth. These no-luxuries-barred 9- to 11-day sojourns in Italy, France and Germany feature cooking demonstrations by world-renowned chefs, long, three-star meals, visits to seldom-seen art collections, private estates, and wineries.

ANNEMARIE VICTORY, 136 East 64th Street, New York, NY 10021, (212) 486-0353.

Jane Grigson, the noted English cookbook writer, and Madhdur Jaffrey, the equally well-known authority on Indian cuisine, have both taught at the Ballymaloe Cookery School, but the Irish school's reputation springs from Ballymaloe House, a hotel with an internationally acclaimed restaurant in County Cork. The special, 3-day workshops taught by culinary stars at Kinoith House alternate with 1-week intensive courses and 12-week Certificate Courses that are the Cookery School's bread and butter.

BALLYMALOE COOKERY SCHOOL, Kinoith House, Shanagarry, County Cork, Ireland, 011-353-21-646785.

Judith Ets-Hokin, owner of a San Francisco "culinary company," occasionally leads 17-day tours to China. Participants spend 5 consecutive mornings at the Beijing Culinary Academy studying technique with master chefs before taking off to Xian, Hangzhou, Suzhou, and Shanghai for sightseeing.

JUDITH ETS-HOKIN, 3525 California Street, San Francisco, CA 94118, (415) 668-3191.

Oenophiles sign on with the German Wine Academy for intensive, 6-day excursions through the Mosel Valley and other prime German wine growing areas. "We focus on the history and culture of the region, too, and there's little free time; the bus leaves at 8:00 or 9:00 am and gets back to the hotel around 10:00 pm," says a staff member, "but you learn a lot."

GERMAN WINE ACADEMY, 79 Madison Avenue, New York, NY 10012, (212) 213-7036. The fee for a 6-day course includes meals, accommodations and tastings.

Bibliography

Guide to Cooking Schools ($16.95 plus $2 postage, Shaw Associates, Coral Gables, FL, 1991). A substantial and very complete, 326-page guide. Order through the International Association of Cooking Professionals, 304 W. Liberty Street, Louisville, KY 40202. (502) 581-9786.

Painting, Potting and Photographing

There is a heightened sense of community among crafts people and artists that tends to make workshops in the art field especially gratifying. True, those wanting a private room will still pay more, but most supplements are fairly gentle. "I'm single and I know what a hassle it is to pay double for everything," commented a representative from New York's School of Visual Arts. "Our 'Arts Abroad' program is perfect for single travelers because they're not penalized for traveling alone like you are on a cruise. Anyone can sign up for our summer classes overseas, and we get a real range in ages, from 18-year-olds to retirees."

"Most people come alone," and "women out-enroll men, but not by much," said a couple of arts administrators about their programs. There aren't many single quarters on summer campuses. Roommates are a fact of life at many of the sleep-away schools.

Pricing Categories

Inexpensive	Under $75 a day
Moderate	$75 to $125 a day
Expensive	$126 to $200
Very Expensive	Over $200 a day

HUDSON RIVER VALLEY ART WORKSHOPS
Greenville, New York

My group of 16 painters watched intently as illustrator Ferdinand Petri rendered the Presbyterian Church in quick, assured strokes. The demonstration finished, we placed our folding stools under maple trees and, concentrating on Petri's maxim "composition is nothing more than the arrangement of light, dark and one or two intermediate values," got out our watercolors to paint.

Learning a new discipline, or honing an old talent, can be as diverting as lolling in the sun. Workshops, lessons and classes produce new relationships as well as intellectual or artistic stimulation and a change of scene. The Hudson River Valley Art Workshops are held at a turreted Victorian inn in leafy Greenville, a peaceful community in the Catskills. The 5-day, May-through-October sessions offered at the suitably picturesque Greenville Arms take place under gracious auspices. The inn is a nurturing environment for artists and students alike.

Dedicated watercolorists, a couple of non-painting husbands and one rank amateur kicked off the third Sunday-to-Saturday session over sangria on the Greenville Arms' sloping front lawn.

Participants usually arrive independently, which makes the group dynamics more interesting. Congeniality is important; everyone shares each other's company day and night. It's helpful to have a supportive atmosphere: learning to render a balanced composition is demanding work.

Neither chilly days nor biting winds kept Ferdinand Petri's watercolor class indoors. Intrepid painters don't run at the first sign of rain clouds; they capture them in ultramarine blue and Alizarian red. Fired by Ferd's hour-long morning demonstration and sustained by walnut-studded brownies one morning, zesty lemon squares the next, we layered on more clothes, peered at the brooding Catskills, and continued painting.

By the third morning, our talented, affable teacher's "Always think in terms of three values" lesson began to sink in, and the hours spent laying washes began to pay off. Beginners were elated to graduate from straight burnt umber to a combination of burnt sienna and ultramarine blue. If they grew despondent, the agreeable surroundings bucked them up.

Beside the spacious pool enclosure, the tidy changing rooms lettered "Ladies" and "Gentlemen" bespoke a gentler era. Laps in the pool followed by a sunbath behind the neatly clipped hedge rested participants for a return to the easel. The friendly Greenville community is supportive, too. The porch-wrapped Greenville Arms and matching white Carriage House across the creek are an integral part of the neat and leafy town.

Built in 1899, the gabled inn is beautifully preserved. The abacus-style wooden beading at the entrance to the restaurant and front parlor and the original leaded glass panels and varnished oak floors glisten. The octagonal turret room, trimmed in golden oak and papered in a quiet floral, was in decided contrast to its retro bath tiled in orchid and acid green. There are newer, more predictably furnished rooms in the Carriage House.

The Hudson River Valley Art Workshops, created by Laura Stevens, are now run by Eliot and Letitia Dalton who recently bought the Greenville Arms. While the Dalton's have done some redecorating, and have turned the homey dining room into a restaurant complete with chef, the only change they've made in the summer workshops is to enlarge the season and increase their number.

For workshoppers, the change in ownership shouldn't affect the social dynamics, in any case. Friendships were cemented over ample dinners, after which we returned to the Carriage House for more lessons, or informative videos. Then it was up the sturdy oak stairs to dream about new painting techniques.

HUDSON RIVER VALLEY ART WORKSHOPS, Greenville Arms, Greenville, NY 12083, (518) 966-5219. Rates include tuition, meals and lodging. Moderate.

HAYSTACK MOUNTAIN SCHOOL OF CRAFTS
Deer Isle, Maine

I have taken two, 3-week clay workshops at the Haystack Mountain School of Crafts in Deer Isle, Maine. Edward Larrabee Barnes designed the grey-shingled Haystack complex with enormous sensitivity to the pine-fringed site. Walkways and steps connect the expansive dining area to the workshops, dorms and cottages superimposed on a granite cliff that sheers into the bay. Each craft has a specific studio, all of which are open 24 hours a day.

One of Haystack's many merits is that 65 students per session are given every opportunity to work. The teachers, and some of the students as well, tend to be well-known craftspeople. Learning takes precedence over play for most participants, but there is time enough for tanning, touring, swimming in the quarry, lobsters, and fairly serious volleyball games. Another virtue is the exposure to all the crafts. Students can circulate among the various studios.

Single rooms are available, but Haystack matches roommates deftly. I was compatibly paired both years I attended and made good new friends.

Meals are great. The wholegrain breads, copious salads made of sparkling fresh ingredients and simply-prepared but delicious casseroles, chicken dishes, and stews were downright dangerous to those afraid of gaining weight, or so it seemed. In fact, we used up so much energy working, an extra homebaked cookie now and then didn't really matter.

HAYSTACK MOUNTAIN SCHOOL OF CRAFTS, PO Box 87, Deer Isle, ME 04627-0087, (207) 348-2306. Moderate.

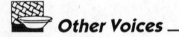 **Other Voices** _____

MAINE PHOTOGRAPHY WORKSHOP
Rockland, Maine

"The instructors are tops. These are world-class guys who really know their stuff," says Darwin, 51, a professional photographer working out of Maine. Nevertheless, he has taken three 1-week courses at the Maine Photography Workshop in Rockland.

"You can go as a rank amateur. The courses run the gamut from basic darkroom techniques all the way up to publishable material. Film is developed overnight, so you see what you've got in the morning. Your work's critiqued, and then you go off on your assignments—everything from studio workshops to architecture, photo journalism, advertising, lighting specialties. I took 'Architectural Interiors' and 'Color in Advertising.'

"There were roughly 20 people in the classes. We'd do some group projects. One day, for example, we had a special lighting day; we used different kinds of natural and artificial lights, with everyone shooting. The next day we broke into smaller groups. My group went to a church, another shot a house. You get more out of it when you work in teams.

"You can live in a dorm, a bed and breakfast or a hotel/motel. I preferred the latter, but someone younger or more social might prefer the dorm. You end up eating lunch and dinner with your classmates.

"It's a fairly social program. A lot of the work is done in teams of two or three, so you get to know people on your team well. I still keep in touch with several people I met there. Evenings, the instructors put on a slide show. You're exposed to the very best work in your field. It's terrifically stimulating."

MAINE PHOTOGRAPHY WORKSHOP, Rockport, ME 04856, (207) 236-8581. Expensive.

GREEK ARCHAEOLOGY COURSE
New York School of Visual Arts International Studies

"We visited museums, famous sites. This was a basic tour of Greece, but because the guide knew so many people, we got into special places no one else can see. We even got to climb the scaffolding on the Parthenon, so we were actually on top of it." Linda, 22, is an illustration major at New York's School of Visual Arts, whose 3-week archaeological tour of Greece she took not once, but twice.

"We covered the two Golden Ages. Unfortunately, not in chronological order, but at first, we were less concerned with the dates than with the art. Then, about half-way through the trip, we wanted to learn about the history. That's when they gave us a fact sheet, and the tour guide, a history teacher, rattled off dates all the time.

"If we liked a site, we'd go back to enjoy it again. This trip is definitely geared for artists. It's very slow and deliberate, not 'Everybody on the bus.' You have free time to do as you please.

"The first year, there were 12 of us, the second time, 8, mostly art students. There was an older couple, a doctor and his wife, on the first trip. You get a grade and course credit for keeping a journal of the trip. Keeping the journal was wonderful. It made you focus on what you were seeing, and when you got back, you had a visual record of the trip.

"Visual Arts also has studio art classes in Italy and China. Because these studio courses are heavily promoted, they probably attract a wider range of people, but they aren't for beginners."

NEW YORK SCHOOL OF VISUAL ARTS INTERNATIONAL STUDIES, 209 East 23rd Street, New York, NY 10010-3994, (212) 679-7350. The rate for the 3-week Greek Archaeology course includes tuition, accommodations and two meals a day. Expensive.

WOODEN BOAT SCHOOL
Brooklin, Maine

For the past 8 summers Stan has traveled from his home on the Connecticut coast up to Brooklin, Maine to spend 2 weeks or more at the Wooden Boat School. Most recently, using the "stitch and glue" method, he constructed a lightweight 14-foot boat. As the retired personnel manager tells it, this probably won't be his last project there.

"I've enjoyed all the courses I've taken at Wooden Boat. I spent my working life in an office, so I wanted to do something with my hands for a change. Boats, if they are well made, are beautiful and attractive, so I started studying wooden boat-building and repair, and I've used a lot of what I've learned summers as a volunteer doing boat repair work at the Maritime Center.

"Building a 20-foot Friendship sloop has been a group project at the school for about 5 years now, and I've worked on that. Last year, though, I took 'Stitch and Glue Boat Building,' with about 14 other guys. The technique involves joining plywood panels, filleting them with a mixture of epoxy and wood dough, and taping the seams. It makes a smooth, very light boat.

"It's a beautiful place to spend a few weeks. The instructors, well-known people, are always good. The Wooden Boat school is housed in a former summer resort right on the water, but you sleep and eat nearer town in the student house. Basically, it's one or two to a room and bath. There's also a game room, TV room, living room, and lounge. I've also stayed at the farmhouse closer to the workshop. Some students bring tents and camp out.

"Everyone eats breakfast and dinner together. Lunch is brought to wherever we're working. Wooden Boat is very well organized, with marvelous equipment and tools. It's a pleasure to work there.

"The popular courses are offered year after year. I'm hoping they'll introduce some new ones."

WOODEN BOAT SCHOOL, PO Box 78, Brooklin, ME 04616, (207) 359-4651. Moderate.

CLEVELAND INSTITUTE
Cleveland, Ohio

Shortly before he retired as a high school English teacher in Cleveland, a colleague suggested that Tom take a drawing course at the Cleveland Institute. The outcome surprised him.

"I had taken no art courses whatsoever. The beginning drawing course met once a week from 6:45 to 9:00 pm. I knew nothing, but I got hooked and discovered I had some talent for it. So I took three more drawing courses.

"For the regular students, the Institute is expensive and highly competitive to get into. Night classes are different. The Institute is situated in University Circle, which is quite a cultural center. You're surrounded by art and music in the cultural heart of Cleveland.

"Most of the students were very serious, even at night. The instructors have been excellent, and very encouraging. Their criticisms are given thoughtfully and positively, which is so important for beginning students. We had homework. Several times, we'd go over to the Museum of Art or other spots to draw. The teacher really pushed us to explore, think, try hard.

"It's been such a gratifying experience that I'm taking Painting and Life Drawing. I'm getting ready for a second career."

CLEVELAND INSTITUTE, 11141 East Boulevard, Cleveland, OH 44106, (216) 421-7000. Inexpensive.

 ## Other Painting, Potting and Photographing Choices

Nearly a thousand students take intensive, 1- and 2-week classes in Painting, Ceramics, Photography, Woodworking, and Furniture Design at the Anderson Ranch Arts Center in Colorado during the summer. Established in a couple of log barns by potter Paul Soldner in 1976, the center now boasts studios, workshops and a residence near the Snowmass Ski Resort 10 miles from Aspen.

ANDERSON RANCH ARTS CENTER, PO Box 5598, Snowmass Village, CO 81615, (303) 923-3181. The meal plan is optional. Moderate.

The Split Rock Arts Program, held on the University of Minnesota's Duluth campus each summer, offers intensive, week-long sessions on a raft of creative subjects from Raku and Choreography to Journals and Diaries. Students, about 80% of whom are women, use the University's pool, health club, tennis courts, and canoes as well as its classrooms, and dine overlooking Lake Superior.

SPLIT ROCK ARTS PROGRAM, 306 Wesbrook Hall, 77 Pleasant Street SE, University of Minnesota, Minneapolis,

MN 55455, (612) 624-6800. Shared accommodations and private bedrooms are available. Moderate.

The rustic Penland School, located in the Blue Ridge Mountains, shares with Haystack the distinction of being one of the top craft schools in the United States. In fact, many of the instructors have taught at both schools. Penland suits its rugged mountain location. "We're 61 years old and run on a shoe-string," declares an administrator. "Rooms are not wonderful, to be honest, but they're clean and no one spends much time in them anyway. Facilities are open 24 hours-a-day and the meals are nice and healthy."

PENLAND SCHOOL, Penland, NC 28765-0037, (704) 765-2359. Rooms are available with or without bath. Moderate to Expensive.

Bibliography

Art in America, 575 Broadway, New York, NY 10012, (212) 941-2800. This magazine includes a comprehensive listing each month of fine arts schools in the United States.

Art New England, 425 Washington Street, Brighton, MA 02135, (617) 782-3008, $3. The October and February issues carry a special "Art Schools, Programs, & Workshops" section.

Exploring Nature

From "gorillas in the mist" to the snowy tips of Antarctica's icebergs, few natural phenomena seem to be inaccessible today. Ecotourism is booming, as travelers in search of nature unvarnished set off in helicopters, safari jeeps and inflatable boats for the least accessible corners of the globe. One person's orchid can be another's daisy, however. Not all nature lovers travel in style. Feet suffice for most, and many travel alone.

"Fifty percent of the people on nature trips travel by themselves because not everyone is interested in nature. Husbands and wives often come separately," advises Wildlife Adventures. A staffer at Wilderness Southeast reports: "About 50% of our clients book singly, and there's no single supplement. We provide the tents." Campers don't pay extra. Opt for a hotel room and there's a modest surcharge. Take a nature cruise and pay up to 200% more than the per person double rate.

Pricing: *The nature of the programs listed in this chapter makes it impossible to compare prices accurately. Contact the organizations directly for up-to-date fee information.*

LITTLE ST. SIMONS ISLAND
St. Simons Island, Georgia

"Quick, there's a piliated woodpecker outside." This cry, from a gimlet-eyed birder, galvanized the group gathered around the hors d'oeuvres table peeling fat fresh shrimp. As one, the 24 guests flocked onto the deck to peer into the branches of a Spanish lob lolly pine, but the bird had flown. Back in the buff lodge on Little St. Simons Island, nature lovers consoled themselves with another drink and accounts of alligators and armadillos sighted.

This 10,000-acre Atlantic Barrier Island in Georgia is maintained as a nature preserve by its owners, the Berolzheimers, an ecology-conscious cedar dynasty. Staffed by trained naturalists, cooks and dedicated managers, this sanctuary has been open to the public for 11 years. The island represents a real bonanza for the naturally inclined and is a companionable haven for the solo traveler.

"Never landed on a sand beach?" asked Buddy, the pilot, as we walked through the Jacksonville Airport toward a Cessna 206 aircraft. "You're in for a treat." It's cheaper to reach the island from Savannah by van, but I chartered the plane. North over Jeckyll Island, home of millionaires past, and Sea Island, home of millionaires present, we flew above serpentine rivers looping malachite-green marshes to a retreat of a distinctly different sort. The plane circled a herd of European fallow deer, startling a great egret into graceful flight, before taxiing to a stop near a small, wooden shelter midway along the island's 6-mile stretch of Atlantic beach. "Welcome to the world's most beautiful airport," said Buddy.

At least three micro-climates comprise Little St. Simons. During the 2 1/2-mile trip in a pickup to the lodges, we traversed the shell-littered seashore, marshlands alive with birds, and the timbered high ground, where Jack the donkey greeted our arrival with a raucous hee haw. Here at the resort proper, live oak leaves crackled under foot and Spanish moss drifted against the sky.

Accommodations are casual, comfortable and varied. During Easter week, multi-generational families filled both Cedar House and River Lodge—two-story houses, each with a screened-in porch, four bedrooms, and a big, cushily furnished living room. Reserve an airy modern bedroom in one of these riverside buildings or an age-burnished room in Hunting Lodge, nearer to the hot tub and pool. There, I occupied a cozy cedar-panelled room with a woodstove, plaid curtains and beige-tiled bath featured twig latches and towel bars to match the twin beds fashioned locally of twigs.

Twenty-one deer heads stared fixedly as I toured the wicker-filled Lodge, built in 1917, overlooking Mosquito Creek. The library, filled with reference works and seashells arranged alphabetically ("Angel's Wing" through "Channeled Whelk") was intriguing, but the lunch gong summoned.

Binocular-draped fellow guests gathered in the dining room as pitchers of lemonade, ice tea and milk were set on two tables for 12.

Nature lovers can be a competitive lot. Especially bird-watchers. As they passed the macaroni and fresh pea salad, hearty corned beef on rye and tasty Scottish oatmeal cookies, birders from Long Island, Philadelphia and Ithaca, New York disputed who had seen which bird, where, and when, but an authority was always on hand to smooth ruffled feathers.

Little St. Simon indulges its guests with folksy home cooking and bona fide naturalists, all three of whom had biology degrees when I was there. During hearty breakfasts of buttery grits and fried eggs and sausage, the naturalists would outline the day's activities. Arrangements for pre-breakfast sorties were made before dinners of crispy fried chicken one night, roast pork and peppery gravy the next.

The resort is dedicated to sharing the island's natural riches with guests. Birdwatchers stalked the marshes at the crack of dawn. Hikers laced up boots to study the maritime forest with a botanist. I rode out on horseback past Myrtle Pond, where the alligators breed, to River Beach, the mating grounds of prehistoric-looking Horseshoe crabs. Oysters squirted in salute and at the juncture of the Altamaha River and the Atlantic Ocean, hundreds of sandpipers skittered and squeaked.

Group activities are the norm, but one *can* be alone in this pristine environment. Take a spin in an aluminum launch across the wide Hampton River. There's fishing in the marshy sloughs, and on the hard-packed beach, thousands of collectable shells.

LITTLE ST. SIMONS ISLAND, PO Box 1073, St. Simons Island, Georgia 31522, (912) 638-7472. All meals and on-island activities are included in the rates.

Other Voices _____

FIELD GUIDES
Expedition to Ecuador

"If you're interested in frogs, these trips aren't for you, but for anyone enamored of exotic birds, Field Guides is a good company to travel with," says Mark, who has taken several birding trips with the outfit. The computer programmer, 32, from Mountainview, California, recalls an 18-day expedition to Ecuador.

"We numbered 14, mostly couples. Field Guides limits the participants in the tropical areas especially. In fact, they often split one trip into small groups, which gives everyone a more personal experience. Most people were in their 50s and 60s, with a few energetic regulars in their 70s. Not everyone was a gung-ho birder. Some came for the scenery in pristine places where nature is still just taking its course.

"The leaders are very knowledgeable and very helpful when it comes to identifying birds. They even bring sound recordings with them to lure birds out of their hiding places. You pick up a lot of tricks on these trips.

"We left Quito by bus and descended to about 6,000 feet, which is absolutely outrageous bird country. There we slept on mattresses in some abandoned buildings. Birds came right into camp. Unfortunately, it rained much of the time, and birds don't come out in that kind of rain.

"Back in the bus, we continued down and east to a fairly tropical zone at about 1,000 feet. We even saw some interesting birds right there in the hotel gardens. People who weren't 100% birders could relax and watch the river go by for a while, take pictures.

"We discovered several birds, including a semi-collared hawk. The only sightings ever recorded are in the west side of the Andes, and here we are on the east side looking at this thing. Wow!"

FIELD GUIDES, PO Box 160723, Austin, TX 78716-0723, (512) 327-4953. The 18-day "General Ecuador" tour begins in Quito and is all-inclusive.

PROGRAMME FOR BELIZE
Belize

"I went to Belize to look at the rain forest maintained by the Programme for Belize and to see how they're trying to protect it," says Jessie, the spunky, 66-year-old from Cape Cod who also described her stay on Cumberland Island.

"I like to travel by myself. Sometimes it's lonely, but it forces you to meet people. It's stimulating. Some people just need more space to themselves. I write and photograph, so I don't really want to be encumbered by another person. Romance? It happens if it happens. It's not something you go looking for.

"I was interested in the Programme for Belize, a multinational conservation effort which is headquartered in Martha's Vineyard. I went down, on my own, under their direction. Belize is an interesting, very hot, Third World country. The coastline is beautiful, not very developed, but travel there is hard because the roads are bad.

"You charter a plane to fly from Belize into Gallon Jug, a farm that's privately owned by a very rich Belizian with his own development theories. From there you drive to Chan Chich Lodge. Chan Chich is a nature lodge right in the rain forest, an enclave of people who are interested in the forest and what lives there.

"The lodge is about 4 years old and can accommodate 12 guests. It's built in the plaza of a Mayan ruin, quite beautiful and so remote the electricity is home-generated. Chan Chich is run non-invasively. The staffers want people to be able to observe the birds and the animals of the forest.

"I also went to Chaa Creek Cottages, another small lodge that's equally kind to the environment. You bathe in the creek. It's just as hard to get to; took me several hours and about $125 cab fare to reach. I was unique; everyone else had come with conservation groups. You eat with the other guests. There's no problem meeting people when you're joined by the same interests."

PROGRAMME FOR BELIZE, PO Box 1088, Vineyard Haven, MA 02568, (508) 693-0856. Reservations for Chan Chich Lodge can be made through the Programme.

CHAA CREEK COTTAGES, San Ignacio, Belize, 011-501-092-2037. Cabin rates include all meals.

SMITHSONIAN ASSOCIATES TRAVEL PROGRAM

"I've always been interested in travel, but being single, I've always found it difficult to find interesting traveling companions. So I put off traveling, waiting to find somebody to go with," explains Robert, 51, an engineer in New Orleans. He traveled to Russia with the Smithsonian Associates in 1975, and he has traveled with them ever since. He tells why.

"I loved the way they handled everything. In particular, I loved the class of people that are attracted by the Smithsonian; travel-experienced, educated, mostly professional people.

"My first outdoor trip was an African camel safari. Then I got into the hiking trips. I hiked in Switzerland; that's a good deal of work. I also hiked in Ireland, Scotland, the White Mountains, three times in Glacier National Park. I rafted through the Grand Canyon.

"You have to be prepared for physical discomfort and you need a sense of adventure for the hiking trips. I was surprised to find more women than men, like a 2:1 ratio. Fine with me! About 75% are traveling alone, or with a friend. The guides and guests on the hiking trips are younger, in their 40s, say. The more active the trip, the younger the group. That's not to say that when I've been straining every muscle on some of these trips, I haven't been passed by a 70-year-old.

"These are naturalist-oriented, not mountain-climbing trips. The guides are naturalists, but they are well-trained in safety as well.

"Stateside trips tend to have about 25 people and last 10 days; overseas trips last a little longer. Some of the hikes are day hikes. Other times, they'll bus you to a trail head and you'll hike all day, maybe over a pass or through a valley to the next hotel. There's always a staff employee along to guarantee that the guides do their job properly, to make sure the accommodations are right and to address any luggage problems and such.

"We never actually camped out, except on the Colorado River trip. In Glacier, we stay in cabins with no heat or running water, no electricity. You get the flavor of the wilderness without having to endure its ferocity. I've always had comfortable roommates. These trips are ideal for a single person traveling alone. The company is wonderful."

SMITHSONIAN ASSOCIATES TRAVEL PROGRAM, 1100 Jefferson Drive, Washington, DC 20560, (202) 357-4700. The 10-day trip to the Waterton-Glacier International Peace Park is all-inclusive. The Associates Travel Program sponsors about 300 trips a year.

VOYAGEUR OUTWARD BOUND SCHOOL
Minnetonka, Minnesota

"It was intense. It was painful; but I really loved being outdoors." Kathleen is the Massachusetts lawyer who also described the Yoga Retreat in the Bahamas. Here she recalls 26 days on an Outward Bound wilderness course in Minnesota.

"I was a city kid, 27, who had never been camping, and I had always wanted to do this. Outward Bound picks you up at the bus station in Ely, Minnesota, and you go right to the National Forest. They put you in canoes and said, 'Paddle.' It's called 'immersion.'

"There were seven of us: three juvenile delinquents on scholarship, a 30-year-old Rochester, New York guy who taught the emotionally disturbed, a 29-year-old woman from Cape Cod, a young college grad, and me. We weren't a very congenial group.

"The second day we had a 3-mile portage with these huge, 50-pound food packs to carry on our shoulders. It was 'Just do it.' Some of us fell behind, and at the end of that haul we got lost. We ended up spending the night on the lake shore. We had food and tents and all, but I was still frightened. The instructor found us next morning.

"That first 6-day trip was all canoeing and portaging. They taught us emergency techniques such as CPR, map reading and the like. Back at base camp we got to sleep indoors and spent a couple of days learning to rock climb on huge boulders at the camp. I have never been so scared in my life.

"We biked for about 10 days, and did more canoeing. One day we had a sort of marathon race. You ran 7 miles and canoed so many miles, competing in groups. I kept thinking, 'God, I can't run another step,' but I did it, and it proved what they said: that your mind gives up more quickly than your body.

"At the end we had a 3-day solo. I loved it. I was so tired of being around people 24 hours a day. You had a little sheet of plastic to make a sort of lean-to and three matches to make a fire. It was cold and raining, in September, and it was such a victory just to get a fire going. They gave us a little food, but I just didn't eat. I wrote a lot. If we were in trouble, we could break rank. We had a whistle system. But no one broke rank. I came away proud of myself."

VOYAGEUR OUTWARD BOUND SCHOOL, 10900 Cedar Lake Road, Minnetonka, MN 55343, (800) 328-2943 or (612) 542-9255. The fee for the 22-day trip includes food, instruction and camping gear.

CAMP DENALI
Denali National Park, Alaska

"Little cabins at about 1500 feet are positioned on a south-facing slope due north of Mt. McKinley. You look out your window at the mountain. This is probably my favorite place on earth." A lawyer in San Diego, Charlie, 41, is speaking of Camp Denali in Denali National Park, Alaska.

"It's easiest to fly into Anchorage or Fairbanks and take the train about 4 hours to Denali Station, where someone will meet you. The camp is near the end of the 90-mile dirt road that pierces the center of the park. I've never made the trip in less than 5 hours. I mean, you're out in the middle of the tundra. You stop and look at animals. Bears and caribou cross the road. Moose follow the bus. If you're real lucky, you'll see a fox or a wolf.

"You go for the beauty. It's a fully-guided vacation, with guides who know a lot—they're naturalists, or birders, geologists. You're in real wilderness. In summer, the longest day is about 21 hours. In spring, the flowers are out. All year, it's a magical place.

"The camp's maximum is maybe 42 guests, and you need to reserve by March or early April for summer. Most of the cabins are one-room affairs designed for a couple or a group of singles. Each has a Yukon stove, a small outhouse and a cold water spigot on the porch. It's a very classy operation for Alaska. Upscale.

"Every day after breakfast two or three guided activities are offered. Some days they have flying trips, sight-seeing. There are bikes and a steep hiking trail behind camp that takes you along the ridge several miles. The guides take people nature-walking or gold-panning. You can hike to the Muldrow Glacier about 10 miles away and walk onto the ice. A rare experience.

"The owners operate North Face Lodge, a more traditional place with indoor plumbing, about a mile and a half away. It's in the same environment but is less guided and less organized. North Face has a more urban feel. It appeals to those who won't like using an outhouse.

"The food at Camp Denali, served in the lodge dining room, is wonderful. It's hearty, always changing, with fresh bread every day. You sit family style at any table you want, and the staff eats with the guests.

"There are propane lights in all the cabins. You can read by them, but no one's very interested in reading at the end of a day at Camp Denali."

CAMP DENALI, Box 67, Denali National Park, AK 99755, (907) 683-2290 (winter: PO Box 216, Cornish, NH 03746, (603) 675-2248). Rates are charged on a shared-cabin basis (No single occupancy), and include three meals a day. Rates for the North Face Lodge also include three meals a day.

Other Nature Choices ────────────

Elderhostel takes pride in the number and scope of its educational offerings. Nature is the focus of many of the modestly-priced excursions. Classes, workshops and lectures, plus, occasionally, participatory sports are the stuff of most tours run by the organization. The over-60 hostelers are housed and fed on campuses, in rustic lodges, retreats, and study centers all over the world.

ELDERHOSTEL, 80 Boylston Street, Boston, MA 02116, (617) 426-8056. Programs in the US cover 6 nights accommodation, all meals, and courses.

Whalewatchers on Intersea Research voyages can sail in Alaska on the state-of-the-art research vessel *Acania*, Constance Bennett's former yacht. "An adventuresome, eclectic group of whale lovers take our luxury cruises," says a staffer. "They're perfect for single travelers."

INTERSEA RESEARCH, PO Box 1106, Carmel Valley, CA 93924, (408) 659-5807.

Questers, a leading nature tour operator, has been putting together painstakingly-researched trips for the past 18 years. Travelers are guided to places of signal interest, spots harboring the rarest birds and botanical specimens, the grandest natural sights, throughout the world.

QUESTERS, 257 Park Avenue South, New York, NY 10010-7369, (800) 468-8668 or (212) 673-3120.

"We teach nature, but our guides, who are well-versed about relationships in the ecosystem, don't lecture, they sneak in information during the course of our trips," explained a Wilderness Southeast representative. Plenty of nature-loving solos sign on for the camping trips to Belize,

Costa Rica, the Okefenokee Swamp, and Great Smokies offered by this nonprofit conservation group.

WILDERNESS SOUTHEAST, 711 Sandtown Road, Savannah, GA 31410, (912) 897-5108.

The Canadian government banned the commercial hunting of baby Harp Seals and now, if you take a Seal Watch trip with Wildlife Adventures, you'll be helping replace the income lost by the seal hunting communities in the Magdalen Islands. Seal lovers are helicoptered onto the ice to pet and play with the "whitecoats" during 4 or 5 night tours each spring.

WILDLIFE ADVENTURES, 1 Sussex Station, Sussex, NJ 07461, (800) 543-8917 or (201) 702-1525.

Students pay $7 a night for a bed in a heatless, waterless cabin and provide their own food when attending classes on Mammal Tracking, Hydrotheral Systems & the Yellowstone Caldera and a raft of other field courses at the Yellowstone Institute.

YELLOWSTONE INSTITUTE, PO Box 117, Yellowstone National Park, WY 82190, (307) 344-7381.

Other Conservation and Environmental Groups include:

SIERRA CLUB, (415) 776-2211.
ADIRONDACK MOUNTAIN CLUB, (518) 668-4447.
APPALACHIAN MOUNTAIN CLUB, (603) 466-2721.
NATURE CONSERVANCY, (703) 841-8776.
THE NATIONAL AUDUBON SOCIETY, (212) 832-3200.

Bibliography

Specialty Travel Index ($5 per issue, 305 San Anselmo Avenue, San Anselmo, CA 94960, (415) 459-4900). Short descriptions of 500 nature and "soft adventure" travel firms.

Learning Vacations, by Gerson G. Eisenberg ($11.95, Peterson's Guides, Princeton, NJ, 1989). Suggestions for 400 trips that better others as well as yourself.

Volunteering to Save the Planet

Keeping trails clean and assisting legitimate scientific research projects (while helping fund them) are among the efforts citizens can take to benefit the planet. These volunteer, or service, vacations are journeys that conservation-minded men and women, in about equal numbers, tend to take by themselves. Sharing or not sharing a tent or bunk room is generally academic; living conditions tend to be primitive. The volunteer vacationer won't find many three-star hotels.

Pricing: *The nature of the programs listed in this chapter makes it imppossible to compare prices accurately. Contact the organizations directly for up-to-date fee information.*

EARTHWATCH
The Mexican Art of Building Expedition

The expedition leader stalked into the lobby of El Presidente Hotel in Oaxaca, Mexico to find 11 Earthwatch volunteers, Team I of "The Mexican Art of Building," waiting.

Architect Logan Wagner shook hands firmly all around, counted heads and announced, "Okay, we're off." Bags stowed aboard three waiting vans, we hit the Pan American Highway for Tlaxiaco, 7,000 feet up in the Northwest corner of Oaxaca State. Once in the isolated Mixteca Alta, Team I would measure and document the area's plazas, churchyards, ball courts, and markets as part of an ongoing survey of early 16th century open spaces led by Wagner and Hal Box, Chairman of the Architecture Department at the University of Texas.

The 1990 Earthwatch catalog listed 111 earth science projects, up from 4 in 1971, when the organization first launched collaborative expeditions for scholars and amateurs. In 1990 I was among 3,000 Earthwatch volunteers who paid a (tax-deductible) share of the research expenses involved in Earthwatch-sponsored programs. "Who Rules the Reef," a study of moray eels and squirrelfish near Tobacco Cay, Belize, and "Rocky Mountain Wildflowers," an examination of the effects of environmental change on Colorado meadows, were also tempting, but "The Mexican Art of Building" won out.

"You'd better be satisfied with the hotel," said Wagner to his volunteers as he nonchalantly negotiated hairpin turns and dodged road-hogging buses. "It's the only one within a hundred miles." When we climbed out of the van 3 1/2 hours later, the Hotel del Portales looked as good as the Ritz. In fact, we grew fond of our clean lodgings once we learned to sleep through the barking of Tlaxiaco's dogs and gear-grinding local trucks.

The fourth annual session of "The Mexican Art of Building" began at about 9:30 am on the roof of the *Palacio Municipal*, across from Tlaxiaco's graceful, yellow sandstone church. Before walking through the Plaza to the city hall, Team I breakfasted, not, as I had imagined, on chilequiles or huevos rancheros, but on tumblers of fresh squeezed orange juice, papaya wedges and big, fluffy flapjacks accompanied by bacon and real maple syrup. Jesus, the manager, had come to the Uni-Nuu ("Three Towns") Restaurant after 5 years at a country club in Greenwich, Connecticut.

Wagner, a down-to-earth and exceedingly articulate man, managed to inspire his mostly-neophyte helpers with his all-consuming interest in 16th century Mexican architecture and to turn them, in fairly short order, into effective researchers. While uniformed *policia*, their rifles laid to one side, shot baskets on the town court below us, Wagner launched into his orientation.

Our team's task was to measure one church complex, together with the contiguous spaces and streets, each day, and to render in ink a plan incorporating the church, the town hall, and other important sites for the University of Texas' archives.

Lunch dispatched in the Hotel del Portales, we straggled back to our *municipio* "office," picked up our equipment, and scattered throughout Tlaxiaco to complete the assignments Logan meted out much to the restrained amusement of the Mixteca people who silently observed our progress.

Team I was singularly purposeful. No one slacked off, unless felled by *microbios* (microbes, causing diarrhea). To ward off that problem, Logan had prudently conscripted Anne, a professional nurse, who was soon baptized Santa Anna del Pepto for her habit of passing around bright pink pills before every meal. We enjoyed a constant stream of Logan's colleagues, who were put to work when they weren't giving us informal talks.

If our group was at all typical, Earthwatch attracts committed solos (over 70% of the volunteers enroll singly). My teammates' idea of diverting themselves was to learn, but certainly that didn't rule out conviviality. Dinners, accompanied by Dos Equis beer, tequila, and decent Calafia wine, were far from somber, and the fare, which included caramelized flan, grilled garlic chicken, spicy beef stews, and great bowls of deeply satisfying vegetable, corn and chicken soups, outdid anything I sampled in Oaxaca.

On a clear, sunny afternoon before I left, Logan was exultant. At San Miguel Achiutla an almost perfect example of the synthesis between pre-Colombian and early Spanish Colonial religious architecture had been found. Miraculously, modern civilization hadn't encroached on the site. Participating in such discoveries is what Earthwatch is all about.

EARTHWATCH EXPEDITIONS, INC., 680 Mount Auburn Street, Watertown, MA 02272, (617) 926-8200. Earthwatch projects cost approximately $800 to $3000.

Other Voices

UNIVERSITY RESEARCH EXPEDITION PROGRAM
Costa Rica and Ecuador Trips

"When I signed on, I wasn't sure what my tasks would be. Basically, the description said we would look at the birds and the bees," which is pretty much what Molly did on two trips to Latin America under the auspices of the University Research Expeditions Program (UREP) at the University of California, Berkeley. A third-grade teacher in San Francisco, 40, she is also an enthusiastic birder.

"My first trip was to Lomas Barbidal, a national park in Costa Rica, with a group of 12, teachers mostly, but also a writer couple from Philadelphia, a DC government worker and a guy from Petaluma. Gordon Franke and his wife have been doing research at Lomas Barbidal for 20 years. They are trying to preserve the park, which is a rare, tropical *dry* forest, not a tropical rain forest.

"I loved it. First, we helped the Frankes with their park planning. Then we split up into groups to help with his bee research. He was testing certain scents to see what attracted the bees. I didn't really enjoy the work particularly, but I did learn lots about bees.

"Mostly, we did PR work within the community; our physical presence gave status to the project. Normally, the locals wouldn't recognize the little park as special. But six of us also got to help a local ornithologist count the native birds. It was fabulous. We kept an inventory, which they hope to use to attract bird watchers to the Lomas Barbidal area. I added 80 new birds to their list in 6 days.

"The following year I took part in an expedition to a tropical Ecuardorian forest 40 miles northwest of Quito. It was a botany expedition with Grady Webster, a world-renowned botanist from the University of California at Davis. We were 10: an English woman collecting ferns for a botanical garden, a banker, two teachers, a doctor from Oakland, a couple of botany graduate students, and a 75-year-old apple farmer from Kentucky.

"We stayed in a kind of hut with a tin roof and just three sides and there was a swimming hole. We divided into groups by plant families: you'd just hike through the woods with three or four other people looking for your family of plants. It was really fun. We had to identify, label and dry plants, but basically only Grady and the English woman were qualified to identify them. So I had extra time to do a lot of bird watching again.

"Certainly there were a few odd moments, or discomfort with all the bugs, bouts of diarrhea, sunburn...but these trips attract people who expect that. I'd give UREP an A++."

UNIVERSITY RESEARCH EXPEDITIONS PROGRAM, Desk-03, University of California, Berkeley, CA 94720, (415) 642-6586. A volunteer's share in the 13-day Ecuadorian Rain Forest trip is all inclusive from Quito.

EARTHWATCH
Lake Baikal, USSR

"It's 180 degrees off the Club Med approach: you know, drink, play volleyball, disco. Earthwatch, you're out there with scientific types interested in problems of conservation or anthropology, whatever, which is a change from insurance salesmen, attorneys and the like." Grant is a scientist, about 60, but, as his remarks make clear, Earthwatch isn't just for experts.

"I've been on a couple of Earthwatches. Some of the trips are very good, others, kind of mediocre. I went on a bird thing in Hawaii, working on terns, daily flight directions and numbers. Not terribly exciting, but the concept is right. Your experience depends on who the principal investigator is.

"The Russian investigation on Lake Baikal was exciting. We traveled as guests of the Russian Academy of Sciences, which footed the bill for us to stay in third-rate Russian hotels and then on the boat. Now, I get along fine in primitive conditions (you've got to be a contortionist to use their johns), but anybody who expects more wouldn't.

"Ken Nealson, from the University of Michigan, was in charge, a super guy. We went looking for bioluminescents in the lake, did some sedimentology, some trace element chemistry and some microbiology. It was part of a joint program between the Institute of Limnology in Siberia and the Center for Great Lakes studies in Michigan.

"We were there about a month, of which we probably spent a good 2 weeks on the lake. The Russians have a good 170-foot research vessel and a bunch of smaller back-up boats. The volunteers would handle depth gear, read computer print-outs on hydrographic parameters and whatever. It wasn't terribly taxing, but the experience was absolutely first-rate. The Russians were just so damn hospitable; they really turned themselves inside out for us.

"You're there to get a job done, but it's a hell of a lot of fun trading songs and that kind of thing. Volunteers range from the real young to the fairly ancient, a few couples, and a lot unattached too, maybe the school teacher type or the student type. You're looking at places that are strange and new in the world instead of the same old resort kind of crap. People do get together. You make a lot of friends."

EARTHWATCH, PO Box 403, Watertown, MA 02272, (617) 926-8200. A volunteer's share of the month-long Lake Baikal trip includes everything except airfare.

NEW YORK BOTANICAL GARDEN
Botany Expedition to French Guiana

"I was really interested in finding new species. I've been a teacher for 20 years, but I really wanted to *do* something with science, like a football coach wanting to play," explains Jane, who teaches high school biology in New Jersey. She joined a New York Botanical Garden expedition to French Guiana to look for new plant species with botanists Scott and Carol Mori.

"We went to Guiana the last week of August, 14 of us, including a French orchid botanist, a data assistant, two computer specialists, a chemist who is active in the Sierra Club, an artist, and a photographer, mixed men and women. After a night in Cayenne, the capital, we flew into Saul, a primitive village in the heart of an untouched forest, where we stayed for 10 days, 5 of us in one house, the rest further out of the village. We slept in hammocks and cooked our own food. Two of the group returned home after 2 days.

"I loved the work. Besides new species, we were experimenting with pheromones and investigating the differing concentrations of sugar produced by flowers to attract hummingbirds and insects. Scott was an excellent leader, patiently explaining everything he was doing. He would take teams of four out several miles to where he was seeking a new species of brilliant, flowering tree. He'd climb 75 to 100 feet up a tree next to it to get clippings.

"Carol's group was figuring out when the blossoms fell. They'd go out every 6 hours at night to check nets and count blossoms. She was also looking for different kinds of hummingbirds. You could work on any of the projects. It was set up so you didn't have the same assignment every day.

"It was hot, hard work, but you can do anything as long as you know when it will end. You got a sense of how primitive it all was. My children may never have the opportunity to see a rain forest like this, and, I did find a new plant, but I didn't know it. They weren't sure until December. For me that was the experience of a lifetime."

NEW YORK BOTANICAL GARDEN TRAVEL PROGRAM, Southern Boulevard and 200th Street, Bronx, NY 10458, (212) 220-8982. The fee for the 2-week expedition in French Guiana includes round-trip airfare from Cayenne to Saul.

OCEANIC SOCIETY
Dolphin Research Trips

"You'd be sound asleep in this tiny bunk in a tiny cabin, and you're suddenly awakened by someone yelling, 'Dolphins!'" says Margi, 38, a therapist from Santa Fe, NM, recalling the first of three, week-long dolphin research trips she has taken with the Oceanic Society.

"You fall out of bed and into the water, where you're surrounded by these large animals, bumping into you. They stay about an hour, but you can see them in the distance all day, and they often return to play for another hour or so in the late afternoon.

"There were about 13 people plus the owners as crew aboard our ship, a 70-foot, steel-hulled sailing vessel. We put out about 40 miles from the Bahamas where the dolphins return year after year. The scientists are trying to identify the different members of the pod, and to learn when the dolphins are born, which ones come back, how long they live, what they do in winter.

"Guests can be as involved or uninvolved in the research as they like. If you know anything about underwater photography, you may help with the filming, which is constant when the dolphins are around.

"But you can't count on their appearance. So there's lots of waiting for the dolphins to show up.... You're experiencing a form of sensory deprivation. All there is is water and sky. Sunsets become immensely important.

"It's kind of a hardship trip, though the food is pretty good, considering what they have to make do with. In the middle of summer it's hot, and the air-conditioning isn't very efficient. The bunk space is pretty cramped. There's little hot water and no privacy. It's worse if the seas get rough, and people get seasick, but many do the trip again and again.

"Being in the water with these dolphins is the quintessential adult play experience. Some paying guests are disappointed to find themselves sitting in the sun, waiting for the next meal and the dolphins. Some find swimming with them a kind of magical or religious experience. Then, for others it just turns out to be the most fun they've ever had playing."

OCEANIC SOCIETY EXPEDITIONS, Fort Mason Center, Building E, San Francisco, CA 94123, (800) 326-7491 or (415) 441-1106. The 6-day volunteer share aboard the Jennifer Marie covers everything but one meal.

SIERRA CLUB

"The Sierra Club caters odd-ball trips for people who like to accomplish good things on their vacations. On my last trip, we probably repaired a half-mile of trail, but each time it's different." Dave is referring to the roughly 65 service trips a year that the Club runs. A computing engineer in San Francisco and a Club volunteer, he has taken more than his share of these jaunts, most recently a 10-day working excursion out of Aspen, Colorado.

"We assembled at the US Forestry Service office, about 16 members and 3 or 4 staff. We were fairly even men and women. This happened to be one of the more strenuous trips; the hike in was uphill all day. As usual, the food, the commissary and trail gear were horsepacked in, while we carried personal and camping stuff in backpacks. High among the conifers, at about 11,000 feet, we made a base camp for 10 days, as we'd be in one place for this trail work session.

"A section of trail was eroding because the underlying support had worn out about a mile from camp. We patched and built water diversion dams, using shovels and pulaskis (half ax, half mattock).

"A majority of the Sierra Club trail repair vacations take place in California and the Rockies, but they're scattered as far away as Alaska and New England. This time we worked 4 or 5 days, hiked in one day, out one day, and took about 4 days off. We might hike to a lake or spend a pleasant afternoon reading or enjoying the view. We took several hikes up local peaks, and everyone took turns assisting the cook. This isn't all work and no play. It's a vacation for most participants. We always aim to have a good time."

SIERRA CLUB Outings Department, 730 Polk Street, San Francisco, CA 94109, (415) 923-5630.

 Other Volunteer Choices _____

Adults and students assisting the Crow Canyon Archaeological Center's excavations of the Anasazi ruins (located in the Colorado's Four Corners area) range in age from 17 to 70 and come from all over the country. Novices work under the direction of the Crow Canyon's archaeology team excavating in the field and analyzing artifacts in the lab.

CROW CANYON ARCHAEOLOGICAL CENTER, 23390 Country Road K, Cortez, CO 81321, (800) 422-8975.

Volunteers take part in nighttime beach patrols to measure tagged turtles, count their eggs and compile other data at the Green Turtle Research Station in Tortuguero on Costa Rica's Caribbean coast. "This is not a tropical vacation; conditions are primitive and volunteers must be dedicated," cautioned the staffer at the Massachusetts Audubon Society, which handles reservations.

MASSACHUSETTS AUDUBON SOCIETY, South Great Road, Lincoln, MA 01773, (800) 289-9504. The fee for a 10-day spring trip in Costa Rica includes airfare from Miami.

La Sabranenque, a nonprofit French group, has been working for 20 years to preserve rural Mediterranean habitats. Come summer, Americans join a multinational band of volunteers in restoring historic villages in Italy and Provence.

LA SABRANENQUE RESTORATION PROJECTS, c/o Jacqueline C. Simon, 217 High Park Boulevard, Buffalo, NY 14226, (716) 836-8698.

When the Sierra Club spokesman described the 60 to 70 service trips this venerable conservation group offers every year [see *Dave,* above], he also could have been describing the trail maintenance programs sponsored by the equally old and respected Adirondack and Appalachian Mountain Clubs. Volunteers usually pack into a base where they set up camp before getting to work clearing trails, picking up the garbage and the like.

ADIRONDACK MOUNTAIN CLUB TRAILS PROGRAM, Box 867, Lake Placid, NY 12946, (518) 523-3480. A small donation is requested each week to pay for food.

APPALACHIAN MOUNTAIN CLUB TRAILS PROGRAM, Pinkham Notch Camp, Box 298, Gorham, NH 03581, (603) 466-2721. A small weekly fee covers cabin or tent and board.

The Smithsonian Institution started a research expeditions program along the lines of the Earthwatch model 5 years ago. Now the Smithsonian fields curator-led forays to 16 or more locations annually, including "Fossil Marine Mammals of Calvert Cliffs," a 10-day expedition in Maryland.

SMITHSONIAN INSTITUTION, 490 Lefant Plaza SW, Suite 4210, Washington, DC 20560, (202) 287-3210. Prices vary.

The environmental field studies program conducted by Wildland Studies at San Francisco State University is concerned with gathering and assessing data in support of various conservation efforts. Team members, under the direction of scientists, collect information on Whale Behavior, Bobcat Preservation, Wolf Habitats, Alaska Wildlands, The Colorado Plateau, and Critical Canadian Environments.

WILDLAND STUDIES, 3 Mosswood Circle, Cazadero, CA 95421, (707) 632-5665. Participants in the 3-week summer program must bring their own camping gear and share in the cost of food.

Bibliography

The Directory of Alternative Travel Resources ($7, published by Dianne G. Brause; available through Co-Op America Travel Links, (800) 424-2667, 26 pages, 1988). Contains a comprehensive list of research and other volunteer organizations plus other travel opportunities.

Helping Out in the Outdoors, A Directory of Volunteer Work and Internships on America's Public Lands ($3, The American Hiking Society, 1015 31st Street, NW, Washington, DC 20007, 92 Pages, 1990). Thorough listing of volunteer jobs available with parks, wilderness areas and environmental groups.

Volunteer Vacations, by Bill Millon ($11.95, Chicago Review Press, 814 N. Franklin Street, Chicago, IL 60610, 1989). A 280-page paperback subtitled "A Directory of Short-term Adventures That Will Benefit You...And Others."

New World of Travel, by Arthur Frommer ($16.95, Prentice Hall, New York, NY, 1990). A first-rate compendium of "Volunteer Vacations" including "Selfless Vacations, the Jimmy Carter Way."

Playing Tennis

There seems to be a correlation between the degree of luxury at America's tennis resorts and sleep-away camps and the singles-to-couples ratio. Elegant, multi-purpose resorts attract far fewer tennis solos than do the collegiate summer clinics that sprout up on campuses all over the US. Less than 10% to 15% of the players at John Gardiners' Tennis Ranch in Arizona arrive alone. Only 20% to 30% of the tennis campers at the Tennis & Life Camps, run by Gustavus Adolphus College in Minnesota, attend in pairs. Topnotch at Stowe, a slick spa, golf and tennis resort in the Green Mountains of Vermont, is an exception. The three tennis weeks held especially for singles in June, July and September are attended by 90% solo travelers.

Pricing Categories

Inexpensive	Under $75 a day
Moderate	$75 to $125 a day
Expensive	$126 to $200
Very Expensive	Over $200 a day

AMELIA ISLAND PLANTATION
Amelia Island, Florida

Encouraging words flew as fast as tennis balls at Amelia Island Plantation in Florida over Memorial Day weekend. Instructors on 8 of the Plantation's 19 Har-Tru courts cajoled and complimented two dozen 25- to 70-year-old "campers" while bombarding them with a steady flow of bright yellow balls. Their encouragement and ebullience took some of the pain out of attempting to relearn the basic tennis strokes and helped keep our minds off the humid, 97-degree day.

The Tennis Singles Weekend at Amelia Island was run by the now-defunct All American Sports. However, the experience is still relevant. Not only does Amelia continue to offer tennis packages, but the program was typical of those offered at most tennis resorts. Even more to the point, a solo jaunt to the enormous Amelia Island complex was illuminating in and of itself.

All American was reputed to deliver quality instruction, and they did. However, I went to the Amelia Singles Weekend with more than tennis in mind. Would a solitary traveler feel overwhelmed at this 1,250-acre complex of hotels, condos, and million-dollar homes spread across a northern Florida barrier island? Would an event arranged especially for singles be fruitful—or fun?

Despite the wide, flat stretch of beach and an exceptionally pleasant and effective staff, this immense property with three eighteen-hole golf courses, six restaurants and three elevator buildings was daunting. For starters, there was a hokey Hawaiian welcome—a lei, an orchid and a plastic cup of insipid punch. Next, the registration clerks had never heard of All American Sports. (Was that an omen?) Nor, at first, had the Racquet Park, where the course was to be held. It turned out, finally, that the placement tryouts for Singles Weekend participants were over, but that latecomers were welcome to come over to the courts and watch the exhibition matches. So I hopped into one of Amelia's endlessly-circling vans to Racquet Park, an impressive tennis-and-spa complex set amidst aged live oaks swathed in gauzy moss.

There were 2,000 people at Amelia over Memorial Day weekend. Still, participants had counted on the tennis program to be a rallying point for singles. We would be a droplet in the stream of conventioneers and festivants, but what matter after a sweaty day on the courts, so long as we found companions with whom to troop off to one of the three Plantation restaurants that served dinner? To their credit, All American tried. Late Friday afternoon, 27 singles, from New York and New Jersey mostly, got together with the staff over purplish punch, beer and cheese. Afterwards, most ended up wandering back to their rooms by themselves.

At 8:30 Saturday morning everyone was back on the courts ready to play. The "Top Seed" program we had elected called for 3 hours of instruction, a half hour private lesson and a round robin doubles tournament the first day, 3 hours of instruction and a videotaped critique the second day and 2 hours, devoted mostly to tennis strategy, the last day.

The program director watched each of us play, and after a drill sergeant-style warm up, she arrayed us on the courts according to ability. Instructors rotated in 30-minute shifts, coaching us in forehand, backhand, service, and volley. With one short break for thirst-quenching orange segments, we played from about 8:45 to 11:30 am. Then came a half hour private lesson before lunch. On Sunday, doubles games followed a review of basic stokes, then our director suggested dinner at the 1889 House in nearby Fernandina Beach for dinner.

Up to this point there was agreement that not enough had been done to see that the singles mingled socially. We also agreed that All American's staff was skilled, but competent teaching does not an exciting weekend make. Except for one lunch, I ate my meals alone.

Judged solely as a resort, Amelia Island has its attractions. The gentle surf and sunflower yellow umbrellas on the fine, firm sand at the Beach Club were alluring. My comfortable, big room in the soaring Sandcastle complex was predictably decorated but pleasing, and if guests didn't feel like walking 3 or 4 minutes to a beach front restaurant, they had a mini-refrigerator stocked with macadamia nuts, cheese, and imported chocolates as well as decaffeinated coffee, soft drinks and liquor. Out under the hot blue sky, or canopied by cedar and beech trees, there were pools, golf courses, and jogging and bicycle paths galore. No resort nicety has been overlooked at Amelia Plantation. At the staid Duneside Restaurant, it's even possible to enjoy a particularly good, prix fixe dinner.

For such a large and complex resort, Amelia Island is exceptionally well-run, but it can be overwhelming for someone traveling alone. This visit confirmed my belief that a solo sojourn is better enjoyed in smaller, more intimate surroundings. Certainly, I'd investigate thoroughly before registering again for a program advertised especially for singles.

AMELIA ISLAND PLANTATION, Amelia Island, FL 32034, (800) 874-6878 or (904) 261-6161. The tennis package includes 2 hours of group instruction, unlimited court time and use of the Health & Fitness Center (no meals). Expensive to Very Expensive.

 Other Voices

TOPNOTCH AT STOWE SINGLES WEEK
Stowe, Vermont

"The singles week at Topnotch at Stowe wasn't like a Club Med vacation, where you eat, drink, socialize, and play tennis with everybody who's there. Not everyone was interested in socializing. So if you went to network or to meet people, you might end up disappointed." John, a 27-year-old Bostonian in computer sales was a bit let down by the social side of the singles tennis camp he attended in Vermont. "However," he points out, "tennis should be the primary reason for going.

"The tennis instruction is outstanding. Topnotch is a resort, but it's also a tennis school, with a fully staffed program. There's a new health spa so you can have a terrific athletically-oriented vacation.

"Maximum attendance is 25 to 30, for 8 outdoor courts. Some people attend by the day. I go 5 days at a time, and I went to one singles week. The instructors are really advanced players who aren't quite up to the pro circuit. Everybody can benefit being around that caliber of player. They divide you into groups of the same ability level, and they rotate the instructors, but I was surprised they didn't have any tournaments or round robins, especially for the singles.

"The accommodations are quite comfortable. Most people stay in the main hotel, and the food is excellent, but none of the tables were set for the group. You have to make your own friends and your own dining plans. Initially, they invited all the guests to the hotel bar to meet the pros, but after a drink or two, everyone seemed to go their own way. It was not unusual to walk into the dining room for lunch and see 10 people from the tennis camp sitting at 10 different tables by themselves. Meals are a la carte during singles week, another mistake.

"I heard that camaraderie was much more evident at the other singles programs that summer. The chemistry of the group has a lot to do with it. Maybe I was just there on a dud week.... There are a lot of things they could have done that would have added to the singles week: organized it better and used some imagination.

"I would definitely go back again, but just to play tennis, and I probably would take someone with me."

TOPNOTCH AT STOWE, PO Box 1260, Stowe, VT 05672, (800) 451-8686 or (802) 253-8585. Expensive.

NICK BOLLETTIERI TENNIS ACADEMY
Bradenton, Florida

Jack, 55, builds computer software and describes himself as a "solid intermediate tennis player." He works at improving his tennis at the Nick Bollettieri Tennis Academy in Bradenton, Florida.

"They group you according to ability. You do various drills, depending on what you want to work on, in half hour segments for 2 hours in the morning, 2 in the afternoon. They rotate instructors, mostly the same people whenever I've been there. Sometimes the instructors serve balls to you; sometimes you're playing with someone else while the instructor watches and critiques. It's a year-round camp, and you can spend from a day and a half to a week there.

"This is not a resort. It's tennis. Bollettieri is on the courts about half the time. He's got about 120 kids who live there, go to high school and play tennis. He's also got a lot of the top, young rising stars, and he has turned out some very good players. Andre Agassi trains there. If you're good, you get to play with the kids.

"You can stay in a hotel or motel in Bradenton, or you can stay on the grounds. The on-campus facilities are okay, two-room suites like you lived in in college. You get cafeteria-style meals there, too, which is convenient because the hotels are too far away to reach for lunch. The food's pretty good. Because of the dormitories and the meals, Bollettieri's is great for singles."

NICK BOLLETTIERI TENNIS ACADEMY, 550 34th Street W., Bradenton, FL 34210, (800) USA-NICK or (813) 755-1000. Moderate.

VAN DER MEER SUMMER CAMP
Sweet Briar College, Lynchburg, Virginia

Carol, a Virginia housewife, age 37, who takes tennis lessons regularly and plays practically every day, reports on the the Van der Meer Summer Camp at Sweet Briar College in Lynchburg, Virginia.

"It was total tennis. We called it 'boot camp' because we were so exhausted by the end of the day. This particular program, in May, was for advanced tennis players. They didn't touch your forehand or backhand, but jumped straight into volleys and running up to the net. Then they keep running the drills, switching you to a different court and a different pro every half hour. By the end of the first day, the instructors knew all our names, about 80 of us.

"They videotape you, and they'll pull you aside if you're not doing something right and spend maybe a half hour with you, just trying to help you get it right. The camp is great. It goes on all summer, with different levels different weeks.

"This Van der Meer [there is another Van der Meer operation on Hilton Head] is especially good for singles. Because you're isolated on a college campus, there's nothing to do but play tennis. You share tables in the cafeteria. Every day I had breakfast, lunch and dinner there, and I met loads of people. You know what they say about college food. I thought, 'Well, I'll go and loose some weight.' But the food was tasty. They served beer, and at night we sat at the tables long after dinner talking, then we'd all play cards, and meet more people.

"And it's just beautiful there at Sweet Briar, nothing but fresh air and mountains. There were more women than men, maybe 50 to 60 out of the 80. A few couples, but not many. Most of the people were over 30, including one 74-year-old man.

"It was so much fun, I'm trying to get all my friends to go back next summer."

VAN DER MEER TENNIS CENTER, Box 5902, Hilton Head Island, SC 29938. (800) 845-6138 or (803) 785-8388. The 4-night, 5-day adult clinic at Sweet Briar includes 25 hours of instruction. Inexpensive.

GRAY ROCKS INN
Quebec, Canada

"I was amazed at how close we all became. The staff encourages people to get to know one another, but everyone's so friendly; they really didn't have to," Dave recalls. A government health researcher, age 32, in Halifax, Nova Scotia, he had spent the second week of September at the total tennis operation run by the Gray Rocks Inn in Quebec Province.

"There were 5 pros for the 22 people taking the tennis week. That's a high ratio, but it was late in the season, which may explain it. We had 22 hours of lessons over the course of the week. I was on the court before breakfast, on my break, late in the afternoon. I played tennis 10 hours a day: hitting at the ball machine, playing against walls, batting balls between ourselves.

"We all ate breakfast together and hit the courts at 8:00 am. Again at night, we'd all meet in the dining area about 7:30 pm to 8:00 pm to eat together. The first night, we ate by ourselves, but after that, it was all of us, one table of 22, at every meal. We'd sit over dinner until about 10:00 pm, then have a drink maybe, and hit the sack.

"There was one casino night in town, but no other organized social events for our group. We shared the dining area with a compressed gas convention—we made plenty of jokes about that—100 of them to our 22, and maybe a handful of other loose guests. There are several accommodations options. I stayed in the main inn, which was fine; not excellent, but my part of the building is to be renovated this year. The rooms are fairly small and close together in that part of the inn, so I imagine they could be noisy if the inn were full.

"The adjective I'd use to describe the Gray Rocks program is 'comfortable.' You couldn't beat it if you were traveling alone. The instructors, the staff, everyone, is willing to help, to advise, to talk with you, and the quality of the food is unparalleled."

GRAY ROCKS INN, PO Box 1000, St. Jovite, Quebec, Canada JOT 2HO, (800) 567-6767 or (819) 425-2771. Use of the tennis courts and private instruction cost extra. Moderate.

JOHN NEWCOMBE'S TENNIS RANCH
New Braunfels, Texas

"I've been happily married for 15 years, and yet my husband rarely goes with me. I dance and sing and play tennis with men from all over, and I have a ball. I've never had a problem or felt uncomfortable," says Cathy, a 35-year-old Houston housewife describing John Newcombe's Tennis Ranch in Texas. "I go to camp there, my children go to camp there."

"It's about 185 miles from San Antonio. They have beautiful condos, some cottages. If you're alone, they give you a single with your own bath. If you're lucky, there will be deer standing on your front steps when you get up.

"There's a lovely dining room in the main lodge, but most of the time the weather is so beautiful you eat outside, dinner especially. No, you never eat alone. If you're a little shy, the pros will take you around a bit and make you feel comfortable.

"The tennis is intense. They have 28 courts, some night-lit. You start off with a welcome reception and cocktails, then dinner. After that they set you in a mixed doubles tournament just for fun. They pair you up according to what you say your ability is (I'm a B player), and you change partners after each set. By the end of the evening you should have played against or with everyone, usually 40 to 50 people, and that's great, because now everyone's met.

"Next morning there's a brief orientation. Newcombe's Australian, and he's got instructors from all over the world. The jokes and wisecracks are really fun. After tips on tennis, you head for the courts, where they break you up into groups of four or six, each with an instructor, for drills until noon. During lunch there's time to sun, swim, hot tub, shower, whatever.

"They videotape you individually during afternoon drills, and the group watches the videos. Everyone cracks jokes; it's not the least bit embarrassing. At 4:00 pm you're back into the mixed doubles tournament, but this time it counts for trophies. Then you go back to your room to freshen up for dinner, thoroughly exhausted.

"Cocktails. Dinner. Awards. Everybody dances and drinks margaritas outside on the deck by the pool, sometimes until 3:00 am. Of course, you're sorry the next morning when you reach the court at 9:00 am. Drills 'til lunch, then a little good-bye party. By mid-afternoon, you're on your way.

"It's the Southern hospitality that makes it so wonderful for people there alone. You'll find players from 18 to 75, senior citizens who've never held a racket before, all having a ball."

JOHN NEWCOMBE'S TENNIS RANCH, PO Box 310469, New Braunfels, TX 78131-0469, (800) 444-6204 or (512) 620-9427. The 5-night, 5-day stay includes 27 hours of instruction, lodging and meals. Moderate.

 ## *Other Choices* _____

The 32-room Inn and Tennis Club at Manitou, 150 miles north of Toronto, is one of the premier tennis resorts in North America. A member of Relais and Chateau, the inn is esteemed for French cuisine, luxurious fireplace rooms with private decks, a brand new lakeside spa, as well as first-rate tennis. No more than 20% of the guests are solos, but the inn is notably friendly, and singles are seated with groups at dinner, unless they prefer a table to themselves.

INN AND TENNIS CLUB AT MANITOU, McKellar, Ontario, Canada P0G 1C0, (416) 967-3466 (winter: 251 Davenport Road, Toronto, Ontario, Canada M5R 1J9). They offer 4- and 7-day tennis packages. Very Expensive.

John Gardiner pioneered all-tennis resorts with the 14-room, 14-court Tennis Ranch in Carmel, California, a bastion of exclusivity today. His latest effort, John Gardiner's Rancho Valencia Resort, a 21-bungalow venture in the hills above Rancho Santa Fe is equally luxurious. The larger, 100-room Scottsdale, Arizona property, John Gardiner's Tennis Ranch on Camelback, is the most appropriate Gardiner clinic for singles. "Socializing is facilitated by the method of instruction—four people plus an instructor on each court—as well as group dining, if you want, and other communal events," reports a reservationist. "By Tuesday, everyone knows each other."

JOHN GARDINER'S TENNIS RANCH ON CAMELBACK, 5700 East McDonald Drive, Scottsdale, AZ 85253-5268, (800) 245-2051 or (602) 948-2100. Rates are all-inclusive. Very Expensive.

"If you wish," states the Tennis and Life Camps brochure, "you are able to spend 15 hours a day in planned and supervised tennis activities." Four different camps, planned to meet different tennis needs, make use of the 12 Plexipave and 4 indoor courts at Gustavus Adolphus College in Minnesota each summer. The staff will pair the mostly-single, mostly-women campers in double dorm rooms.

TENNIS AND LIFE CAMPS, Gustavus Adolphus College, St. Peter, MN 56082, (507) 931-1614. Inexpensive.

Up to 5 hours a day of tennis instruction, rain or shine, isn't the only attraction at the summer clinics held by Total Tennis in the Berkshires. Volleyball games, a swim party, movies on Tuesday and Friday nights please the 20 to 45-year-olds—about a third arrive alone—who make up the majority of the players who flock to the Williston Northampton School, where the tennis program is held. You'll find group seating at meals, single and double rooms (Total Tennis will match you with a roommate), even a health spa.

TOTAL TENNIS, Box 1106, Wall Street Station, New York, NY 10268-1106, (800) 221-4696 or (718) 636-6141. Moderate.

See also CLUB MED PARADISE ISLAND in CARIBBEAN.

Bibliography

The UNITED STATES TENNIS ASSOCIATION, 707 Alexander Road, Princeton, NJ 08540, (609) 452-2580, distributes three publications free: printed guidelines for selecting an appropriate tennis camp; a booklet called *1992 Tennis Publications*; and "Tennis Camps and Clinics," an annual directory.

The World's Best Tennis Vacations, by Roger Cox ($12.95, Stephen Greene Press, Viking Penguin, Penguin USA, New York, NY 10014, (212) 366-2000, 1990). An excellent, outspoken guide. Cox is an expert and his opinions ring true.

Dude Ranches

Riding, roundups, rodeos, and roping are great levelers. The four Rs of ranching (once there were five, but "roughing it" is still in style only on working ranches) ally guests of all ages, backgrounds and partnership states.

The trend today is toward diversification. The hot tubs that coddle a rider's sore rump in summer bubble in winter for the cross country skier. White water trips are sure to be part of the fun if the ranch encompasses a river swift enough for rafting. Llama treks are *de rigueur* on certain spreads, and there is almost always fishing.

During July and August most traditional dude ranches are filled to their pine lodgepoles with multi-generational families and summer-vacationing kids. Those who prefer mingling with couples and other loners should plan to visit earlier or later in the season.

There will be fewer children and more solos, even in high season, at a no-frills, working ranch where guests saddle up and help drive the cattle. A custom designer of western itineraries believes working ranches are particularly appropriate for singles because "everyone mucks in together."

The resort-style ranch is also a possibility. "Singles do well at the bigger, multi-faceted ranches, where there are plenty of people and activities to choose from," remarks Dave Wiggins, owner of Old West Dude Ranch Vacations.

Ranches are also integral to many "Combo Vacations." Those who are unsure whether or not they want to be stuck at one ranch should simply add a pack trip, canoe voyage or both to their vacations.

Pricing Categories

Inexpensive	————	Under $75 a day
Moderate	————	$75 to $125 a day
Expensive	————	$126 to $200
Very Expensive	————	Over $200 a day

CIRCLE Z RANCH
Patagonia, Arizona

The Circle Z Ranch, turquoise-trimmed and brightened by vibrant ovals of emerald green grass, may be the lushest spread between Tucson and the Mexican border. In January, the honey beige ranch houses hung with chile ristras and sprays of juniper, are a cheerful contrast to the sere, wintry hills. Here, for aficionados of Southwestern style, is the real thing.

Tucked between rocky Sanford Butte and Sonita Creek at an altitude of 4,000 feet, the Circle Z opened for guests in the twenties. Sixty-five years later, with riding, tennis, a solar-heated pool, trap shooting, and shuffleboard, it caters to 40 guests and is one of the oldest dude ranches in Arizona. Mission-style buildings fashioned of adobe bricks made on-site and timeless Mexican furnishings are only part of the 880-acre ranch's authentic charm. The 90 mostly-ranch-bred horses and the little-touristed location are equally compelling. Devout Western riders inspired by resolutely Old West landscapes ("Red River" was filmed here) should find the Circle Z especially pleasing.

Riding's key; the horses are tops. Our mounts stayed put, reins on the ground, as we washed down mesquite-seared hamburgers with beer during the traditional Saturday cookout. They didn't pause to drink while fording streams or munch on grass along the trails. The foreman made assignments, noting that "Everyone wants a small horse with rocking-horse gaits."

Guests were grouped by ability into posses of seven or eight. "Medium" rides offered loping; a "slow" ride means trotting at most on the 2 1/2-hour daily rides. The wranglers were pleasant enough, but not too talkative. Circle Z regulars acted as guides, pointing out red-tailed hawks, barrel cacti and spiky ocotillo, stands of cottonwoods and silvery mesquite.

The riding is sociable, the atmosphere's Western casual, and the hospitality's unstinting at the Circle Z. It took me all of an hour to feel at home. First-timers on the bargain weekend plan offered sporadically November through January were indistinguishable from the weekers. The ranch attracts families and is ideal for single parents with kids.

Before dinner guests can read and play board games by the stone fireplace, but most wander up to the cantina to fix their own drinks. Wedged around the oblong bar, everyone crunches roasted corn kernels and chats until a flick of the lights signals dinner at 7:00 pm sharp.

Back in the lodge's colorful dining room, succulent roast pork was dished up one night, gratineed chicken breasts in a winy cream sauce the next. We heaped on accompaniments from the terra cotta buffet and sat at colorfully set tables for six. Fridays, Pancho cooks Mexican—all day. At dinner, lightly battered, fresh Anaheim chiles were stuffed with jack cheese, and the zucchini casserole was flecked with corn, onions and cheese. Weather allowing, guests lunch outside on the grassy patio.

The weather is highly unpredictable in late winter and early spring. Temperatures can veer 40 degrees in one day. Bring clothes to layer on or strip off. Old Circle Z hands dressed for dinner in wool, designer sweaters and down vests.

Frost covered the ground each morning, but my inviting salmon pink and blue room in Casa Rosa was toasty. Forced-air heat flooded the large, spotless room and handsome, beige-tiled bath. Mexican tiles topped the dressers, an oval braided rug and locally silk-screened cushions on the white wicker furniture composed the pleasing decor.

Sunday, the horses' day off, is a good time to explore the formidable countryside. Several worth-the-detour shops include Graham & Wrays, an emporium stocked floor-to-dusty-ceiling with bargain-priced Mexican glasses in Nogales, Arizona and El Changarro at Elias 91-93 Nogales, Mexico.

This top-notch source for fine Mexican antiques and artifacts ships to US customers via UPS. You can also drive 20 miles north to Tubac, a folksy shopping mecca and former garrison town. Except for the Tortuga bookstore's astute collection of regional books and cards and the primitive, hand-painted animals and furniture at Jonathan Shriver's, the Latin-accented Tubac stores were predictable. For outstanding watercolors, jewelry and other local handcrafts, visit Mesquite Grove in the town of Patagonia.

CIRCLE Z RANCH, Patagonia, Arizona 85624, (602) 287-2091. Rooms come with either shared or private bath. Moderate.

 Other Voices _____

ABSAROKA RANCH
Dubois, Wyoming

"Evenings, they turn all the horses loose on the range. Every morning at about 5:00 am the wranglers round them up. It's just beautiful to watch, as the sun comes up, the horses running in." An office manager in Cincinnati, 43, Joanne was looking for a remote, out-of-the-way place to relax. She found it at the Absaroka Ranch in Wyoming and returned a second year. She tells why.

"They met me at the airport in Jackson Hole, a couple hours' drive from the ranch, the end of June. It's way off the beaten path, at an elevation of 8,000 feet. Perfect for riding the high country. The lodge, with a backdrop of mountains, accommodates a maximum of 16, and the food is out of this world. Emmy Betts, co-host of Absaroka with her husband Budd, oversees it all.

"We'd get up and have breakfast about 8:00 am. The horses would be saddled up and ready to go by the time we finished. Everybody ate together; the guests, the help, the owners, everybody, and you got to know people sitting around that big, round table. We'd ride 'til lunch, come back and eat at the ranch, or sometimes they'd pack our lunch and we'd take all-day rides high up into the mountains.

"They divide you into different levels of riding, according to your ability. The groups were of three or four people, so you could make some really close friends or you can just hang loose. You can fish, hunt, and they will take you out on several-day camp-outs. You have your choice.

"The guests included a couple of families with kids. If you're by yourself, it's best to go before school's out or in September. There were other singles, but it was mostly couples. I didn't feel the least bit out of place, never thought about not having a mate with me."

ABSAROKA RANCH, Star Route, Dubois, WY 82513, (307) 455-2275. Moderate.

G BAR M
Clyde Park, Montana

"It was nice meeting people from all over the world at the G Bar M in Montana, but I really wanted to meet the people who lived there, the locals," explains Andrea, 26, an office services manager from Maryland.

"The G Bar M is a family ranch with a plain but homey ranch house, no pool or tennis courts. It's the Leffingwells' home. At the most, there were eight of us, mostly couples, so you all sit around the big table in the kitchen. There are a few bedrooms in the house, and a few cabins for people with kids or if you just want privacy.

"Everyone gets their own horse, and George Leffingwell is very concerned about how comfortable you are with your horse and your saddle. You don't have to work unless you want to. It's very down to earth, nothing fancy.

"I did get up early and go out first thing and watch the animals come to water. I saw deer and assorted little animals. I'd come back from my walk to a huge breakfast: pancakes, eggs, sausage, toast, the works, all of us together. Then we'd all go out for a morning ride into different areas of the mountains, every day a different view. Montana is pastoral and just gorgeous.

"You'd come back and have lunch at 12:30, a big feed. You could go out again for another ride in the afternoon, or fish or something else, maybe take it easy later. Dinner's at 6:30. It's a real family, and they made you feel like you belonged.

"I left with a sense of what's really important in the big scheme of things. It was a combination of the vastness and beauty of the earth and how much this family, who has worked the ranch for generations, how much they respect the land and each other, how decent they are."

G BAR M, Box AE, Clyde Park, MT 59018, (406) 686-4423. All meals are included in the rates. Inexpensive.

SKYLINE RANCH
Telluride, Colorado

"Even on the morning ride you pass through some pretty tough terrain. Reminds you of a John Wayne western...in fact, a number of movies have been filmed around Telluride where the ranch is located." Paul, age 31 and a commodities broker in New York, describes the Skyline Ranch in Colorado.

"I did things there I never thought I would do, like climbing a 14,000-foot peak, going on horseback trips...the whole horse bit. The last time I stayed there, in late winter/early spring, Sherry and Dave Farny, the owners, took me to canyon country in Utah. I didn't know that kind of pristine environment still existed in the US. Visiting the ranch exposed me to new adventures, and a new appreciation of the wilderness, and a concern for it.

"The Farnys aren't the kind of people who like to see you sitting around doing nothing, even though they say okay, sure, it's fine. They really want you out riding and climbing, cross country skiing and rafting. Dave's the horse guy. Sherry will drive you into town at night to a classical concert, and tell you the names of all the wildflowers.

"Basically the summer activities are horses, hiking and square dancing. At night, we all sat around drinking beer and doing this silly square dancing stuff, but it was great. There was no pretentiousness about it.

"The ranch is a wonderful place to meet people, assuming you're not a total introvert. The Farnys work hard to see that everybody mixes. Skyline's for those who want to try new things and see things they never expected, not for those want to play bridge or sit around and watch TV."

SKYLINE RANCH, PO Box 67, Telluride, CO 81435 (303) 728-3757. Rates are all inclusive. Moderate.

RANCHO DE LOS CABALLEROS
Wickenburg, Arizona

"Rancho de los Caballeros is a quiet place with a largely over-50 crowd." Emmy, a recently widowed New Yorker, describes the 6 weeks she spent at this luxurious ranch resort.

"The ranch is in a charming little town, Wickenburg, and beautifully done. The accommodations were superb; there are old one-story adobe buildings and a new section that's more modern-looking but southwestern inside. Like most, my room had a beehive fireplace in the corner and a patio overlooking the hills. Lovely.

"They have a gorgeous golf course right there on the grounds. Beautiful tennis courts. Skeet shooting. I did a lot of walking and painting on my own. The riding at Los Cab is wonderful. Most of these ranches have very reliable horses that are sure-footed but kind of plodders, but Los Cab seemed to have a much better breed of horse. The riding program is well supervised, with different rides; slow, medium and fast.

"You make your own way there, do your own thing—bridge-playing, pool, movies, and lectures at night; in general, pretty standard ranch fare. The help is friendly, intelligent, anxious to help and to please. They were marvelous with the single ladies, of whom there were quite a few.

"The dining room seats 100 or more, and is family-style. You're assigned a seat at a large table. I just enjoyed myself immensely. There were single men, and two elderly gentlemen who I went out to dinner with.... This was a marvelous bunch of people. I'd do it again."

RANCHO DE LOS CABALLEROS, Wickenburg, Arizona 85358, (602) 684-5484. Rates include all meals. Moderate.

C LAZY U
Granby, Colorado

"A well-established dude ranch in Granby, Colorado, the C Lazy U is family-run. They make a special effort to introduce you around if they know you're single," reports Robin, 31, a vice president of a major New York City bank.

"You eat family-style, so you can sit wherever you want and always meet new people. In fact, the food is the best I've ever eaten. Breakfast is buffet, lunches outside near the pool. You'll have a couple of barbecues during the week and planned group activities such as square dancing, or a talent show, or someone singing.

"The people who go there are all horse-lovers, on different levels. You don't have to be a good rider since they have three levels of trail rides. The horses are great, about 150 good cow ponies. You have people from all over, many repeaters. Of a maximum of 100 to 110 guests there might be 8 to 10 single women and 4 or 5 single men, but you don't go there for a fling.

"Over the course of 30 to 40 years, the ranch has added a variety of accommodations: old cabins that stand alone, where you have your own bedroom and fireplace, newer structures with a couple of bedrooms for families, or you can have a small room and private bath in the main lodge. These are the least expensive, but they're cheerful and every room has a picture window looking out at the mountains and the ranch.

"Children aren't allowed in September, so you get a smaller crowd with more singles, but in summer the kids, even though they're in a special camp during the day and don't even eat with the adults, add to the excitement and fun. The people seemed nicer in family times; the September guests were more serious horse people.

"The ranch closes after September and reopens in winter with some great cross country skiing and even some downhill trails, but you can't ride. It's not cheap. This is a five-star, five-diamond ranch, so most of the guests are professionals."

C LAZY U, PO Box 378B, Granby, CO 80446, (303) 887-3344. Expensive.

Other Dude Ranch Choices _____

Sixteen guests (about 10% of them solos) share 2,300 acres and an unusually wide range of activities at Busterbach Ranch, a resort with a cattle operation. There's windsurfing, kyacking and canoeing on nearby Lake Alturas and mountain biking at the informal eight-guest-room spread that runs a Nordic ski center in winter.

BUSTERBACH RANCH, Star Route, Ketchum, ID 83340, (208) 774-2217. Expensive.

A maximum of 40 guests may sleep in old log cabins at the Circle Bar Guest Ranch, but they socialize and dine in a modern, Western-elegant lodge. Registered quarter horses comprise half the saddle herd and riding is key, but there are hayrides, cookouts and fishing too. "Sara Hollatz, the owner, writes musical comedies and has a way with her guests. That's why I recommend the Circle Bar Ranch to solos," says one pro.

CIRCLE BAR GUEST RANCH, Utica, Montana 59452, (406) 423-5454. Moderate.

The Focus HT, a working ranch, has been taking on about 30 guests to help move cattle, check fences, open irrigation ditches and demolish beaver dams for over 35 years, but the cowboy wannabes dismount occasionally for sightseeing trips, hikes, picnics, fishing in the Little Snake River and for steak cookouts, square dances or a baseball game now and again.

FOCUS HT, Slater, CO 81653, (303) 583-2410. Moderate.

Guests can ride, fish, hike, and be as dudish as they like at High Island, a 91,000-acre, operating cattle ranch. In June guests can also help drive the cattle 35 miles from the lower ranch to the upper (dude) ranch at 9,000 feet; in September they can help drive them down again. Camp out and dine from a horse-drawn chuck wagon during roundup. Guests can also take part in branding week during June.

HIGH ISLAND, Box 71B, Hamilton Dome, WY 82427, (307) 867-2374. Moderate.

Saguaro, ocotillo and rolly-polly barrel cactus grow on the second oldest ranch in Arizona, the notably friendly Kay El Bar. Twenty guests sleep in ancient adobe buildings there; ride out to the Hassayampa River and enjoy the blandishments of their hostesses, two sisters who bought the homey ranch 10 years ago and run it with an assist or two from their husbands.

KAY EL BAR, PO Box 2480, Wickenburg, AZ 85358, (602) 684-7593. Moderate.

Quoting *Dude Ranches of the American West*, Tack Van Cleve, an owner of the 26,000-acre guest and cattle ranch, says the Lazy K Bar is "One of the oldest and most beautiful dude ranches in the country." There are Yellowstone trips, dips in the pool and top-notch riding, but life is unstructured on the 110-year-old ranch where up to 45 guests help with the cattle operation if they wish.

LAZY K BAR, Box 550, Big Timber, MT 59011, (406) 537-4404. Moderate.

Set between the snow-capped Wind River and Absaroka ranges in a valley 19 miles long, the exceedingly scenic Lazy L & B is surrounded by limitless land. The up-to-30 guests, usually including several solos, can opt for a change of scene and spend a couple of nights on the upper ranch camping in tents at this traditional Western dude ranch.

LAZY L & B, Dubois, WY 82513, (307) 455-2839. Moderate.

Tennis courts, modern bedrooms and a fitness center are a few of the resort-like wrinkles that have earned Mountain Sky, an old ranch with a new owner since 1986, the Triple

A's 4-Diamond Award. Families predominate in July and August, but in June and September solos account for about 50% of the 65 guests.

MOUNTAIN SKY, PO Box 1128, Bozeman, MT 59715, (800) 548-3392 or (406) 587-1244. Expensive to Very Expensive.

 Reservations Services _____

OLD WEST DUDE RANCH VACATIONS, PO Box 1486, Boulder, CO 80306, (800) 444-3033 or (303) 494-2992. Represents 40 western ranches, 22 of them in Colorado, and also offers a number of "combo" vacations.

OFF THE BEATEN PATH, 109 East Main Street, Bozeman, MT 59715, (800) 445-2995 or (406) 586-1311. Western trip planning specialists who draw up detailed itineraries, book guides and make reservations for their clients for a fee.

Bibliography

Dude Ranches of the American West by Naomi Black ($12.95, The Stephen Greene Press, Lexington, MA, 1988). Handsome color photographs illustrate this study of 29 classic dude ranches.

Farm, Ranch & Country Vacations by Pat Dickerman ($12.95, Adventure Guides, 36 East 57th Street, New York, NY 10022, (212) 355-6334, 1990). An annotated and illustrated guide that's been updated annually for the past 41 years.

Ranch Vacations by Eugene Kilgore ($18.95, John Muir Publications, PO Box 613, Santa Fe, NM 87504, (800) 888-7504, 1989). A hefty compendium of guest and resort, fly-fishing and cross-country skiing ranches.

Adventure Travel North America by Pat Dickerman ($15.95, Adventure Guides, 36 East 57th Street, New York, NY 10022, 1990). Has information about combo vacations.

Riding Horses

Trek inn-to-inn astride a Morgan horse in Vermont. Ride tent-to-tent on a cow pony in the Rockies or, in New Mexico, follow pack mules to sacred Anasazi Indian sites. Riding vacations are a flourishing travel genre for the novice and the accomplished equestrian alike.

Outfitters estimate that between 30% and 50% of the participants on their rides are solitaries, a good portion of them women. Cowgirls, then, (and cowboys, too) should be pleased to know that most outfits charge a per person rate for their horseback trips. As well they might, considering that riders often bunk together in tents. Single supplements are levied only when participants opt for a single room at the ranches or inns they visit en route.

Pricing Categories

Inexpensive	Under $75 a day
Moderate	$75 to $125 a day
Expensive	$126 to $200
Very Expensive	Over $200 a day

RAPP GUIDE SERVICE
Durango, Colorado

The air was autumn-crisp as I rode into the Colorado Rockies astride a mannerly Apaloosa behind guide Jerry Rapp and a string of five pack mules. Second Box Canyon was still 8,500 feet up in the San Juan National Forest. A faint breeze stirred the golden, aspen leaves, while the spiky new tips of a million spruce trees glowed iridescent blue.

174

From mid-September until mid-October, Jerry Rapp, or his colleague Mark, shepherd four to eight pack-trippers up to the base camp, a collection of beige canvas tents and a makeshift corral tucked into a Sandy Creek bank near the junction of the river. This leisurely, 4-day, camping-and-trail-riding trip was slotted between the high altitude (11,000 feet or more) summer pack trips Rapp leads and the mid-October to mid-November elk season, when hunters fill Jerry's wall tents.

From the start, my association with Rapp Guide Service, arranged by Off the Beaten Path, was straightforward and pleasant. But slick or dudish? Hardly.

Thursday morning Jerry hoisted me into a somewhat battered flatbed truck. We lumbered off through a wide, pastoral valley tinted yellow by the cottonwoods and ringed on three sides by the snow-capped Rockies. The grandeur of the stately mountains engulfed us for the next 4 days.

Saddled and tied to Ponderosa pines, the animals waited at the end of the dirt access road into the Park. With little wasted motion, the waterproof pack bags were filled and strapped onto the mules with diamond hitches. By the time the other riders arrived, we were ready to hit the trail. Jerry led off with the string of mules and the rest of us fell into line. Two hours later, we filed across a river-rimmed meadow into our camp beneath pines and Douglas firs.

The interiors of the two big tents were a bit dusty, but changes have since been made. Tarps now cover the floor of the cook tent, oilcloth has been tacked to the tables and in the sleeping tent, there are colorful flannel "Indian Blankets" on every cot. The tents were of small account in any case, considering the admirable get-up-and-go of our healthy horses, the bonhommie that sprung from shared adventure and the attention Rapp paid to making sure we got the best out of every ride.

On a high, windswept meadow we were perfectly still, except for Rapp, who was attempting to call an elusive elk. The notes, half bugle, half wailing sax, pierced the forest surrounding Lone Tree Park. Suddenly, a bull elk answered, but remained hidden stage right.

Famished and tired after the excitement of the ride, we fixed turkey, salami and cheddar sandwiches and fell asleep on the sun-warmed grass. Behind us jutted the jagged, white peaks of the Continental Divide.

"Be sure to bring a bathing suit," Anne Rapp had said. Hot springs had been discovered in the Piedra. The third day out, we snapped ourselves into long yellow cowboy slickers and in a light rain rode downstream to two large tub-shaped pools. Stripping down in the 45-degree air was small penance for the long, hot, soak that followed.

Breakfasts were hearty, pancake-French-toast-and-bacon affairs cooked in Dutch ovens on two portable stoves. Equally leisurely dinners of the grilled steak and barbecued chicken variety were also cooked in the cast iron pots, sometimes over the crackling bonfire. I learned much about the area from Jerry and my companions, read by the light of faintly hissing Coleman lanterns and got 11 hours of sleep a night. Good fellowship and knockout scenery combined with Western-style riding provided a heady 4 days.

Anyone taking the high altitude, summer trips should spend 24 hours in Durango beforehand acclimating themselves, according to the Rapps. For the 8,000 to 9,000-foot fall trip, 16 hours was sufficient. The night I arrived, Durango—part false-fronted frontier town, part Victorian west—looked especially cheerful. The wide, downtown streets were brightly lit, as were The General Palmer House and the Palace Grill, a comfortable stained-glass and oak restaurant. Next door is the station for the Denver and Rio Grande train that makes the scenic 6-hour round-trip to Silverton over narrow gauge tracks. The engine's hissing steam and mournful whistle add a touch of verisimilitude to the overly recreated, Gay Nineties complex. More satisfactorily authentic is the three-story brick Hotel Strater and the eye-watering hot chiles rellenos served at the Durango Diner for breakfast.

Western Outfitters, located directly across Main Avenue, sells rakish straw cowboy hats for the trip. A few blocks south is the O'Farrell Hat Company, ten-gallon hat-makers par excellence.

RAPP GUIDE SERVICE, 47 Electra Lake Road, Durango, CO 81301, (303) 247-8923. Moderate.

Other Voices _____

RICOCHET RIDGE RANCH
Fort Bragg, California

"I don't like to travel alone at all. I hate walking into a restaurant and sitting by myself," explains Linda, a painter, 36, and art teacher in New York City. A 1-week horseback trip that began at Ricochet Ridge Ranch on Northern California's Redwood Coast eliminated the restaurant problem.

"I flew to San Francisco, then took a bus up to Fort Bragg where Lari Shea met me. The first day she asked about our riding experience in order to assign each of us the proper horse. Some riders were definitely beginners, some were more advanced, and some chose western saddles although most rode English. My horse turned out to be really fast; we'd go flying up the hills, but a couple of riders grumbled about their mounts.

"Beautiful countryside along the Northern California Coast; the beaches are just gorgeous. The first night out we stayed in a hotel, had a cookout and shared a hot tub, which was a good way to get to know each other. There were about 22 people from all over, including a mother and daughter, two middle-aged married couples, other singles (more women than men), but I'd have preferred a smaller group.

"One night we camped out after riding up and down mountains all day. It had been a real endurance test, and there I was in the middle of the forest with my tentmate and her Louis Vuitton luggage. The horses kept getting loose, and we had to wash in the stream, but actually, this wasn't a Girl Scout affair. A cook was brought in to grill salmon and steaks; it was all done very nicely.

"Otherwise we stayed at inns along the way where corrals had been arranged for our horses. Mornings Lari would lay out cold cuts, granola mix and drinks, and we'd pack our own lunches. It was also our job to saddle and unsaddle our horses. In New York City your horse comes down the ramp all ready to go. I had no idea how to put a bridle on, but I learned.

"These trips combine something I like to do, riding, with a way of seeing the surroundings that you can't get on your feet, and you end up being friends with people you wouldn't think you'd choose."

EQUITOUR, PO Box 807, Dubois, WY 82513, (800) 545-0019. Very Expensive.

KEDRON VALLEY STABLES
South Woodstock, Vermont

"Paul Kendall, the proprietor, is very careful in matching you up with a horse, taking your weight, height and riding experience into consideration. He has a variety of horses and has been around animals all his life." Alan, a 47-year-old executive from Massachusetts, was discussing the inn-to-inn rides operated by Kedron Valley Stables.

"The first morning, after dinner and the night at the Kedron Valley Inn, you drive over to the stables, get on your horse and set out for the day. Your bags end up, via truck, at the Inn at Weathersfield, which is the best of the four inns you'll sleep in. The other two (Inn at Long Last in Chester and the Echo Lake Inn in Tyson) are fine; they just don't have as much atmosphere as the Weathersfield. It's homey, very intimate, with excellent food. The owner is a cherub. He plays the piano and sings during dinner. Then he becomes a trivia person and raconteur. Great.

"Each day the stables meet you along the route with a picnic lunch. You take 45 minutes or so to eat, then you ride all afternoon, along dirt roads, logging roads, through fields. Paul's a Woodstock native. He knows all the people, all the trails, and the scenery is so gorgeous. Even in the rain, you enjoy the beauty of it: the trees, meadows, the stone walls, the birch trees."

KEDRON VALLEY STABLES, PO Box 368, South Woodstock, VT 05071, (802) 457-1480. Moderate.

TETON CREST HORSE TREK
Victor, Idaho

"We packed into the Jeremiah Smith Wilderness on the Idaho side of the Tetons, where there are fewer regulations than in the national park. I wasn't with a group. It was just me and a guide named Phil Majors from an outfitter called Teton Crest." This is Andrea, 26, the office services manager from Maryland (see DUDE RANCHES).

"I had no idea what to expect or even what I wanted. All I knew was that I wanted to get into the wilderness, see the mountains and get away from everything. Julie Davies of Off The Beaten Path planned my whole trip West. I really think it's worth the extra 5% on the cost of your vacation to have them help you. Its almost like an insurance policy. They get to know you, and through a range of questions, can really figure out what things to do and the ranches you'd like most.

"On this pack trip part, we were out 5 days. Majors had a camp set up already that we used for 4 nights. We had three mules, two horses and his dog. In retrospect, it would have been more fun with a few more people along. The country was spectacular. If you're afraid of heights or squeamish, it's not a good ride. Some of the mountainsides were terribly steep. We were at an altitude of about 8,000 feet, I think. You really have to trust your horse, but the animals were incredibly sure footed and well-behaved.

"Basically, we took four 1-day trips from base camp. The landscape was very green, since the Tetons had had plenty of rain, and the wild flowers were rife. The weather in late June was perfect, and there was snow. The lake was frozen over. We saw bear tracks and loads of deer. A moose even came into our camp in a wide open meadow near a stream. The sky was beautiful.

"The outfitter supplied a cot, a sleeping bag, the tent, a little shower device, everything, and Phil cooked every night. He even baked bread."

OFF THE BEATEN PATH, 109 East Main Street, Bozeman, MT 59715-9943, (800) 445-2995 or (406) 586-1311. Moderate.

BAR-T-FIVE COVERED WAGON TRAIN
Jackson Hole, Wyoming

"The covered wagons you see in the movies are longer, but these are pretty big; they can take 10 people easily." After 16 straight years, Marilyn is a devotee of the wagon train, which offers the choice of riding horseback or riding in the wagon. A banker, 65, from Washington State, she travels with the Bar-T-Five covered wagon train out of Jackson Hole. She tells why.

"The Thomases take wagoneering very seriously, trying to give people an idea of what it was like when the owner's great-grandfather came through the pass in a wagon 102 years ago. Bill Thomas is consumed with the land and environment.

"We head for the first camp Monday about noon. We'll camp three times: twice on a lake and once on Calf Creek in the Targhee Forest. About 4:00 pm we arrive, set up, get the fire started and begin cooking. Those on horses go for rides and some hike up the mountain.

"The food is delicious. I go on a diet 2 weeks before I leave. There are full breakfasts: French toast, hot cakes, hash browns, bacon, and all. Lunch varies. One day, tacos and fresh fruits and salad, another it's sloppy joes. For dinner, there's always some kind of potato, and bread, vegetables and a salad or coleslaw, as well as fish, steak or chicken and cowboy beans. The hands help with the cooking.

"The wagons are pulled by one team of horses each, the chuck wagon requires two teams. Bill Thomas has several wagons, most of which he built himself. You can either sleep in the wagon or in the tents, which are group tents. You can get a single tent if you really want it.

"The program starts June 25, and goes till the end of August. I've traveled by myself 4 out of the 16 times I've gone. I really need that week by myself to unwind, and this trip is the best thing I've ever found."

BAR-T-FIVE COVERED WAGON TRAIN, PO Box 3415, Jackson, WY 83001, (307) 733-5386. Moderate.

EVERETT RANCH
Salida, Colorado

"I went to the Everett Ranch for the cattle drive and the calving." This may seem an unlikely vacation for a British diplomat stationed in Washington, but it wasn't James' first stay on this working ranch.

"The ranch is a lovely place, gorgeous countryside in the foothills of the Rockies about 3 1/2 hours from Denver. You have a mixture of aspen and spruce forest and open plain, all above the valley of the Arkansas River, but what I like especially is that Everett doesn't make any concessions at all for vacationers. They do just what they would be doing if you weren't there, which is cattle ranching.

"This last visit, early in the year, there was only one other guy and me as guests. Another time there were a school teacher and his girlfriend from San Francisco, a trucker from Michigan, and four French Army officers....

"The accommodations are pretty basic, which is exactly what I want. You're in an old cabin. No electricity, no plumbing, gas lights, wood-burning stoves, and good home-cooking. There's a spring for water. You're by yourself. Owls hooting. It's remarkably peaceful.

"You really work, and it's hard work. You ride all day, maybe 8:45 am to 6:00 pm. That's a lot of hard saddle, and the cattle don't always go where you want them to go. You don't need to be a good rider, but you do need to have a fair amount of push. Otherwise, if you stand there looking feeble, the cow will just stare back at you, and then wander off into the woods.

"Jeanie Everett does all the cooking. You come back and eat a huge meal. Then you play cards, somebody plays the guitar maybe, and then you hit the bed. You get up pretty early.

"The Everetts and the ranch hands are all extremely nice, and they're slightly intrigued that anybody should want to pay a bit of money to get to do what they do."

EVERETT RANCH, 10615 County Road 150, Salida, CO 81201, (719) 539-4097. Inexpensive.

Other Riding Choices _____

A 5-day "Sierra Singles Trail Ride" is only one of the 20 trips that occupy the 135 horses belonging to the Rock Creek Pack Station, an outfit that has been headquartered 10,000 feet up in the Sierras for over 70 years. Participants fish, hike and ride through the John Muir Wilderness accompanied by cooks, mess facilities and separate-sex dorm tents.

ROCK CREEK PACK STATION, PO Box 248, Bishop, CA 93514, winter: (619) 872-8331; summer: (619) 935-4493. Inexpensive.

Kristina Calabrese recently began 4-day inn-to-inn treks on the sure footed small (13 to 14-hand) Icelandic horses she raises. "Because of their easy, singlefooted stride, the gaited and purebred Icelandics are excellent for novices and experienced equestrians alike," explains Kristina, who often leads the Vermont Icelandic Horse Farm riding tours through the Mad River Valley herself.

VERMONT ICELANDIC HORSE FARM, RR 376-1, Waitsfield, VT 05673, (802) 496-7141. Expensive.

Once a year in late spring a maximum of 16 guests, about 50% of them solitaries, gather at the Cataloochee Ranch bordering Great Smokies National Park for 7 days of riding. Spend 3 nights at the Ranch and 4 at a base camp where ranch cooks fix cornbread and biscuits, country ham and other hearty southern dishes for famished riders back from day-long sorties inside the park.

CATALOOCHEE RANCH Route 1, PO Box 500, Maggie Valley, NC 28751, (800) 868-1421, (704) 926-1401 or (704) 926-0737. Moderate.

Today when they circle the covered wagons in Montana's Flathead River country it is to protect Old West Adventures' wagoneers from the wind, not from Indian attack. In mid-July and again in early September, Doc Hammill takes a maximum of 20 participants on authentic, 2 or 3-night wagon train trips from Whitefish, Montana near Glacier Park.

OLD WEST ADVENTURES, PO Box 1899, Whitefish, MT 59937, (406) 862-0626. Expensive.

From June through mid-October Press Stevens, an outfitter located in Dubois, Wyoming, teams up with another packtrip organizer, H. A. Moore of Gardner, Montana, to offer riders customized trips through three ecosystems: The Big Horn Mountains, Greater Yellowstone and the Absarokas, and the Wind River Mountains. Stevens arranges packtrippers into compatible, five to eight person groups.

PRESS STEVENS, Beaver Creek Road, Shell, WY 823441, (307) 765-4377. Moderate to Very Expensive.

"More and more, as adventure travel catches on, our clients are singles, mostly from the East," reports Smoke Elser, co-author of the authoritative *Packing in on Mules and Horses* (Mountain Press) and an outfitter in Montana's Bob Marshall Wilderness for over 25 years. Elsner's Wilderness Outfitters runs 8 to 12-day summer trips a dozen riders at a time; the 2 fall trips are limited to 6 or 8 people.

WILDERNESS OUTFITTERS, 3800 Rattlesnake Drive, Missoula, MT 59802, (406) 549-2820. Moderate to Expensive.

 ## Reservations Services _____

EQUITOUR, PO Box 807, Dubois, WY 82513, (800) 545-0019 or (307) 455-3363. Represents a global assortment of 30 trips.

FITS EQUESTRIAN, 2011 Alamo Pintado Road, Solvang, CA 93463, (805) 688-9494. Offers rides in 21 foreign countries and in 12 different states and makes travel arrangements for its clients.

AMERICAN WILDERNESS EXPERIENCES, PO Box 1486, Boulder, CO 80306, (800) 444-0099 or (303) 494-2992. Books wagon train and packmule trips.

OFF THE BEATEN PATH, 109 East Main Street, Bozeman, MO 59715, (800) 445-2995 or (406) 586-1311. Western trip planners; they arrange customized pack trips and riding itineraries.

Bibliography

Western Horseman, PO Box 7890, Colorado Springs, CO 80933-7980, (719) 633-5524, $5 for a back-issue. "Horseback Vacations" are covered in the special February issue.Equus.

Equus, 565 Quince Orchard Road, Gaithersburg, MD 20878, $4. Also publishes its travel issue, featuring riding holidays for English and Western saddle enthusiasts, in February.

Adventure Guides Inc., 36 East 57th Street, New York, NY 10022. Send a stamped, self-addressed envelope to receive their 4-page *Cattle Drives and Roundups* newsletter.

Cycling

Ten years ago, cycling trips were something teenagers did in summer; today, they're adult terrain, and sweeping the globe. Biking vacations have come of age. In Maine, come August, adult bikers are as thick as black flies in June.

Inn-to-inn journeys have replaced camping trips as the industry standard. Offerings among this country's estimated 140 bicycle touring companies include "Off the Road" tours for mountain bikers, bike-and-hike, bike-and-sail, bike-and-raft combos, and glamorous wheel safaris to the most *recherché* corners of the world. Lycra-skinned cyclists aren't the only space-age aspect of biking. Tour operators with spiffy "sag," or support, wagons and optional vegetarian meals are also very much up-to-date.

"Sixty percent," responded All American Tours, a biking and hiking reservations service, when asked how many of their clients were single. "Without a doubt, people who sign up by themselves account for 50% to 60% of our business," said a Backcountry Bicycle Tours representative in Bozeman, Montana.

Backcountry also had a tip for those traveling alone. "Savvy solos ask about a trip's makeup before signing on. They say something like 'I've been considering three different tours for the third week in August. What's the composition of your group?'"

Pricing Categories

Inexpensive	Under $75 a day
Moderate	$75 to $125 a day
Expensive	$126 to $200
Very Expensive	Over $200 a day

The intimate size of most inn rides—12 to 15 people seems about average—is determined by the lodgings chosen, which tend to be small and cozy. Expect to pay extra for a single room on inn-to-inn trips. Single supplements are seldom imposed on camping trips where participants sleep in tents.

VERMONT COUNTRY CYCLING
Tour of Virginia's Tidewater Country

The trip leaders worked the room like a couple of professional vaudevillians the night before VCC Four Seasons Cycling tour of the Tidewater Country in Virginia. With rapid-fire one-liners, they shattered the barriers between the 13 strangers scrunched together in the parlor of the Ravenswood Inn sipping cassis and white wine Kirs. Effortlessly, it seemed, we exchanged names, revealed backgrounds, and generally connected before we trooped to the buffet to sprinkle grated cheese and other condiments on the spicy, meat-laden tacos our hostess, Sally Preston, had made for dinner.

We had at least one thing in common: everyone had elected the 2-day weekend tour of Virginia's Chesapeake Bay-fringed shore for it's flat terrain. This boded well for the less experienced bikers. That not everyone was a pro became clear as we took turns describing our cycling experiences after polishing off the last crumbs of Toll House pie. Although the two fit young women from Maryland were experts, the two men from Texas had just graduated from excercycles.

Most arrived with bikes perched jauntily on the back of their cars. Four of us rented bikes from Four Seasons Cycling, a Virginia outfit now affiliated with Vermont Country Cyclists. Our leaders sketched out Saturday's trip. Sally said she'd fix box lunches and the nine cyclists sleeping at Ravenswood stumbled upstairs to bed. The overflow, including a family from North Carolina, two physiotherapists from Maryland, a Baltimore doctor and our leaders, headed 2 1/2 miles up the road to the Riverfront Inn.

Most of the rooms in the two small inns have double beds, and I had a room to myself. Normally, singles share twin bedded rooms or pay a surcharge. My tidy private bath and carpeted, grey-blue room at the back of the house may not have had a view over the sweeping lawn to the water, but it looked out on cedars and a magnolia tree, as well as the inn's nascent vineyard.

Saturday was overcast, and during the breakfast of eggy potato and onion fritata slathered with Jack cheese, I was wary of what lay ahead. A sometime cycler, I had never used a gear shift, or ridden further than Central Park. At least there were options. We could ride for 16.7 miles, 41.8 miles or 57.3 miles. Ken would lead on the first leg and Jim would follow in the van. Everyone agreed to take the 16.7 loop to a crafts outlet, where Sally was to deliver lunch.

I needn't have worried. Ken adjusted our snappy 12-speed rental bikes, showed us how to fasten our styrene helmets and slipped the trip map into the plastic pocket that rested atop the handy zippered case attached to the handlebars. Within minutes of reaching the web of country roads that comprised the first leg of our trip, I realized that bike touring is fairly easy and companionable.

An experienced fellow biker helped refine my gear-changing technique as we peddled beside sedge colored grasses, Scotch pines, and newly-turned fields. Gulls and crows wheeled overhead searching for the choicest grubs, and we ganged up four abreast as we pedaled a deserted stretch before heading for Mathews Public Beach.

The trips offered throughout the US by VCC Four Seasons Cycling are as varied as the nation. Other bike tours include the opportunity to shop for antiques in New England, take in the New Orleans sights, hop from island to island in the San Juans, or sleep aboard a four-masted schooner between day trips around Maine. I chose the Virginia tour as much for the Spring landscape as for the lack of hills.

After lunch, most opted for the Mobjack Loop, but a few pedalers hitched a ride in the blue Four Seasons van rather than bike in a light rain. Upon returning, some chose to soak their sore bodies in the magnolia-shaded hot tub. Others sought out the services of an outstanding masseur. By 6:00 the living room floor was littered with bikers involved in an impassioned environmental debate.

This weekend was particularly refreshing. Bikers may well be a kinder, gentler tribe, or maybe we were just exhausted. We were certainly calmer and less anxious the second night than the first, but Sally's dinner of mesquite grilled chicken and asparagus fresh from local fields was just as delicious as her previous effort, and afterwards, the laughter rang just as loud and true.

Sunday morning after crisped and syrup-drenched croissants, my suitably, but not slickly, dressed companions and I headed into the fresh, fragrant day for the 19.4 mile round-trip to Gwynn's Island.

Hymns issuing from the distinctive, four-spired Baptist churches and the pre-summer tranquility of Gwynn's Island compensated for the heavy traffic at the start and finish of Sunday's ride. By then we sailed along, able to mostly ignore the speeding cars. Back over the dirt road to Ravenswood we bumped, in time for farewell pictures. Cameras at the ready, bikers took turns snapping the group, which needed no prompting to smile.

VCC FOUR SEASONS CYCLING, PO Box 145, Waterbury Center, Vermont 05677-0145, (802) 244-5135. The "Chesapeake Bay Weekend" package includes all but the bike rental fee. Moderate.

 Other Voices _____

TIMBERLINE BICYCLING TOURS
Mountain Bike Trips

"Last time we went to Split Rock and Canyon Land in Utah. It's a natural Disney World. The hills and curves and big boulders seemed designed as the perfect course for mountain bikers." According to Morel, a Los Angeles dentist, 45, Timberline Bicycling Tours caters to the sturdy, experienced biker. "I like Timberline's adventurous spirit. This outfitter is a little more rugged and rigorous than most. I took the Fryingpan Mountain Biker trip. We did Durango, Telluride, Cinnamon Pass, and Aspen in 5 days. Had some really heavy weather out

there, including a hail storm. One guy actually got hypother-
mia. Another complained that it was too strenuous.

"You travel with a sag wagon, which carries all the supplies and water. The groups average 8 to 10 people, mostly
men, but always a few women, and 2 guides. Basically we
stay on trails. On the Santa Fe-Taos-Red River ride, my first
and a gorgeous trip, the owner went along. He's an attorney
who quit to become a professional mountain biking guide.

"We camped 2 nights along the Colorado River on the
last trip, but usually we stay in hotels or motels. These aren't
quaint little inns; they are mostly Best Westerns. Generally,
we eat in restaurants. They pay for all your meals, except for
drinks, and you can order what you want. The riders do
everything as a group, so that lots of friendships develop. We
all exchange pictures after each trip."

*TIMBERLINE BICYCLING TOURS, 7975 East Harvard, #J,
Denver, CO 80231, (303) 759-3804. The 5-day Fryingpan trip
fee includes all lodging and meals. Moderate.*

BREAKAWAY VACATIONS
Biking and Hiking Trips

Allison is a computer systems programmer in Connecticut,
25, and an experienced bicycle tourer. She talked about one of
her favorite outfitters, Breakaway travel.

"What I like about Breakaway is that they're not
extremely regimented. You really can do your own thing. I've
been on Breakaway trips where some people just relaxed or
did a little sightseeing, while those of us who really liked to
ride fast put in the miles on the country roads. Breakaway
finds the most picturesque routes, not too difficult, and away
from heavy traffic.

"There are usually about 20 in a group and the composition varies. Some trips are entirely women, and others are
almost all couples. I would say, on average, 50% are single,
and there are universally more women than men.

"I've also done a few Breakaway hikes, but I'm primarily
a biker. They offer a few trips that are strictly hiking or
strictly biking as well as a few that have both options.

"I went on a combined hiking-biking trip in western Virginia. You just roll through the hills past beautiful estates and thoroughbred horses. One of the hikes on Old Rag Mountain in the foothills of the Blue Ridge was fairly strenuous, steep and rocky, but at the top there is the most spectacular view of the Shenandoah Valley.

"We stayed at a wonderful former plantation run by a very outgoing couple. All the inns on these trips are nice, and the hosts feed you to death, which is everyone's biggest complaint. Lots of the single women bikers are dieting, but you don't go on these trips to lose weight."

BREAKAWAY VACATIONS, 164 East 90th Street, 2Y, New York, NY 10128, (212) 722-4221. Moderate.

BACKROADS BICYCLE TOURING
Singles' Tour of Italy

"Tuscany is all hills, and we probably averaged 35 miles a day. We were definitely doing the back roads of Italy." Nan, a printing sales person from San Francisco, had admittedly "never spent much time on a bike before," but after a satisfying California wine country trip with Backroads Bicycle Touring, she signed on for a singles' tour in Italy.

"The routes each day varied. You could take the long route, the longer route, or the mega-extended route. Cycling, everyone goes at his own pace. We took off at the same time in the morning, but I didn't really see the guides or the group again until dinner. I would chug into town about 3:00 pm, shower, and, depending on the town, go exploring. We all stayed in the same place, but we didn't necessarily eat there. Dinner began at 8:00 and would take 3 hours, with lots of wine and many courses. The food was sumptuous and, with one exception, the accommodations were great.

"There were 22 in the group.... No interaction at all between the 11 men and 11 women.

"The hills. There were some that took me 3 hours to climb. Of course, going back down was wonderful, and every day you got better. The biggest thing for me to overcome is that it wasn't a race, that it didn't matter what time I checked into my hotel that night.

"They had a guide on a bike and one in the van. He went ahead with all the luggage, checked us in, got our room assignments, and then would come back and make a sweep. That sweep took a long time. You might have to wait 3 hours. Easier to just keep pedaling.

"I wasn't terribly impressed with the 2 leaders, men, each about 25. I would have enjoyed a little more historical background, some guidance, but then, this was the first year for this trip. All in all, I had a wonderful time, and I'd certainly do it again."

BACKROADS BICYCLE TOURING, 1516 5th Street, Berkeley, CA 94710-1740, (800) 245-3874 or (415) 527-1555. Very Expensive.

ARROW TO THE SUN
Yucatan Peninsula Trip

"We rode 1,084 miles from San Diego down and around Baja California in 18 days, and we only spent 4 nights in hotels. I loved the camping out." Dallas is a business executive, 55, from Minneapolis with a penchant for endurance biking. He describes two Arrow to the Sun trips he has taken in Mexico.

"There were just five guys and the leader on the Baja trip. To attract more people I think they would have to stay in motels. We could camp in Baja because we had a support wagon carrying all the equipment. Mike Sobrero, the owner and leader, did most of the cooking. Lunches, we ate loads of peanut butter and jelly sandwiches; at night he'd buy beans and make tortillas or something.

"We took Highway 1 down along the water on both sides of the peninsula. Once, we stopped and watched a whale. Another day we went aboard a trawler and bought some fish. We really winged it.

"The second trip was 2 weeks in the Yucatan, starting in Cancun. The sand was so beautiful. Mike couldn't bring his wagon along with all the gear, which meant we all had to bring our own bikes and gear. He did rent a supply wagon down there, so there was someone sweeping in back. Mike mapped out each day, and everyone peddled at his own pace.

"The group was a potpourri of people and ages; a family with 2 sons, 10 and 12, a couple of single women, a couple of single men, one woman and her 25-year-old son. It was a trip to see the Mayan ruins, actually. We swam in fresh water *cenotes*...it was a wonderful sightseeing journey, but we didn't work terribly hard. The Baja trip was more my style."

ARROW TO THE SUN, PO Box 115, Taylorsville, CA 95983, (916) 284-6263. Moderate.

BACKCOUNTRY BICYCLE TOURS
Bryce and Zion Canyons Tour

"Utah reminded me of Colorado; a lot of open space, some sandy areas, little canyons, Navaho red rocks. They chose the most scenic routes and told us stories about them." The 5-day ride Kathy, a 28-year-old lawyer in Denver, took through Bryce and Zion Canyons with Backcountry Bicycle Tours was her first bike trip.

"Eighteen of us from California, Canada, Colorado, and other Western states set out in St. George, Utah. There was an older man and one guy from Colorado who were also single. The rest were couples, or paired off in some way. They were mostly professionals, in their 20s to 50s. Sometimes the average age is even higher. People retire and climb on their bikes.

"Our first day, in May, it snowed and we were glad to sleep at a cozy bed and breakfast that night. A couple of nights we stayed in big open lodges with fireplaces in the national park, and one night we rented a whole A-frame. Always we had homecooked meals and cheerful tablecloths.

"The two guides were so good, real professionals and fun, too; they worked at getting everyone to interact. The guides knew so much about the wildlife and flowers and they discussed the routes ahead of time, so you knew what to look for. We'd break around noon for lunch, and they put a lot of creativity into the picnic fixings. One guide would go on ahead and set up for a 2:00 pm break, while the other rode behind. You're never alone.

"I just wished we could have spent another day in Zion National Park. One night and one day weren't enough, even though we hiked really high up, a cliff-hanging type of climb, and picnicked with the Park in full view."

BACKCOUNTRY BICYCLE TOURS, PO Box 4029, Bozeman, MT 59772, (406) 586-3556. Sign up 60 days in advance to avoid being charged a single supplement. Moderate.

BICYCLE ADVENTURES
San Juan Island Trip

"The nice thing about biking is that if you have a well-arranged tour—and this was a well-arranged tour—it doesn't matter whether you're a person who thinks 50 to 60 miles a day is just about right, or whether you think 20 or 30 is more like it. You have both options." Connie likes to peddle long and hard despite her 59 years. A financial planner in Minnesota, she tells about a 6-day Bicycle Adventures trip to the San Juan Islands in Washington State.

"After Labor Day, you don't get that many folks; we had 18 in our group, which was nice. We bicycled on three islands, Lopez, Orcas and San Juan, riding the ferry in between. Then we cycled around La Conner, one of the biggest tulip-growing areas in the world, on the mainland about 30 miles north of Seattle.

"Mt. Constitution is a bicycle mecca, where cyclists go to test their toughness. This was the most outstanding bicycling we did on that tour. I got about two-thirds of the way, where most people turn off, but three people from our group made it up the really steep grade to the top.

"Our tour included people from all over, and the guides were just terrific. There was nothing they wouldn't do to help you. This touring outfit is very well-managed. There was a wagon, for example, with space for everyone and all our bikes. Had it rained, we could all fit in the van, and that's important for people who get tired or don't have the muscle to cycle up steep hills."

BICYCLE ADVENTURES, PO Box 7875, Olympia, WA 98507, (206) 786-0989. Expensive.

Other Cycling Choices _____

The National Office of American Youth Hostels (AYH) in
Washington, DC and the New York Council, the largest of
AYH's 39 Councils worldwide, are both noted for their
cycling trips. While teen tours outnumber adult rides 5 to 1
at the New York branch, the over-20 set has a choice of low-
cost camping and hosteling rides here and abroad, as well as a
70-day coast-to-coast camping trip.

*AMERICAN YOUTH HOSTELS, 891 Amsterdam Avenue,
New York, NY 10025, (212) 932-2300; PO Box 37613, Washington, DC, 20013-7613, (202) 783-6161. Rates vary depending on the trip.*

  Blyth & Company, an Ontario-based firm with an
assortment of 8-day European trips, runs a provocative 5-
night tour that passes through the potato fields and aged fishing villages of Prince Edward Island, "Anne of Green Gables"
country, before ending where it started, in the capital at the
landmark Charlottetown Hotel.

*BLYTH & COMPANY, 1 Rockefeller Plaza, New York, NY
10019, (212) 265-9600. Expensive.*

  The venerable Sierra Club organizes rides over 10,000-
foot passes in the High Country of Colorado, across the Aval-
on Peninsula in Newfoundland and cross-country on mountain bikes through New York's Adirondack Park. Rates are
reasonable because bikers carry their own gear (no sag wagons) and sleep in sleeping bags rather than four posters
although a few of the more expensive trips use inns.

*SIERRA CLUB OUTING DEPARTMENT, 730 Polk Street,
San Francisco, CA 94109, (415) 923-5630. The High Country
of Colorado trip takes 12 days, the Avolon Peninsula trip, 8
days, and the 5-night New York Adirondack Park trip
includes 2 nights in inns. Inexpensive.*

Eight-day bike tours of the Outer Banks of North Carolina and, from mid-January to mid-March, 14-day tours of New Zealand are the specialty of Paradise Pedallers, which also leads a couple of trips each summer to Switzerland and Germany for good measure.

PARADISE PEDALLERS, PO Box 32352, Charlotte, NC 28232, (704) 335-8687. The fee for the 14-day tour of New Zealand include air fare. Moderate and Very Expensive.

Vermont Bicycle Touring (VBT) pioneered inn-to-inn cycling 20 years ago and, utilizing Vermont's well-maintained roads and top-notch hostelries, this illustrious outfit continues to grow. New are 2-night "Fly & Cycle" packages arranged by VBT's in-house travel agents.

VERMONT BICYCLE TOURING, 711, Bristol, VT 05443, (802) 453-4811. Moderate.

 ## Singles Only Trips _____

BICYCLE ADVENTURES, PO Box 7875, Olympia, WA 98587, (206) 786-0989. Offers a dozen singles outings to the Juan Islands and Puget Sound.

BACKROADS BICYCLE TOURING, 1516 5th Street, Berkeley, CA 94710-1740, (800) 245-3874 or (415) 527-1555. Runs weekend jaunts for singles in Northern California as well as longer journeys through the Rockies, Hawaii, Ireland, and Italy.

 ## Reservations Services _____

ALL ADVENTURE TRAVEL, PO Box 4307, Boulder, CO 80306, (800) 537-4025 or (303) 939-8885. A 4-year-old agency specializing in bicycling and hiking vacations.

Bibliography

Bicycle USA, Suite 209, Baltimore, MD 21207, (301) 944-3399. The March/April "Tourfinder" issue, available for $5 from the League of American Wheelmen, 6707 Whitestone Road, contains short, factual descriptions of commercial tour operators and non-profit organizations.

The Cyclists' Yellow Pages, published by Bikecentennial, PO Box 8308, Missoula, MT 59807, (800) 835-2246 or (406) 721-8719. A trip planning guide with details about 150 tours.

Walking, Hiking and Trekking

Outdoor travel is booming. New walking, hiking and trekking tour operators flourish, as do pioneers such as the Appalachian Mountain Club, the Adirondack Mountain Club and the Sierra Club. The industry has passed the fledgling stage and now a number of excellent companies provide imaginative trips for an increasingly discriminating public.

Hiking tent-to-tent or hut-to-hut was for years the forte of the mountain clubs. Walking went upmarket with the introduction of inn trips. Now CEOs trudge through the Loire Valley with their spouses chateau-to-chateau.

No self-respecting adventure travel firm would be without its esoteric hikes in international climes. In the US, biking companies once offered walking trips as a sideline. Now, walking-hiking-trekking is fast becoming a travel category unto itself. Vermont Hiking Holidays and Four Seasons Walking Vacations, for example, are owned by Vermont Bicycle Touring and the fast-expanding VCC Four Seasons Cycling, respectively.

Day rambles tend to be sociable. This is less true of rigorous hikes. It's hard to catch one's breath, much less talk, when trekking in the Himalayas. Still, count on camaraderie come

Pricing Categories

Inexpensive	Under $75 a day
Moderate	$75 to $125 a day
Expensive	$126 to $200
Very Expensive	Over $200 a day

evening with fellow solos who, tour operators estimate, comprise between 30% to 40% of their clientele.

Participants tend to share rooms or tents; count on paying a supplement for a private room if there are any available. Some of the small inns don't have space for single sleepers.

CRAFTSBURY CENTER AND INN ON THE COMMON
Craftsbury Common, Vermont

Spring erupted in Vermont over Memorial Day weekend and a group of 17 walking enthusiasts explored its glories from the Craftsbury Center, a camp for adults located near the Canadian and New Hampshire borders.

Craftsbury Common, an austere and exemplary New England village that crests a rise facing Mount Mansfield, is home not only to the Center, which offers programs in sculling (see CANOEING), skiing, running, walking, and mountain biking, but also to the Inn on the Common. Outdoor enthusiasts have a choice. They can occupy a dorm-like accommodation at the Center or settle into one of the 18 meticulously furnished rooms at the handsome Inn.

Sunday morning at 9:00 am a group of 20 to 60-year-old walking buffs, fanny packs and canteens strapped around their middles, met at the Center, where our leader outlined the route. At a civilized 2 mph we set out down hard-packed dirt roads to Greensboro, 11 miles away.

Chatting idly, we strode under a faultless blue bowl of sky. After a pit stop at The Old Forge, a source for handknit British sweaters in East Craftsbury, we headed toward sparkling Caspian Lake and lunch. Out of the Center's waiting van came tuna and potato salads, sandwich fixings and gooey date bars. Thus fortified, the hearty continued 4 miles to Greensboro. The rest of us rode back to the Center in the bus.

Most of my companions, from as far away as Alaska and Savannah and about a third of them unattached, elected to stay in bootcamp-like quarters at the slightly ramshackle Center where doughty scullers and mountain bikers happily mixed it up. A couple of Bostonians said they particularly enjoyed the conversational give-and-take during substantial homecooked meals in the dining shed overlooking Big Hoesmer Lake. By 7:00 pm when the blue-jeaned crew at the Center was settling down for an ecology lecture, those of us who'd opted for refinement at the Inn on the Common were making small talk with fellow guests over drinks.

The Center and the Inn offer a very real choice. Lazy lake swims or dips in an elegant pool? Communal bathrooms and make-your-own-beds or immaculate private baths and antique beds covered with handstitched quilts in prettily wall-papered quarters? Tuna-noodle casseroles, yogurt and wheat germ or zesty pureed pimento soup, rabbit in garlic cream and almond-raspberry tartlets?

The rabbit might have been a tad dry but the atmosphere at the Inn's two long, formally-set tables was as sparkling as the shell-patterned silver plate. The low, firelit room looking over a lovely formal garden hummed.

Penny and Michael Schmidt are the somewhat starchy hosts. These veteran innkeepers, who began assembling the three late-18th century clapboard buildings that comprise the inn 16 years ago, definitely know what's nice: for starters, separate sitting areas in each bedroom and thick terry robes after a bubbling, post-walk soak. The cypress-bordered gardens with a croquet lawn and a clay tennis court are stunning. Then, for getting together, there are pool-side loungers, a library, a moire-and-velvet living room, and a recreation room with over 200 movie titles in the South Annex across the street.

The Inn and the Center are poles apart in terms of luxury, and about 2 1/2 miles in distance. At the inn, you'll need wheels. The Center can meet guests at the Burlington Airport, but they will try to hook up those arriving on the same flight; it's cheaper to share a rental car.

INN ON THE COMMON, Craftsbury Common, Vermont 05827, (802) 586-9619. Rates include 2 walks and 2 lunches under the Center's auspices and 2 breakfasts, 2 dinners and 2 nights lodging at the Inn. Very Expensive.

THE CRAFTSBURY CENTER, Box 31, Craftsbury Common, Vermont 05827, (802) 586-7767. Rates include 2 walks and all meals and lodging for 2 days. Moderate.

Other Voices _____

ELK RIVER VALLEY LLAMA COMPANY
Clark, Colorado

"Llamas are better natured than camels, I found, because they're better treated. Most of the llama packers have $10,000 to $15,000 invested in an animal, so they don't tend to abuse them." Dave was discussing the latest hiking accessory: llamas as pack animals. A freelance photographer and travel writer, he sampled llama packing with a day trip in the Zirkle Wilderness. (Peter Nichols' Elk River Valley Llama Company usually runs 5-day trips.)

"Peter's been at this since 1982, so he's got a lot of experience, good professional gear, and he knows how to guide, camp and cook out. They use first-rate food, thick steaks and rainbow trout. He scouted a fine site for his base camp, about a 6-mile hike straight up from Clark. You camp near the Continental Divide, and hike out from there to lakes and other scenic spots during the day. You're not stumbling around in the dark looking for a camp.

"A typical group would be a dozen people, sleeping in tents. It's not that strenuous a hike, feasible for just about anybody. He's had plenty of octogenarians, in fact. The llamas carry the gear, up to 75 pounds. They're strung together so they don't wander off independently.

"The day I hiked with Peter, he took along a pair of new llamas that he was just breaking in. They were a bit stand-offish and jittery when I came around. His regular llamas are generally very docile and obedient; they don't spit at you.

"Because llamas walk more gently than horses, they do less damage to the land. They're cute animals, fun actually. I never got tired of watching them, and it's handy to have someone toting your pack."

ELK RIVER VALLEY LLAMA COMPANY, PO Box 674, Clark, CO 80428, (800) 562-5262 or (303) 879-7531. Expensive.

NEW ENGLAND HIKING HOLIDAYS

"I really like the people who take these hiking trips; educators, professors, professional people. I find them stimulating and refreshing." Susan, an educational specialist, 40, in Virginia, has taken three 5-day hikes with New England Hiking Holidays.

"I can't get over the lovely lunches the tour guides carry in their knapsacks. They shop the night before, so instead of getting just a sandwich, we get fresh fruit and all kinds of cold cuts. They even carry all our drinks. The trips are beautifully planned, and you're really cosseted. If you want your ankles taped, the guides will tape them. If you forget something, they run to the store and get it for you.

"Sixteen people are the maximum on these trips; on the Colorado trip we had nine from all over: England, Iowa, New York. Most of the singles are women. There were 2 women from Kansas, 63 and 65 years old, who kept right up with the group.

"Everyone takes the morning hike. Then, after lunch, decisions are made about what to do next. One of the guides will push on with those who want to hike farther, and, if part of the group wants to do an easier trip, the other guide will lead them. If you want to go to town, they'll drive you. Everything is done for the individual.

"Hiking up the mountains was amazing. In Colorado, we only covered a few miles a day because we had trouble adjusting to an altitude of 8,000 feet. At Acadia National Park in Maine we averaged about 9 miles a day. This is real hiking. You have to be prepared and train for it.

"The food is absolutely wonderful. In New England, we stayed in carefully chosen inns without dining rooms. Special arrangements were made so we could eat anything we wanted in restaurants. In Colorado we stayed in two wonderfully western-style lodges, very rustic, with high ceilings, log beams and a big fireplace. These are superb trips."

NEW ENGLAND HIKING HOLIDAYS, PO Box 1648, North Conway, NH 03860, (603) 356-9696 (or (407) 778-4499 between December and April 15). Moderate.

OUTWARD BOUND
Hurricane Island, Maine

Before moving to Michigan from New York City, where she worked on a magazine, Susan, 27, took her second Outward Bound course, a 28-day, hiking/rock climbing/canoeing trip to Hurricane Island, Maine.

"From basecamp on the mainland they drove us up into the mountains, I guess to expose us to all the elements of camping, hiking, packing, and to get to know each other. There were eight of us, five women. The age difference kept us a little divided, since four were college students and four were already in the work force. There was a difference in motivation.

"Normally I like hiking, but you couldn't see in front of you for the clouds of mosquitoes. They covered us. It was hot and muggy and sticky, and we had to dress head to toe in nylon because they were so vicious. I couldn't wait for that phase to end.

"We next spent a few days on a lake learning canoeing, including white water techniques, before paddling down the Penobscott River about 120 miles, two to a canoe. At the mouth of the river we did a 4-day solo out in the woods alone with a tarp, water, an apple, a handful of nuts and raisins and a granola bar. I guess we were supposed to fast and contemplate life. Again we were bombarded by mosquitoes. At night, I'd lay there and hear beavers running past me to get to the river, bumping into my tent. You did get in touch with the wildlife.

"We returned to a huge meal, and more canoeing. We also spent a day working with a retarded adults' group home. This interesting experience was designed to show you how lucky you were and how to give of yourself.

"At this point our canoes were exchanged for a giant rowboat with a sail. We literally left civilization for 10 days on this boat. It was very strenuous; we sailed at night and rowed all day to meet our goal, which was to reach a distant island. Learning to set goals for yourself is the emphasis of the program.

"I was grateful to return to Hurricane Island, where we tackled rock climbing. I was deathly afraid but rock climbing turned out to be my favorite part of the trip. We climbed in a quarry with straight sides and ledges. They train you exceedingly well. It couldn't have been more fun."

OUTWARD BOUND, 384 Field Point Road, Greenwich, CT 06870, (203) 661-0797 or (800) 243-8520. The fee for the multi-element course is all-inclusive. Moderate.

COUNTRY WALKING HOLIDAYS
Pacific Northwest Tour

"We stopped at La Conner, an artists colony, for lunch before taking the ferry to Orcas Island in the San Juans, where we stayed at the swanky Rosario Resort." So began one of the Country Walking Holidays led by Douglas Caldow in the Pacific Northwest. Arnold, a retired language teacher from Long Island, had already taken an 8-day walk with Caldow in England before signing on for the 12-day walk.

"We hiked on Orcas Island and took a layover day there, which we spent day tripping to Friday Harbor, which has English and American military camps dating from the War of 1812.

"From Rosario Resort, we ferried to Victoria on Vancouver Island, which was just beautiful, for several days. Then on to Whistler, Canada's Vail, a little mountaintop town, very new and planned, with a Swiss feeling. The weather cleared just long enough for the planned helicopter ride to the top of Mount Whistler, which was quite scary.

"Just outside Vancouver we left the bus to hike to Caldow's house for a party. Doug and his wife are Americans, but they live in Vancouver, and every Pacific trip ends there. Caldow personally leads all the trips. He has staked them out with a view toward scenery and history. Each leg is accompanied by a local guide who talks about the flora and fauna and local history.

"A bus accompanies the hikers, up to 25 of them, with the luggage. Doug picks the best accommodations, some of them rather luxurious. I usually pay extra for a single room, but there are provisions for sharing."

COUNTRY WALKING HOLIDAYS, 1122 Fir Avenue, Blaine, WA 98230, (604) 921-8304. Expensive.

NORTH WIND HIKING TOURS
Vermont-New Hampshire Hike

"The routes they chose are exclusive. In fact, we changed our plans one morning when we found two other vans parked at the base of the mountain. We drove to another spot, and then returned the next day so we could be alone. I have a lot of respect for this program." An attorney in Ottawa, Terry had just returned from a 5-day Vermont-New Hampshire hike with North Wind Hiking Tours.

"Dae and Clif Todd, the owners, are excellent leaders, and very nice people as well. The six other hikers, two couples and a pair of women, all had some hiking experience and were good companions. The weather was great right after Labor Day, never too hot.

"We slept at the Mulburn Inn in Bethlehem, before being vanned next morning to the beginning of the hike. These hikes weren't extremely difficult, and the views were always quite good. The Todds know the wildlife and plants, so we learned lots along the way. We covered mountainous terrain every day but Franconia Notch, where we spent 8 hours on the mountain, was the only difficult hike.

"The inns were all very nice, especially Rabbit Hill Inn in Waterford, Vermont, which had great food. By and large, the meals were good throughout the trip, and we all ate together.

"There was a nice mixture of pleasant people from Baltimore, North and South Carolina, three of whom were grandmothers. Everyone kept up, no one whined, but then, I'd be hard-pressed to think of anything to complain about on this trip."

NORTH WIND HIKING TOURS, PO Box 46, Waitsfield, VT 05673, (802) 496-5771. Moderate.

 ## Other Walking, Hiking and Trekking Choices _____

The contact for the New York Chapter of the Adirondack Mountain Club (ADC) assures people that "Linking up with ADC is as safe a way of meeting new people as going to church." To participate in hikes and other activities, join one of the Club's 28 Northeastern chapters. Information, publications and details about the Adirondack Club's two mountain lodges are available from the Lake George Headquarters of the 17,000 member group.

ADIRONDACK MOUNTAIN CLUB, RR 3, Box 3055, Lake George, NY, (518) 668-4447.

Hiking forays to three National Parks in the Rockies, called the "Mountain Parks West" trips, are among the adventures offered by the Washington headquarters of American Youth Hostels.

AMERICAN YOUTH HOSTELS, PO Box 37613, Washington, DC 20013-7613, (202) 783-6161. Participants in the 22-day "Mountain Parks West" trip stay in dormitory-style hostels and shared tents. Inexpensive.

Thanks to *Appalachia*, the magazine published by the Appalachian Mountain Club 11 times a year, members of each of the club's 12 branches can find out about the activities offered by all the clubs. Furthermore, in *Appalachia*, the "Major Excursions" (defined as trips lasting more than 1 week, or more than 500 miles from the home chapter) offered by the 36,000-member club are detailed. Expeditions include trips abroad as well as US selections.

APPALACHIAN MOUNTAIN CLUB, 5 Joy Street, Boston, MA (617) 523-0636.

Lots of cycling companies also offer hiking trips. Breakaway Vacations, a tour operator with a heavily single, heavily New York clientele, is one such firm. Small, intimate Breakaway groups hike, as well as pedal, around New England inn-to-inn on weekends and week-long vacations.

BREAKAWAY VACATIONS, 164 East 90th Street, 2Y, New York, NY 10128, (212) 722-4221. Moderate.

The "Walking" and "Hiking" inn-to-inn trips and "Backpacking" forays offered by Hummingbird Nature Tours to Vancouver Island, northern New Mexico, Spatsizi Plateau Wilderness Park in British Colombia and Washington's Olympic National Park in Washington are carefully researched and particularly provocative.

HUMMINGBIRD NATURE TOURS, #31-22374 Lougheed Highway, Maple Ridghe, British Columbia V2X2T5, (604) 467-9219. Moderate to Expensive.

Among the backpacking, horse trailing and trekking courses offered by Outward Bound's North Carolina-, Minnesota-, Maine-, Oregon-, and Colorado-based schools are trips especially for couples, parents and children, families, and women. Some of these demanding and rigorous courses include rock climbing.

OUTWARD BOUND National Office, 384 Field Point Road, Greenwich, CT 06830, (800) 243-8520 or (203) 661-0797. They offer 5- and 9-day courses. Moderate.

Of the trips described in *Sierra Club Outings*, 23 are hikes and climbs from base camps located primarily in the West but also in the Virgin Islands, North Carolina, Tennessee, West Virginia; 83 are backpacking expeditions through the Sierra mainly, and 16 are western treks accompanied by pack horses, llamas or burros.

SIERRA CLUB OUTING DEPARTMENT, 730 Polk Street, San Francisco, CA 94109, (415) 923-5630. Choices for trips include 10 days based at a camp 8,000 feet in the High Sierra, 10 days backpacking around Kings Canyon Park in California, and a 10-day trek of the Oregon Cascades (with llamas). Inexpensive to Moderate.

Spiffy accommodations in elegant old hotels, inns and seaside cottages are the specialty of Vermont Hiking Holiday's "inn-to-inn" vacations. Five-day tours to New Brunswick and the Bay of Fundy, Nova Scotia as well as several spots in Vermont attract walkers and hikers in search of a vacation.

VERMONT HIKING HOLIDAYS, Box 750-C, Bristol, VT 05443-0750, (802) 453-4816. Singles share, or pay double the rate. Moderate to Expensive.

 ## Singles Only _____

SIERRA SINGLES, 6014 College Avenue, Oakland, CA 94618. Offers a number of hikes, as well as horseback rides, canoe trips and bike rides.

THE ELK RIVER VALLEY LLAMA COMPANY, (800) 562-5262 or (303) 879-7531. Offers a 5-day llama trek for singles every summer.

 ## Reservations Services _____

ALL ADVENTURE TRAVEL, PO Box 4307, Boulder, CO 80306, (800) 537-4025 or (303) 939-8885. Represents about a dozen hiking tour companies as well as biking firms.

Bibliography

1988 Walking Almanac ($3.95 from *The Walking Magazine*, 9-11 Harcourt Street, Boston, MA 02116, (617) 266-3322). Lists tour operators and has a directory of walking clubs organized by state. Also check the ads for walking, hiking, and adventure trips.

Backpacker (Rodale Press, 33 E. Minor Street, Emmaus, PA 18098, (215) 967-5171). Carries ads for walking, hiking and adventure trips.

Running Rivers

Rafting is exceptionally companionable, whether hurtling down a turbulent river in a four-man boat or drifting along a wide, calm stream on a large pontoon craft. River trips, like other adventurous outings, foster conviviality. Once the stretch of water has been selected—the Colorado through the Grand Canyon, the Middle Fork of the Salmon in Idaho, Oregon's Rogue River and the Tatshenshini in Alaska are classics—the next decision is the type of boat.

The traditional choices are pointy-prowed wood or aluminum dories that hold four people and a rower; motor-powered J- or S-rigged pontoon rafts that carry groups of around 8 or 15; guided, inflatable paddle boats that 4 to 6 people paddle themselves; and larger, inflated oar boats rowed by trained crews. Options include paddle-and-oar combinations, called "hybrid" trips, and inflatable kayaks called variously "sportyaks" and "funyaks."

Financially, rafting is solo-democratic. Singles pay no more than pairs for the privilege of sleeping on soft, sandy beaches and using tented, hand-dug latrines.

Pricing Categories

Inexpensive	Under $75 a day
Moderate	$75 to $125 a day
Expensive	$126 to $200
Very Expensive	Over $200 a day

COLORADO RIVER AND TRAIL EXPEDITIONS
Rafting Through Canyonlands National Park

The boatman checked my life jacket, handed me a can of beer and commanded "Jump!" With that I leapt into the Colorado River to bob along in the wake of an inflated raft with three fellow rafters. Our buoyant, 2-mile drift was a marvelous release after a tense 2 hours spent shooting Satan's Gut and other rapids in Cataract Canyon. This 16-mile stretch of white water in southwest Utah, rating 8 on a 1 to 10 scale of difficulty, was the most dramatic experience in a 2 1/2-day run through Canyonlands National Park to Lake Powell.

Around 9:00 am we broke camp in a canyon of red Navajo sandstone. Having served up strong coffee, whopping slabs of cheddar omelettes and limitless bacon strips, our guides lashed half a ton of gear to the steel deck of our pontoon craft. This second day of our 95-mile odyssey was to be the high point of a raft trip that set in at Potash, near touristy Moab.

In fact, the bucketing ride through churning rapids and the paddle in the gentle current that immediately followed was boisterous fun, but I found floating quietly through the tortured, ever-changing sandstone cliffs equally engrossing. In spite of the fact that our group started out as disparate strangers, this trip proved my theory that shared adventure breeds camaraderie between strangers. "Who'd have ever thought we'd be discussing the survival of the fittest over breakfast," said a father to his son as we packed up camp the last day.

Our random foursome reaped the rewards of an undersubscribed trip. The outfitters often run two or three full rafts, with one boatman each, on their Cataract Canyon trip. Resting against waterproof packs, we motored down river with an experienced boatman plus a helper at 5 mph on a 24-foot pontoon raft designed for 8.

The river, which peaks in May, had reached its height. (Motor trips are run only when the river's full; in July, when the river drops, oars lengthen the time to 5 days). Temperatures hovered in the low 80s. Mosquitoes were rare, and the night before our departure provided an exceptional omen: a blue moon.

The second full moon of the month rose, bright-as-day, above the dark canyon walls. We slept on a sandy patch beside roaring Indian Falls, a bugless, water-cooled haven. After a steak dinner accompanied by home fries and red cabbage slaw, cooked beside the river, we lugged our bedding 45 minutes up to the waterfall and bathed in the chilly, reddish water.

Twisted rock pinnacles and arches etched against the cerulean sky held us rapt as our raft navigated the now-placid water. Before casting off we had studied petroglyphs carved in sandstone and, after an on-board sandwich beneath sienna walls, we hiked up the canyon sides to inspect more glyphs and the Anasazai Grainery, where 1,000-year-old corn cobs have been found. Not even the Grand Canyon-like grandeur of our second night's campsite near Clearwater Canyon could compete with the beauty of that first Canyonlands leg of our trip. The vastness of our surroundings the second day produced a sense of insignificance that was utterly liberating.

The journey ended on the barren red-ochre shore of Lake Powell where, assaulted for 2 hours by 96 degree heat, we got a taste of what the river must be like in mid-summer. When our boat was finally unpacked, we were loaded into the back of the outfitters truck (Colorado River & Trails offers the basics; other companies provide frills like air-conditioned mini-buses to transport rafters back to base) and dropped off at the canyon rim, where a single-engine plane waited. It had taken us 52 hours to travel the Colorado's twisting course from Moab to Lake Powell; Red Arrow Air retraced the route in 40 minutes.

Alpine Airline's Salt Lake City to Moab flight is also to be commended, as are the simple charms and the tasty meals at Pack Creek Ranch, a grassy desert oasis where I spent the night. There is a bird's-eye view of the snow-capped Wasatch Mountains and the surreal Utah tablelands from the co-pilots seat on Alpine Aviation. The Pack Creek Ranch, as welcoming a compilation of farm cottages and barns as is likely to be found in Utah, also offers 1- and 2-night pack trips into the La Sal Mountains that jut up behind the ranch. Plan to stay at Pack Creek before or after a Canyonlands trip, but only if arrangements can be made with the ranch and the outfitter for transportation between the airport, the ranch and the Moab parking lot where the rafters congregate. In Moab, there are no taxis.

COLORADO RIVER & TRAIL EXPEDITIONS, 5058 South 300 West, Salt Lake City, Utah 84107-7575, (801) 261-1789. The 4-day motor trip package includes the air fare for the Red Tail flight from Lake Powell to Moab. Moderate.

ALPINE AVIATION, PO Box 691, Provo Utah 84603, (801) 373-1508.

PACK CREEK RANCH, Box 1270, Moab, Utah 84532, (801) 259-5505. The rate for a room with bath includes breakfast and dinner. Inexpensive.

 Other Voices

ECHO
Rogue River Oar Trip

"One night the guides built a sauna with tarps and fire-warmed rocks in the sand. You could sit in that and then jump in the cold river. That was great fun," recalls Wendy, a 35-year-old world traveler and former New York arbitrageur. A veteran river runner, Wendy took the 5-day Echo oar trip on the Rogue River and recommends it for solo travelers.

"It's a wonderful kind of trip for someone traveling alone because you're in a boat with a number of people but not necessarily the same boat every day. You're going down the river looking at the scenery, the wildlife, learning about the area, and you have all these different people to talk to.

"On the Rogue you could either be a passenger in one of the oar boats, rowed by a guide, or you could paddle inflatable one person kayaks. On any river, your activities are determined by the water flow. If you were on a safe section of the Rogue, you could then move back and forth, have water fights or just have a lazy time enjoying the scenery. The boatmen let people fool around. If there were rapids, I'd get in my funyak and paddle, otherwise, I'd just lie there and relax.

"We slept under the stars on sandy beaches we camped on at night. One of the guys on the trip brought a banjo. He'd drag it out and we ended up dancing on the beach. Maybe people pursuing that kind of outdoor experience are more open, more out-going and friendly. I found it very easy to make friends."

ECHO, 6529 Telegraph Avenue, Oakland, CA 94609, (415) 652-1600. Moderate.

HOLIDAY RIVER EXPEDITIONS
San Juan River Trip

"It's *the* way to see the Utah canyons, often just about the only way," says Jay, 29, a journalist recapping his 3-day, 3-night trip down the San Juan River to Lake Powell with Holiday River Expeditions. There's no stopping for a close look, as he explains.

"The San Juan River is noted for dropping more in a shorter distance than any other river in the Southwest. It moves really fast. You can see why getting caught in the rapids is so dangerous. The rocks are all smooth, there's nothing to hold onto. The water just rushes through. On portions of the trip we could not get out of the boat.

"Don't get sick. One of the guys fell ill almost immediately after we started off. There was nothing for him to do about it, and it was incredibly hot.

"I felt very comfortable; the Holiday people are real professionals. The equipment is great and the guides, all young, were very impressive, especially the woman leader. I'd take another trip with Holiday in a minute.

"Holiday vanned us to the put-in an hour south of Green River, Utah, along a very beautiful road bordering the San Juan. Our group was like the cast of 'Thirtysomething.' Everybody was good-looking, and everybody but me was traveling with someone else.

"Meals were well done, and the guides did all the work. You could volunteer, but there were no real expectations. The trip was really economical too. Excellent."

HOLIDAY RIVER EXPEDITIONS, 544 East 3900 South Salt Lake City, UT 84107, (800) 624-6323 or (801) 266-2087. Moderate.

UNICORN EXPEDITIONS
Five-Day Maine Adventure

"Trying to figure out how to go to Maine by myself is how I ended up going rafting," explains Diane, a how-to writer, 41, from New Jersey. Her experience with Unicorn Expeditions is especially instructive for the novice.

"I went for a 5-day trip: 2 days rafting on the Penobscot, a day off, then another 2 days rafting the Kennebec River. The week before Labor Day the nights were cold, 47 degrees. If it hadn't been for the campfire at night, I might have frozen.

"Rafting was a little different from what I'd expected. We weren't on the river all day; there's a certain amount of carrying the raft and setting up. You camped outdoors, which was very comfortable. You have to unpack at night and pack up again the next morning, otherwise Unicorn took care of the equipment.

"I was very impressed with the people who ran the out-fit. We had 2 rafts, 12 to 16 people, for the week. It was a nice-sized group and very congenial. The two leaders knew the river and they knew what they were doing.

"You paddled. It was very important that you be an active participant and do what you were asked to do. No holding on with both hands in the rapids; that could endanger the boats. They showed us how to wedge our legs under a strap and under the pontoon so we were wedged in pretty well. The rafts are bendy and flip around. Being somewhat short-legged and not in terrific shape, when we went through the first rapids I was scared. I wasn't prepared for this level of rafting difficulty....

"If you could handle that, it was the most exciting thing in the world, but I was genuinely terrified of getting thrown out. After the first two days, I elected not to go again. I stayed on the bus and transported stuff down a wooded path through a beautiful gorge. In fact, it was my favorite day of the trip.

"The food with this outfit is not fancy, but it's very good. The one day off, we stayed in a motel-like place in a ski area. You could take the chair lift up the mountain, pick blueberries, hike, buy homemade ice cream.... That was Unicorn. In terms of quality I'd recommend them highly."

UNICORN EXPEDITIONS, PO Box T, Brunswick, ME 04011, (207) 725-2255. Inexpensive.

ROCKY MOUNTAIN RIVER TOURS
Salmon River Trip

"The guides' skill and their whole dedication to the wilderness philosophy, their knowledge and their extreme courtesy to everyone made the trip the most comfortable and enjoyable possible," marvels Chuck, a businessman, 35, from San Francisco, who booked his 6-day rafting trip on the Middle Fork of the Salmon River with Rocky Mountain River Tours.

"I was a bit nervous. You begin at a spot that has a most peculiar meteorological phenomenon: 15 frost-free days a year. On June 19 it was snowing in the parking lot. We looked at each other, 'This is crazy. This is not going to be fun.' You descend 100 or more feet that first day, and it warms up considerably. It did snow the first night out, but then got really quite comfortable.

"This outfit's raft trips are at the upper end of the scale. They are excellent on many levels; the food is extraordinary. It's quite spectacular what they can do in the wilderness; the baked goods are amazing. I could have done with a little less waiting, much of their stuff was elaborate. The whole food thing got to be an obsession, and we must have gone through a half case of wine a meal.

"The guides were great. Many of them are serious naturalists, so you can learn a great deal. They're charming people, with a good sense of humor. They get their share of cantankerous folks, but they're courteous and diplomatic all along. Basically, you come first. Last year was my introduction to rafting. Now it's become my obsession."

ROCKY MOUNTAIN RIVER TOURS, PO Box 2552, Boise, Idaho, 83701, (208) 344-6668. Expensive.

GRAND CANYON DORIES
Grand Canyon

Many people do the whole 18-day trip, but there are those who get on, or off, at Phantom Ranch and Irene, a 57-year-old law school dean, chose to hike down 9 miles from the Canyon's South Rim and board the Grand Canyon Dories near the Ranch on the canyon floor. "Personally, I'd rather hike than spend so much time on the river," says Irene, but she highly recommends the dory trip.

"The dories are very small wooden boats, with an oarsman and only two or three passengers. Five boats traveled together, so we had a cook and an assistant cook and someone to row the supplies along. They have a schedule, but they're flexible, depending on the weather and what people want.

"The oarspeople, both men and women, are naturalists, campers, hikers, and the like and quite knowledgeable about the area. They encourage you to ride with different guides each day so you learn different things. They have maps and books to teach you about the canyon, and you learn a great deal. We saw some wild sheep and all different kinds of cactus and vegetation and rock formations.

"We usually spent 4 or 5 hours on the river, stopping for lunch. A couple of days we hiked all day. One woman sprained her ankle, and even she enjoyed herself reading and sitting in the scenery since she couldn't hike. The food was excellent; we even got wine with dinner. After dinner the head oarsmen talked about what we'd be doing the next day, or they'd tell stories of disasters and exciting trips they'd had.

"Almost every day—this was the last week in May and early June—there were rapids and some were pretty exciting. No one capsized, but one day we did have to stop and repair some damage to the boats. Some rapids were too rough to ride through.

"At that time of year nearly everyone on the trip had some sort of connection with a university, having planned their trip to come right at the end of the school year. There were a few lawyers. Almost everyone was 25 to 40, but it didn't matter that I was so much older because everyone was so compatible."

*GRAND CANYON DORIES, PO Box 67, Altaville, CA
95221, (209) 736-0805. Expensive.*

WILDERNESS RIVER ADVENTURES
Grand Canyon Expedition

"The third day out, I was wondering, 'Oh, why 8 days?' Then
by the seventh day, it was, 'Oh! You mean we only have one
more night?' It was really an adventure." Kiriki is an English
teacher from Woodstock, New York, who traveled throughout the Grand Canyon on a motorized raft with Wilderness
River Adventures.

"We put in at Lake Powell, stayed at a hotel there for
orientation the night before we left. They taught us how to
pack our duffel bags, then we met in the morning and boarded two motor-powered boats (S-rigs) with a crew of two per
boat. We were 28, split into 2 groups. A crowd had come from
California and, in fact, we've gotten together since for a
reunion and to show pictures....

"Then there were the buddies from the South, real
macho, loud-mouthed, beer-drinking exhibitionists.... We
weren't out an hour before the captain got annoyed and hove
to. 'This is for fun,' he said, 'and you can drink beer and carry
on, but I am the captain, and there are rules. If you don't keep
them, I'll send you home.' This captain was a young kid in
his 20s. Those river guides are just fantastic.

"They were also wonderfully dramatic. Our motor cut
out one time, and we got caught on a rock. All kinds of
excitement happening....

"The food was wonderful. We always had a full breakfast; eggs, sausage, toast. Lunch included fresh salad and all
kinds of sandwich makings. Dinner was not gourmet food,
but it was very good camp food.

"The best part was finding all the little flowers and the
fauna, and then, gliding down this incredible cut, the guides
gave us a booklet and talked about the area. They pointed out
the strata in the rock, told us about the plans for more dams.
You gained from them a feeling of how precarious this ecology was and how terribly important it was to preserve it."

WILDERNESS RIVER ADVENTURES, PO Box 717, Page, AZ 86040, (602) 645-3296. Expensive.

 Other River Choices _____

Arizona Raft Adventures (AzRA) runs complete, 225-mile Grand Canyon trips, from Lee's Ferry to Diamond Creek, that take 8 days on 32-foot, motor-powered rafts (maximum 16 passengers), 13 days by oar and 14 days for pros who want an all-paddle adventure. Partial, as well as special trips for hikers, natural history buffs and gourmets, also on AzRA's agenda, which includes hotel, rental car and discount airline reservations for clients.

ARIZONA RAFT ADVENTURES, 4050 E. Huntington Drive, Flagstaff, AZ 86004, (602) 526-8200. Moderate.

A noted outfitter, respected for excellent food as well as meticulous attention to detail, Grand Canyon Expeditions specializes in 8-day motor-powered expeditions on 37-foot S-rigs (maximum 14 passengers). Longer voyages? There are 14-day oar trips powered by accomplished rowers. River historians, ecology experts, geologists, archaeologists, and photography instructors accompany the special-interest journeys.

GRAND CANYON EXPEDITIONS, PO Box O, Kanab, UT 84741, (800) 544-2691 or (801) 644-2691. Moderate.

Don't investigate the Middle Fork of Idaho's Salmon River for a motor trip; engines aren't allowed. The 6-day raft and paddle trips run by Kurt & Gayle Selisch's Middle Fork Wilderness Outfitters merit praise.

MIDDLE FORK WILDERNESS OUTFITTERS, PO Box 4682, Ketchum, ID 83340, (208) 726-2467. Expensive.

The 10-day Tatshenshini River trip arranged by Sobek gets high marks. The river travels through the Yukon's St.

Elias Range, becoming ever wider as it joins with the Alsek River before emptying into the Gulf of Alaska. The sight of building-sized icebergs calving off the glaciers is, apparently, unforgettable. The meals were said to be terrific, too.

MOUNTAIN TRAVEL SOBEK, 6420 Fairmount Avenue, El Cerrito, CA 94530, (800) 227-2384. Tent accommodations. Expensive.

"River Canyons not only overflow with beauty and excitement, they also glow with great healing energy," according to Whitewater Voyages. This outfitter offers "Inner Voyages:" holistic trips on five California rivers and Oregon's Rogue with vegetarian meals and time to practice T'ai Chi. Numerous traditional runs on "more rivers in California than any other outfitter—including nine National Wild and Scenic Rivers" are also offered.

WHITEWATER VOYAGES, PO Box 906, El Sobrante, CA 94820, (415) 222-5994. Moderate.

 Reservations Services _____

THE RIVER TRAVEL CENTER, PO Box 6-R, Point Arena, CA 95468, (800) 882-7238 or (707) 882-2255. Represents over 200 Western rafting companies.

FRIENDS OF THE RIVER, Fort Mason Center, Building C, San Francisco, CA 94123, (415) 771-0400. A booking service as well as a group dedicated to saving endangered American rivers.

A number of ecologically-concerned groups sponsor raft trips, most accompanied by naturalists as well as guides. They include:

OUTWARD BOUND, (800) 243-8520.

SMITHSONIAN INSTITUTION'S STUDY TOURS AND SEMINARS, (202) 357-4700.

THE NATURE CONSERVANCY, (704) 841-5352.

Bibliography

River Runner magazine, PO Box 697, Fallbrook, CA 92028, (619) 723-3638, $5. The annual February Travel issue surveys the prime rafting rivers and the outfitters that run them.

Whitewater Rafting in Western North America by Lloyd D. Armstead ($13.95, Globe Pequod Press, 138 West Main Street, Box Q, Chester, CT 06412, (800) 243-0495 or (800) 962-0973, 1990). Describes 140 river voyages.

Whitewater Rafting in Eastern North America by Lloyd D. Armstead ($9.95, Globe Pequod Press, 138 West Main Street, Box Q, Chester, CT 06412, 1989). A companion to Whitewater Rafting in Western North America; lists 49 river runs.

Adventure Travel North America by Pat Dickerman ($15.95, Adventure Guides, Inc, 36 East 57th Street, New York, NY 10022, 1991).

Paddling

Canoeing and kayaking, those most indigenous of North American water sports, are avidly practiced today. While the original birchbark and sealskin craft have been replaced by fiberglass and aluminum, modern canoeists and kayakers still paddle alone or in pairs, at least during the day. Come nightfall, the boats are beached and paddlers unite at lodges, inns and camps.

Touring in bigger, tandem canoes and two-person touring kayaks needn't present a problem for the partnerless. Walt Durrua of the Jersey Paddlers, a kayaking and canoeing store, says novice singles are often put in double kayaks with a stronger paddler. He also says that, overall, solos account for about 50% of the participants on the adventurous paddling trips he favors. Several outfitters assured me that if they couldn't pair me up, I would paddle with the guide. That's exactly what happened on my trip with Gunflint Northwoods Outfitters.

Unlike cycling, camping is still commonplace on canoeing and kayaking tours. The only supplements solos face are for those trips that meander to lodges or inns.

Pricing Categories

Inexpensive	————	Under $75 a day
Moderate	————	$75 to $125 a day
Expensive	————	$126 to $200
Very Expensive	————	Over $200 a day

GUNFLINT NORTHWOODS OUTFITTERS
Boundary Waters Canoe Area

A paddling excursion in the 2-million-acre Boundary Waters
Canoe Area (BWCA) along the Minnesota-Ontario border is a
potent remedy for urban toxification. Fall is especially
vibrant, as long as one is willing to chance 25 degree nights
and squally weather. The lodge-to-lodge trip run by Gunflint
Northwoods Outfitters, about 150 miles north of Duluth,
Minnesota, was a brisk introduction to the BWCA and canoeing. Three and a half days in this watery immensity are sure
to leave one invigorated, but don't forget to bring long johns.
In September, the Northwoods are chilly.

Gunflint runs BWCA excursions from July to mid-
September. I arrived September 10th for the last trip of the
season. Saturday's hearty, wild rice and spit-roasted pig supper was comforting after the 4-hour drive from Duluth, and
the trip itself had been a treat. A guide from the Lodge had
motored me and two other Gunflint-bound canoeists along
the birch-and-aspen-studded shore of Lake Superior, the
largest lake in the world.

Five days later, my experience paralleled that of a North
Carolinian who had finished her Boundary Waters canoe
adventure the day I flew in for mine. "I set off by myself with
strangers," she told me, "and had the most wonderful time."
Between our arrival and departure nights at Gunflint, we
slept one night at the Chippewa Inn, a fisherman's camp, and
two nights in nylon tents. At the Lodge, my fire-warmed
cabin, made decades ago by Justine Kerfoot, the 86-year-old
doyenne of Gunflint, was carpeted and comfortably rustic,
except for the new pine paneled bathroom and sauna.

Our adventure began, officially, when we met for a roast
turkey and Swedish meatball dinner in the Lodge's lake view
dining room Sunday at 6:30 pm. "We" were a newsletter pub-
lisher from Reno, a Minnesota agronomist and his wife, who
made their own cedar strip canoes, a couple from Denver, and
me. Brian, a poised college graduate who proved to be an
exceedingly able guide, outlined our 34-mile trip. There
would be 10, 20 to 110 rod (a rod measures 16 1/2 feet)
portages, but all we *had* to carry were our blue, 20- to 30-

pound packs. If necessary, Brian would heft each canoe onto his shoulders and walk it over the stony paths that by-passed the rapids.

Monday morning, Mr. Reno and I joined Brian in a three-man canoe, after the two couples' packs had been stowed into two 50-pound Kevlars selected from Gunflint's 250-boat fleet. At 9:45 we paddled onto Gunflint Lake bound for Gneiss Point, 10 miles and 5 portages distant. This first day was our most intricate passage, the scenery the most intimate of the trip. The lakes and rivers through which we passed were, for the most part, narrow. We could study the lichen that clung to the pinkish granite boulders and the veins in the yellow-tinged aspen leaves, they were that close.

Expecting to have a hard time keeping up on this, my canoe debut, I was relieved to be in a three-person boat and astonished to discover that, with a minimum of shoulder pain, I could manage the pace. The unison paddling was mesmerizing. We reached our destination slowly. There was time to listen for loons, to spot a bald eagle, to distinguish between a stand of spruce and a clump of fir. Portages provided diversion, at least for the women. All we did was lug our packs. The men, first time portagers all, carried their own canoes, often over treacherous ground. Beyond that, Brian and Andy, our cook and packer, took meticulous care of us.

Gliding down Gneiss Lake we spied a spiral of smoke, then a colony of spring green tents that turned out to be ours for the night. Andy had everything under control. Sleeping bags lay neatly on air mattresses. Water boiled on a sturdy iron grate that the US Forest Service provides, together with molded plastic latrines, at the 100-odd campsites it maintains in the Boundary Waters Canoe Area. Some of us layered up and sipped tea in a mossy, sunstruck glade while those with swimsuits braved a pre-dinner dip.

Gunflint meals are an instant cure for anemia. Our first lunch had been disappointing, but that evening, a tasty, freeze-dried rice-and-vegetable mix accompanied the marbled, 10-ounce steaks Andy grilled to order. Tuesday morning we feasted on a hearty camp breakfast after a night spent squirming into more socks, another pair of pants, an extra sweater. While we reveled in the brisk fall days, the cold nights took adjustment.

We spent the third night of the 6-night trip at the far-from-aristocratic Chippewa Inn, or "Dorothy's." The sky was grey and threatening, and the rain came pelting down just as we landed our canoes. In retrospect, Dorothy's was almost too primitive, but at that moment everyone was profoundly grateful for this somewhat bizarre and isolated haven. We tested the back-breaking mattresses before choosing rooms upstairs in which most of the color-coordinated furnishings had been sewn on a treadle-powered sewing machine by Dorothy herself.

Of necessity (Dorothy's is 125 miles from the nearest Canadian town) most of the fixings for our turkey dinner and pancake-bacon-and-eggs breakfast were packaged or canned, but portions were copious to a fault. Flashlights illuminated trips to the outdoor privies. Protected from the weather, we all slept like logs.

Wednesday heralded glorious, Indian summer weather. Sun-warmed, we paddled happily through this longest, most arduous day of the trip. Lunchtime found us stretched out on a sloping granite boulder munching apricots, pumpkin seeds and banana chips, while Brian toasted bagels for a slathering of cream cheese and jelly. At 4:30 we made landfall at a marvelous campsite on a finger of spruce-rimmed grass sloping into Seagull Lake.

Everything came together that last night. Campfire smoke rose straight up into the still air. We had forged an easy camaraderie, and my only regret was not having witnessed a display of Northern Lights.

Jim saw them first: sheets of icy white light shot up, then down, then up again, even higher, from a brilliantly glowing base on the southern horizon. Spellbound, we huddled together in front of our tents to take in the spectacular show.

GUNFLINT NORTHWOODS OUTFITTERS, HC 64, Box 750, Grand Marais, MN 55604, (800) 328-3325. Moderate.

Other Voices _____

CANOE USA and WILDERNESS SOUTHEAST

"Canoeing isn't nearly as strenuous as hiking or climbing up rocks, and there's always somebody nice around to pick up the canoe and put it in the water." Kay ought to know. This game, 80-year-old retired pediatric allergist from Virginia took two, 5-day canoe trips last year with Canoe USA, not her first by a long shot. She also took her own canoe along on a houseboat-canoe trip in Florida with Wilderness Southeast.

"There's quite a bit of instruction before you set out with Canoe USA. They get you a partner on the inn-to-inn trips, but if you want to paddle by yourself you can. Usually one or two guides accompany 12 people in 6 canoes.

"We canoed for 5 days in Northern Florida the first trip I took with them, and we stayed at inns. I had a big suite with a sitting room in Ocala at the Seven Sister Inn. They gave us a real fancy dinner. In Maine, we did five or six rivers and stayed in historical old houses. The accommodations were very nice, and we had lovely, big breakfasts and gourmet picnics. Sometimes we ate dinner at the inns; one night we had a lobster bake.

"On these trips they van you to the put-in, towing the canoes in trailers. You canoe during the morning, then they meet you for lunch.... Then at the end of the day they van you back to the inn. Oh, those were elegant trips. I wish I lived that way all the time.

"Wilderness Southeast trips are heaven. This nonprofit group's aim is to take people out into the wilderness and teach them about trees and wildlife. They're very careful about conservation. The leaders are trained naturalists, mostly with degrees, and they train volunteers to help out. You get people from all over, young people, a few couples, all ages; 20-year-olds up to me.

"On the houseboat trip we were 5 days on the St. John's River and the lakes not far from Deland, Florida. We had 2 houseboats, each holding 8 to 10 people. The canoes went on the roof. We slept and had all our meals on the boats. It was close quarters sleeping but nobody minded. Everybody helped with the cooking and we ate all together on one boat.

"During the day, the houseboats followed the canoes. We visited the manatees in a big spring near the St. John's. Some people didn't canoe; they just read, or sunbathed, or went swimming with the manatees. They're very peaceful creatures. You ought to try that sometime."

CANOE USA, Box 610-BR, Waitsfield, VT 05673, (802) 496-2409. Single occupancy rates vary each year depending on the inns they use. Expensive.

WILDERNESS SOUTHEAST, 711 Sandtown Road, Savannah, GA 31410, (912) 897-5108. Inexpensive.

SLICKROCK ADVENTURES and BAJA EXPEDITIONS
Kayaking in Belize and Baja, California

"We didn't even take sleeping bags, just tents and sheets. Sometimes we'd string hammocks between palm trees. Very few bugs down there in Belize." The 45-year-old owner of Jersey Paddlers near Point Pleasant, New Jersey, Walt puts together groups for scores of paddling trips. He's talking about a recent, 2-week kayak trip to Belize with Slickrock Adventures, with some added remarks about Baja Expeditions.

"We flew from Belize City to Placentia to pick up our boats. Placentia's a beautiful seaside town with just a handful of people. Very primitive....

"Our trip was offshore to the cays that cap the world's second longest barrier reef. There were four or five kayakers from Jersey Paddlers, plus a few others that had signed on separately with Slickrock. We lived out of the sea kayaks for a week with no problems at all. Our guides brought plenty of food but we caught fresh fish, ate fresh palm hearts and the like. You could live off the land there if you wanted to.

"The islands are small, so you can cover one quickly. Inside the reef the water is pretty calm, although we paddled the rougher waters outside the reef some. There was a girl who'd never been in a kayak before, and a man in his

50s...who was overweight but had no trouble at all. One couple from California used a double sea kayak.

"Cully Erdmann, Slickrock's owner, is a good outfitter. He's been doing sea kayaking for a while, so he's really relaxed. His Belize trip is a little more primitive than some of the trips you can take, but that's the beauty of it. There are kayak trips where everything's done for you, gourmet meals every day.

"Who runs fancy trips? Baja Expeditions, out of San Diego, for one. They follow you around carrying everything, and they tailor the trip to the group. They get people who like to be waited on. They use a panga, sort of an ocean-going row boat, to carry gear and food and set up for you in advance.

"Sea kayaks are inherently safe. They won't sink. You can pair up with someone more experienced and use a double. There is always a guide in front of the pack, a guide in back, and one in the middle. If the leader blows the whistle, everybody groups together. The guides tell you what to do if you run into trouble.

"All ages go on these kayak trips, about 50% of them single, and the ratio of men to women is pretty good, too. The guides are very knowledgeable, so if you want to know about the birds, or stars, hiking in the desert, whatever, they can tell you about it. If all you want to do is lie on the beach or grab a line and fish, you can do that, too.

"There's always a sunrise or a sunset. The sky is clear, you can see all the stars. I've never had anyone come back and not rave about the beauty."

SLICKROCK ADVENTURES, INC., PO Box 1400, Moab, Utah 84532, (801) 259-6996. Moderate.

BAJA EXPEDITIONS, INC., 2625 Garnet Avenue, San Diego, CA 92109, (619) 581-3311. Moderate.

EXPLORERS AT SEA
Kayaking Along the Maine Coast

"You have all those islands around you, a flock of birds settled on the water by my bow. I've done plenty of cruising on sailboats, but this kind of intimacy with the water was phenomenal." Nancy's enthusiasm was prompted by two, day-long kayak trips along the Maine Coast with Explorers at Sea, when the 50-year-old Maine real estate broker paddled her own sea kayak.

"My introduction to paddling took place Memorial Day weekend. We had 3 instructors for 10 people, an excellent ratio. We launched from Stonington into a watery thoroughfare protected from the open water by all these little islands. The staff is very careful. You must paddle in a group. You don't get tired because there's a lot of stopping for rests in coves. It was trial by fire, and it gave me long-lasting confidence.

"Our itinerary included crossing a big channel to get to an island, where we were going to picnic. When we reached the channel, there were these huge waves with white caps! I didn't get the slightest hint from any of the instructors that this was a heavy sea or that it wasn't doable. This being my first time in a kayak, I thought, 'Well, this is what kayaking is all about, I guess. Just go with the flow.' It was work just to paddle, but I had all these other people around me, and the instructors, so I wasn't discouraged.

"Some had done more paddling than others, but some had never been in a kayak before. It was just enough of a challenge to be exhilarating. Had it been any longer, I would have tired and felt it was beyond me. I was very pleased to get to the island. The experience gave me tremendous respect for the kayak, that it could take these big winds without turning over. I didn't feel vulnerable.

"The second time out was totally different. The water was like glass. It was just so beautiful! But that time I got restless. I wanted to paddle ahead, and I didn't want to stop in all the little coves.

"I learn by doing, and this program was just ideal."

EXPLORERS AT SEA, PO Box 469, Main Street, Stonington, ME 04681, (207) 367-2356. Offered are 2-, 3- and 5-day sea kayaking/tent camping trips, including several for women only.

NANTAHALA OUTDOOR CENTER

"I've canoed all my life, but I've outlived all my canoe partners, so I took up kayaking," explains Spike, a 76-year-old out-
doorsman who runs a Christian youth camp in the Missouri
Ozarks. Having shot the rapids in the Grand Canyon in a
canoe with the Nantahala Outdoor Center at the age of 72, he
chose them again when he decided to try kayaking.

"Nantahala offers all kinds of trips. I took a 5-day beginner course in kayaking 4 or 5 years ago, then went back to
North Carolina a couple of months later for more. They have
what they call a Week of Rivers for good paddlers, and they
take trips to Chile, or the Scottish Highlands, or to Mexico.
After paddling for about a year I went on their Grand Canyon
deal. Oh, my goodness, I had so much fun.

"...This was what they called a raft-supported trip. The
Outdoor Center had booked about a dozen paddlers, and
another five or six came on their own. Sleight [the outfitter]
supplied the food, supplies, tents, kayaks, and 4 oar rafts, and
we just kayaked for 2 weeks.

"We put in below Grand Canyon Dam at Granite Creek,
which is on an Indian reservation near Lake Powell. Some of
the people hiked in and met us about halfway through.

"...A true kayak, like the Eskimos use, is enclosed and
has a skirt, so you can roll. That's what I used. I did hurt my
shoulder and had to ride the raft for 2 days while it got better.

"The food was unbelievable. I mean candlelight and
wine, the whole thing. On the river. You don't have to be a
paddler to enjoy those things.

"The Grand Canyon is the ultimate trip in the US for
rapids because it's so long, with so many big rapids. In 226
miles, the Colorado River has something like 160 rapids of
various sizes, and lots of class 5s and 4s. There's a lot of flat
water too, and the river moves well. In the long stretches of
flat water you can just lay back and watch millions of years
go by. Oh, it's a spectacular experience."

*NANTAHALA OUTDOOR CENTER, Box 41, Bryson City,
NC 28713, (704) 488-2175 or (704) 488-9221. Moderate.*

CRAFTSBURY SCULLING CENTER

"I always assumed that rowing was elitist. You had to go to a really expensive private school or something. Then I read that you could take sculling lessons at the Craftsbury Sculling Center, that they taught absolute beginners how to scull. I thought, 'Here's my ticket.'" Arthur, a 24-year-old graduate student and a native of the Bronx, took a week's course at the Craftsbury Center 2 years running. Now he has his own shell and plans to row in New York City.

"...At Craftsbury, you get a little coaching and try to do what they tell you from 7:00 to 9:00 am. After breakfast, there's another 2-hour session. The coaches videotape you so you can see what you did, which turns out to be different from what you thought you did. Next day you make your corrections. By the time you leave you have a visual picture of how you should look and feel if you're sculling correctly. You know when you've got it right. You can feel it.

"The accommodations are spare, but frankly they could set me up in a little hut and it wouldn't matter. All you think about is rowing. There are about 20 people in a session. They've got the right ratio of coaches to scullers, so you get lots of personal attention. In fact, most people try to row away from the coaches because they're always critiquing something. They're implacable.

"Without question, besides the rowing, the best part is the people. It takes a certain kind of mind to say, 'Okay, I'm going to go to rowing camp.'...You get positive, friendly people of all ages who are also physically fit, confident, outgoing.... You get one of everything.

"I learned a lot going back a second time. I saw significant improvement and really felt like I was meant to do this...."

CRAFTSBURY SCULLING CENTER, Box 31, Craftsbury Common, VT 05827, (802) 586-7767. The fees for 3-day and 1-week sessions include lodging, 3 meals a day and coaching. Inexpensive to Moderate.

Other Paddling Choices Outfitters ——

The Canoeing Inn-to-Inn trip Arthur Sharkey initiated on the Connecticut River 10 years ago hasn't attracted a lot of singles, but I mention this package because the 30-mile voyage to 3 little inns is so appealing. Some solos take part in kayaks or one-person canoes; occasionally the Sharkeys can pair up singles; otherwise couples rent two-person canoes for the Monday-to-Thursday jaunt.

CANOEING INN-TO-INN, c/o Stone House Inn, North Thetford, VT 05054, (802) 333-9124. Rates include all meals and lodging. A single supplement is levied only when all the inns are full. Inexpensive.

Canoeists, kayakers, rafters, and fishermen, too, are ably served by Dvorak's Expeditions. This outfitter runs 10 rivers that course through 29 canyons located in three countries. Notable are 1- to 12-day instructional canoe and kayaking seminars held on rivers in New Mexico, Utah, Texas, Idaho, and Arizona, plus Colorado's own Arkansas, Dolores and Colorado.

DVORAK'S EXPEDITIONS, 17921-AG US Hwy 285, Nathrop, CO 81236, (800) 824-3795 or (719) 539-6851. Inexpensive to Expensive.

Renting canoes and equipment in the Adirondacks accounts for two-thirds of St. Regis Canoe Outfitters' business. Those who've longed to take to the woods alone now have a chance. When not out portaging light-weight Kevlar canoes by themselves, solos, who comprise about 20% to 30% of the Cilley's clientele, sign on for guided tours in the Adirondacks and Maine as well as through Florida's Everglades in winter.

ST. REGIS CANOE OUTFITTERS, PO Box 318, Lake Clear, NY 12945, (518) 891-1838. Moderate.

Wild and Scenic Expeditions offers all-Sportyak trips on both the San Juan and Green Rivers in Utah, but canoeists who tire of paddling solo can climb aboard the oar-powered raft that accompanies the fleet of 7-foot skiffs.

WILD AND SCENIC EXPEDITIONS, PO Box 460, Flagstaff, AZ 86002, (800) 231-1963 or (602) 774-7343. Moderate.

The following are outfitters that accessorize their trips with inflatable kayaks.

ECHO, (415) 652-1600 (see Rafting), DVORAK EXPEDITIONS, (800) 824-3795 (above), and WILD AND SCENIC EXPEDITIONS, (800) 231-1963 (above).

 ## Other Choices: Schools

The Nantahala Outdoor Center teaches a variety of skills at its base camp in the Southern Appalachians; hiking, backpacking and rock climbing in the rugged mountain terrain; canoeing and kayaking on the Nantahala and Ocoee Rivers. Those who have learned to play the river and roll, are ready for one of Nantahala's "Weeks of Rivers" trips in Georgia, Tennessee or West Virginia. The Outdoor School also arranges challenging whitewater tours on Mexico's Usumacinta, Chile's Rio Bio-Bio and other fabled rivers around the world.

NANTAHALA OUTDOOR CENTER, Box 41, Bryson City, NC 28713, (704) 488-2175 or (704) 488-9229. Fees for courses include instruction, equipment, shared lodging, and all meals. Moderate.

The National Outdoor Leadership School (NOLS) pioneered wilderness education 25 years ago. Among NOLS' 38 offerings are 14-day sea kayaking courses for the "25 and Older" set in the Sea Of Cortez and through the green islands and glaciers of Alaska's Prince William Sound. There's also a 14-day "25 and Older" River Kayaking course in the Arctic

National Wildlife Refuge located in the Alaska's Brooks
Range.

*NATIONAL OUTDOOR LEADERSHIP SCHOOL, PO Box
AA, Lander, Wyoming 82520, (307) 332-6973. Moderate to
Expensive.*

Grouped by ability into four classes, kayakers learn and
perfect their whitewater techniques under the tutelage of
experienced guides on the California Salmon River at the
Otter Bar Lodge. The glass-and-hardwood-sheathed lodge
shelters no more than 10 people and attracts "plenty of singles: healthy, active people of all ages, about 40% women,
60% men," explains Kristy Sturges, who, with her husband
Peter, runs an operation deluxe enough to make hard-boiled
kayakers gush. Strawberry daiquiris in the hot tub. Indeed.

*OTTER BAR LODGE, PO Box 210, Forks of Salmon, CA
96031, (916) 462-4772. The rate for the 7-day trip is all-inclusive. Moderate.*

The Outdoor Centre of New England gives an exceedingly comprehensive selection of kayaking and canoeing
courses. There are separate courses for women beginners and
over-40-year-olds. Solo canoeists can take instruction in
either open or decked canoes at the Outdoor Centre's classrooms in the town of Millers Falls in North Central
Massachusetts and on the (sometimes low) Millers River
nearby.

*THE OUTDOOR CENTRE OF NEW ENGLAND, 8 Pleasant
Street, Millers Falls, MA 01349, (413) 659-3926. They offer
optional accommodations: a bed in the Centre's mixed-sex
bunkrooms. Moderate.*

Teaching river kayaking is Sundance Expeditions' forte.
A 10-mile stretch on the Rogue River on Oregon serves as a
class room for their Nine Day Basic Kayak School: 5 days of
instruction plus a 4-day downriver trip. Sundance also offers
a 5-day Advanced kayaking trip on Wild & Scenic portion of
the Illinois River (in Oregon), and 3 intermediate classes on

the North Umpqua where kayakers overnight at the Steamboat Inn (see INNS). Sundance is about as plush as paddling gets. Choice wines and inventive dinners are served where participants sleep, in scenic River House perched high above the Rogue.

SUNDANCE EXPEDITIONS, 14894 Galice Road, Merlin, OR 97532, (503) 479-8508. Moderate.

 ## Canoeing and Kayaking Reservations ——

RIVER TRAVEL CENTER, Box 6, Point Area, CA 95468, (800) 882-7238. A reservationist here explained why they booked far more sea kayaking (and rafting) than river kayaking trips: "Rafting is the entry-level river sport. Open water kayaking is next up the ladder in difficulty. Novices can easily master the long tracking sea kayaks used for touring and cruises, but river kayaking is a lot trickier. You need classes and good skills before you're ready to go out. River kayaking outfitters are less likely to list with us because they want to be sure their clients know what they're doing." Many adventure firms and various conservation groups also offer a wide selection of canoe trips.

SMITHSONIAN INSTITUTION'S STUDY TOURS AND SEMINARS, Rm. 3045, 1100 Jefferson Drive, S.W., Washington, DC 20560, (202) 357-4700.

MOUNTAIN TRAVEL SOBEK, 6420 Fairmont Avenue, El Cerrito, CA 94530, (800) 227-2384.

Bibliography

Canoe, 10526 NE 68th Street, Kirkland, WA 98033, (206) 827-6363, ($4 for back-issues). Publishes an annotated list of "North

America's Foremost Paddling Schools," as well as an "Adventure Paddling Directory" (culled primarily from their advertisers).

The National Association of Canoe Liveries and Outfitters, PO Box 1149, Murdock, FL 33938-1149, (813) 743-7278. Will provide a list of the 12-year-old association's members.

The Big Book of Adventure Travel by James G. Simmons ($14.95, New American Library, New York, 1990). Contains good descriptions of leading outfitters, but discount coupons for trips offered by most of these companies compromise the book editorially.

Adventure Travel North America by Pat Dickerman ($15.95, Adventure Guides, NY, 1991).

Learning to
Sail

Catering to novices and old salts alike are a raft of learn-to-sail schools. Study navigation or cruising at a single-focus school or learn to sail at a branch of one of the large, multifaceted teaching facilities. Participants can take lessons, line up crews or a crew job as well as socialize at clubs. Classes more nearly resemble vacations when sailing offshore. About half the facilities described in this chapter offer learn-aboard cruises.

Spending a day on the water learning to sail, or honing skills already acquired, is about as congenial as learning experiences get. However, it may be lonely at night when on something other than a liveaboard. Of the schools listed here, only Wooden Boat and the Offshore Sailing School have housing "on campus." Other facilities provide lists of local lodgings, or, make reservations at selected inns or motels.

Pricing: *The nature of the programs in this chapter makes it impossible to compare prices accurately. Contact the organizations listed for up-to-date tuition and accommodation rates.*

ANNAPOLIS SAILING SCHOOL
Annapolis, Maryland

Rain. The Saturday morning sailing class, 1 of the 4, 2-hour periods scheduled on the water, had been canceled due to atypical thunder and lightening. There were those who hoped the afternoon sailing classes would be canceled, too. Forget it. Annapolis Sailing School staffers rounded up all the foul weather gear they could find. At 2:00 pm, crackling in yellow plastic, we set out to practice what our two instructors had, that morning, so lucidly taught.

Muttering the trinity of sailing basics according to teacher Bob—"Where is the wind coming from? How shall I steer the boat? How should the sails be set?"—our foursome of three women and one man began unbuckling halyards, freeing sheets, and performing other salty tasks. Under the watchful guidance of one sailing instructor per boat, all 12 crews cast off and sailed into Maryland's Severn River.

Water squished out of our boat shoes as we clambered out of our little sail boats onto the rain-soaked docks around 4:00 pm. We'd been tested and survived.

The Annapolis Sailing School, founded in 1959, is the oldest and largest sailing school in the US, with teaching facilities in St. Petersburg, St. Croix; Clear Lake, Texas; Key West, Florida; Charleston, South Carolina; Greenport, Long Island; as well as Maryland. Still, the school manages to escape standardization and the other pitfalls often associated with being "big."

Students registered for the "Become a Sailor in One Weekend" course at the white colonial school headquarters at 8:30 am and dashed back out through the deluge with maps detailing the way to the school's Marina at the confluence of Back Creek and the Severn River. Once reunited at the boat-storage-with-classroom shed, we placed our catered lunch orders and broke into 2 sections of 24 each. Shortly after 9:00 am, our teacher handed around the school's explicit primer and then lit into a bow-to-stern description of our training vessel, the Rainbow Sloop.

After a rigorous morning of terminology, theory and technique in the classroom, we were divided into groups of four, couples intentionally split into separate boats. The classes were lively and personal. We all benefited from patient, one-on-one lessons once aboard the 24-foot Rainbows. In 2 days the sailing instructors were able to drum the basics into my hands and head.

Saturday evening, my pleasant, warm room in the Maryland Inn was an appropriate haven from the miserable weather. Elect the accommodations option offered by

Annapolis Sailing and be housed in one of the five handsome 19th century buildings collectively known as the Historic Inns of Annapolis. All are located in the heart of Maryland's red brick capitol.

Those arriving after dark can use the luminous white State House dome, built in 1771, as a beacon to find Governor Calvert House, the check-in hotel for most of the Historic Inns. A hotel manager is on hand to register me, summon a valet for my car and direct me past drifts of bridal-wreath and dogwood to the Maryland Inn with its inviting, small town ambiance. The furniture and bathroom tiles evince the hotel's unglamorous past, but the soft French blue wallpaper that match the curtains and spreads is evidence of a more gentrified present. The smiling, can-do service is also most appealing.

The waiters are attentive, as they serve satisfying dinners of, say, salt-cured salmon, grilled swordfish and Opera cake at the Treaty of Paris restaurant housed in the basement of the Maryland Inn. Sunday, a valet delivered my car, and I set off for a second round of classes after a pleasant breakfast at the Treaty of Paris (superior to the help-yourself, sailing school buffet offered at the Governor Calvert House) on a truly glorious day.

The atmosphere on my boat our last day was upbeat and convivial. The fleets of moth-like, small boats that race where the river joins the Chesapeake Bay give Annapolis Sailing School students wide berth. Severn River sailors know that a Rainbow patch on the mainsail indicates a beginner on the helm. Not that this dampened our spirits; it just made us feel safer.

Cheers and laughter erupted late Sunday afternoon as diplomas were handed out to a vigorous complement of 48 students hailing from North Carolina, Virginia, New Hampshire, and New York, among other spots. We may have accepted our certificates with wry amusement, but there was genuine pleasure in our accomplishment as well. Downing beer and Coke in celebration, students filled out school evaluation sheets at picnic tables beside the two-story metal classroom shed. Though not everyone had aspired to becoming a helmsman—some wanted to be better crew, others had enrolled to please a friend or beau—our group seemed satisfied. We'd become adept at handling the sloops and we had been effectively taught.

ANNAPOLIS SAILING SCHOOL, PO BOX 3334, Annapolis, MD 21403, (800) 638-9192 or (301) 267-7205. Beginning, intermediate, advanced, racing, and navigation courses are offered. The 2-day "Become a Sailor in One Weekend" package at Annapolis includes 2 nights lodging and Continental breakfasts.

 Other Voices _____

"I wanted to learn sailing for such a long time," reports Maggie, 27, "and finally decided to so something about it." This sales manager for a San Francisco hotel shopped around the San Francisco Bay Area and chose the Olympic Circle Sailing Club in Berkeley, California, where she was an enthusiastic member of 2 months standing when interviewed.

"A membership is $1500 for the year, and you're given a $2000 credit [the extra $500 is a club-issued bonus]. It's like a bank; you use that "money" for classes or trips with the club. It's expensive, but you'd spend more money than that just chartering boats.

"The clubhouse, a really nice facility, is at the Berkeley Marina. The owners are very involved in what goes on there, and the members are serious about sailing; many of the other clubs seemed to be more social. Olympic offers all kinds of seminars—navigating, for instance—during the week that are free to members. People go to learn, but at the same time they are interested in meeting and getting to know you.

"We sail Cal-20s and J-24s, with three people and one instructor per boat. I like learning with other people, watching what they do wrong and what they do well. You proceed at your own pace. I've got to pass a test to enter the advanced class. A couple of guys I met organized a study group of friends on my level who need to pass, too. It's neat.

"There *is* a social aspect to the club, but it's not over-bearing. I mean, I'm single, so I'm always interested in meeting new friends, but I also wanted to learn to sail.... I don't think I'd join a group or club just for singles...."

OLYMPIC CIRCLE SAILING CLUB, 1 Spinnaker Way, Berkeley Marina, Berkeley, CA 94710, (415) 843-4200. The Club also offers a number of liveaboard cruises in the Bay Area and Europe.

SAILING FOR SINGLES
Manhasset, New York

Joe is a 27-year-old bachelor in financial services in the New York metropolitan area, and he talks about Sailing For Singles, a club he joined.

"It's a well-educated group: doctors, lawyers, programmers. ...The club doesn't own any boats; they charter them. We usually sail to a destination, take a break, then sail back. Last weekend we sailed a 36-foot ketch to Greenwich, Connecticut. I think there were nine of us on board, and it was a little tight.

"I took an 8-day sail to Martha's Vineyard, a special event. The sailing club's organizer chartered a 62-foot boat, and it was one of the best trips I've ever had. We stayed at inns every night....

"Three factors can determine whether you have a good trip or not. First, the weather, and we had 8 days of sunshine. Second, the people. People did fight on board, but it was fairly constructive. I mean, sailing is dangerous. You have a big boat with some people who know what they're doing and some who don't, so there's lots of yelling and screaming. If you can't deal with that, you don't belong. If the boom swings the wrong way, you'll get your head knocked off; when someone yells at you, it's for your own safety. There were seven on the trip, a good number.

"The third consideration is the captain. You really need a strong leader, a strong mediator. Where should you head? Some people want to go sightseeing, some want to sail. Do we stick to the original charter, or do we vote on it, or what?

If you vote on it, everyone should come out feeling like they were treated fairly. On this trip the owner of the boat was the captain, and he was good.

"I'm not going to buy my own boat. I'll sail anywhere with other people. A boat is no use without a crew; that's why Sailing for Singles was founded. Bringing a 60-foot boat into a harbor you need help. Anyway, two people on a boat by themselves is boring."

SAILING FOR SINGLES, Box 1043 Manhasset, NY 11030, (718) 279-2680. The 12-month membership comes with either 3, 5 or 10 free daysails. Joe's 8-day cruise to Martha's Vineyard and back was a special arrangement. The fees for typical 1-week trips include breakfast and dinner, but not marina fees.

SEA SENSE
New London, Connecticut and St. Petersburg, Florida

"I want to be a really good sailor. To that end, I've gone on 3 trips in the past year for a total of about 5 weeks with a sailing school for women only called Sea Sense, which sails out of New London, Connecticut in the summer and in St. Petersburg, Florida in the winter." Sally is a graphic designer, 38, from Massachusetts. She seems to typify the single-mindedness of the women attracted to Sea Sense.

"With Sea Sense we sail a chartered Pearson 32.4. It's a gorgeous sailboat and truly seaworthy, with air-conditioning and radar, so you're learning how to be an up-to-date sailor.

"I signed up for a 7-day trip around Long Island with 5 others: an older woman with her college-age daughter, a 58-year-old from California and a 38-year-old woman, a very interesting group. Everyone really wanted to learn, and we worked tremendously hard. We sailed from New London into the Harlem River, down the Hudson to the Atlantic. It took us about 2 1/2 days to reach Montauk. Then we came around and had dinner at Port Jefferson. They cook very simple meals en route: spaghetti, barbecued chicken, whatever.

"Sea Sense is run by Patti Moore and Carol Cuddyer, both in their late forties, and both licensed for years by the

Coast Guard as master captains aboard motor, as well as sailing, boats. The owners also give courses on motor boating, and they've just started a business teaching people how to sail or motor their own boats. They fly all over the country doing this. These two women are superb. They keep their cool, and they make the most wonderful teachers. I've been out with other women's sailing groups; they can't touch the quality, the time, the commitment these women give.

"Carol and Patti entered the Ft. Lauderdale-Isla Mujeres [on the Yucatan Peninsula] race with their students as crew. They came in third out of 26 boats in the Cruising Class, a remarkable feat with a novice crew. I flew down and crewed back with four others. We ran into very, very heavy weather, terrible days of high seas. It was a harsh trip, yes, but it didn't stop me. I'm absolutely hooked."

SEA SENSE, 25 Thames Street, New London, CT 06320, (800) 332-1404 or (203) 444-1404. Offers powerboat and sailboat classes for women in New London, Florida and offshore, at sea.

J WORLD
San Diego, California

Charley, 28, in San Diego real estate, wanted to race his own boat, but didn't feel confident of his skills. "I've sailed, but strictly as a crew person. The whole reason to take the J World course was to become a racing skipper.

"I took Racing II with three others...My friend, who had never raced before, was placed in Racing I. The two groups, Racing I and II, competed against each other all week.

"Every day, we had a lecture from 8:00 to 10:00 am. Then about 11:00 am we'd go out on the water after rigging the boats. We were usually in by 4:00. Then it was up to the bar for a drink and kind of a debriefing with the instructors of each boat.

"This was January, and the San Diego J World gets sailors from the East Coast and the Midwest who come to get warmed up for their season 2 months later. Others in Racing I and II included a guy and a couple from Washington State and one from Chicago. Out-of-towners put up at the Kona Kai Resort right next to J World's marina.

"The instructors are just great. I wouldn't recommend the class for cruising sailors, it's really geared toward racing. Fortunately, the boats aren't too big. Larger boats can be a real problem, they get out of hand. Smaller boats are more responsive to little things, and that's how you learn.

"The instructors say the students with the least experience are the easiest to teach. The ones who've been sailing a long time say, 'Well, this is how I've always done it.' I guess that's why I was so pleased with what I got out of the course. I went in with a pretty clean slate."

J WORLD, 12921 Candela Place, San Diego, CA 92130, (800) 666-1050 or (619) 259-3836. J World also offers many courses at their Newport, RI and Key West, FL locations.

STEVE AND DORIS COLGATE'S OFFSHORE SAILING SCHOOL
Chatham, Massachusetts

"I was a very active racing sailor several years ago, but I didn't have much confidence. I called [the] Colgate's Offshore Sailing School and signed up for a summer course on Martha's Vineyard in Massachusetts." So reports Diane, the how-to writer from New Jersey, 41, and a fairly eclectic solo traveler, whose experience as a novice rafter is described in RAFTING.

"...We all stayed at the same hotel in Edgartown, where they matched me up with another woman. We spent a pleasant week together. [Offshore recently moved its Massachusetts base from Edgartown to Catham, MA, on Cape Cod, where students stay at the Wequassett Inn. However, there has been no change in their teaching method].

"I took the 'Learning to Sail' course. They gave us classroom work in the morning, and these lessons were pretty good; rules of the road when sailing, the parts of the boat, how things work, the basic principles of sailing. The afternoon was spent on the water in 27-foot Solings, four in a boat rotating tasks under the guidance of an instructor. Classes over, you were on your own, for meals and socially.

"It was the first time I'd been to the Vineyard, and there was plenty of time to go exploring. Certainly you got to know the sailing conditions of the area, but what I learned, mainly, was how much I already knew.

"The school had it all together. They didn't go out of their way to be friendly, but the course was well-organized and the equipment was in good condition. The Offshore course wasn't cheap, but sailing isn't inexpensive. I thought it was good value."

STEVE AND DORIS COLGATE'S OFFSHORE SAILING SCHOOL, 16731 McGregor Boulevard, Ft. Myers, FL 33908, (800) 221-4326 or (813) 454-1700. The 5-day, 4-night package at the Wequassett Inn on Cape Cod includes lodging, classes and two parties but no meals. Classes are also offered in Captiva, Florida, and at three Caribbean locations.

 Other Sailing Choices _____

Since 1983, 3,500 sailors have learned cruising skills (no spinnaker handling, no racing tactics) in classic 36-foot Pearsons and Catalinas at Bing Murray's Adventurer Sailing School. "Bing," reports one authority "has a fine reputation as a teacher and is excellent at instructing women." There are never more than five people in a class, and students, about 50% of whom come by themselves, choose their own lodgings from a list the school provides.

ADVENTURER SAILING SCHOOL, 1 Lagoon Road, Portsmouth, RI 02871, (401) 683-3852.

The Argosy Sailing Center just south of Seattle is one of over 100 teaching facilities affiliated with the American Sailing Association (ASA). Classes at ASA member schools conform to uniform standards, so a student graduating from, say, a beginner's class at one ASA school is qualified to enter intermediate sailing at another ASA affiliate. Students completing one of Argosy's 1- to 5-day courses receive an ASA certificate as well as a log book. (J World, above, and the New York Sailing School, listed below, are also ASA members).

ARGOSY SAILING CENTER, 22536 6th Avenue S., Des Moines, IOWA, 98198, (206) 878-3226. A 5-day class is composed of 24 hours of instruction and lots and lots of practice.

"The Heavy Weather Sailing School" is one name for the 3- and 4-day teaching cruises held in the Channel Islands off Santa Barbara by the Pyzel Navigation and Cruising School. Mike Pyzel, a veteran of the first Singlehanded TransPacific race, has been teaching reefing, anchoring and other cruising skills to two to three students at a time in the same Cal 28 for the past 12 years. Coastal navigation is Pyzel's other specialty.

PYZEL NAVIGATION AND CRUISING SCHOOL, PO Box 4217, Santa Barbara, CA 93140, (805) 640-0900.

The New York Sailing School has won the American Sailing Association's "School of the Year" Trophy a record-breaking three times. This school, situated on City Island right on Long Island Sound, offers accelerated 3-day "Master's Courses" (beginner-intermediate), and "Coastal Cruising," for advanced students. Those who don't commute stay at the Ramada Inn or the New Rochelle Hilton.

NEW YORK SAILING SCHOOL, 560 Minneford Avenue, City Island, NY 10464, (212) 885-3103.

The Seamanship Classes taught at the Wooden Boat School located on prime sailing waters in Maine are special. Six-day "Craft of Sail" courses are held on a 32-foot Friendship sloop and a 35-foot ketch. The teachers are deeply involved in yacht design and history, as well as boat handling. Students who take "Cruising Boat Seamanship" classes learn while living aboard the 50-foot schooner Mary Harrington.

WOODEN BOAT SCHOOL, PO Box 78, Brooklin, ME 04616, (207) 359-4651. Tuition for "Craft of Sail" is separate from the fee for shared room and board at the Wooden Boat School. Campsites are also available. Berth, board and tuition are all icluded in the fee for "Cruising Boat Seamanship."

Sailing Clubs for Singles _____

Sailing appears to have spawned more singles clubs than any other sport except skiing, but these facilities can be hard to find. Check your local yacht club for names.

Sail magazine, Charlestown Navy Yard, 100 First Avenue, Charlestown, MA 02129, (617) 241-9500, will print out a list of the sailing clubs in your area upon request. Thanks go to a *Sail* editor for contributing the following list.

MARINA SINGLE SAILING CLUB, PO Box 9876, Marina del Rey, CA 90295.

POLARIS SAILING SOCIETY, PO Box 86256, San Diego 92138-6256.

SINGLE SAILORS OF SOUTH FLORIDA, PO Box 70391, Fort Lauderdale, FL 33307, (305) 523-9849.

SAILING FOR SINGLES, Box 1043, Manhasset, NY 11030, (718) 279-2680.

SINGLES ON SAILBOATS, a branch of the SINGLES CLUB OF RESTON, PO BOX 363, Great Falls, VA 22866, (703) 709-8542.

WOMEN ON WATER, c/o Metropolitan Yacht Club, 55 Embarcadero Cove, Oakland, CA 94606, (415) 536-7450.

Bibliography

Cruising World, 5 John Clarke Road, Newport, RI 02840, (401) 847-1588. Compiles a comprehensive, six-page "Directory of North American Sailing Schools," and will provide the list at no charge upon request.

The American Sailing Association, 13922 Marina del Rey, CA 90292, (213) 822-7171. Contact them to request their membership list.

Scuba Diving

Interest in underwater diving has exploded since scuba first became popular some 20 years ago. Divers, avid for new frontiers, are pushing the global envelope. Few reefs or atolls will be left unexplored as enthusiasts search for sites of unassailable purity. Meanwhile, as long as they remain sightly, the great and famous dive sites will continue to thrive.

In the beginning, divers lived on boats a la Jacques Cousteau. Liveaboard cruises still remain the backbone of the industry, but resorts are becoming equally popular.

Today's diver has a choice: ever-less Spartan liveaboards or resorts that run the gamut from bunk-room basic to Hilton plush. "Cruises are only for those who want to dive their brains out," said one agency reservationist. "You don't get cabin fever at resorts. You can dive and still experience the local culture." She might have added, dive resorts are usually cheaper.

Scuba is unique among participant sports in that you must be certified to practice it. That means classes, out of which may emerge a nucleus of diving companions. Furthermore, divers don't just plunge into the deep by themselves, they usually dive with a partner.

Certainly, a number of divers travel alone. Estimates from scuba reservations agencies state that singles range from 20% to

Pricing Categories

Inexpensive	Under $75 a day
Moderate	$75 to $125 a day
Expensive	$126 to $200
Very Expensive	Over $200 a day

50% of the clientele. Join a group and expect to share a room or pay the supplement; traveling to a resort by yourself automatically means a single room and a higher rate than twosomes. There is little choice on the liveaboards, where most cabins are outfitted with two bunks or beds.

SMALL HOPE BAY
Andros Island, Bahamas

Small Hope Bay, located on Andros Island in the Bahamas, is infinitely benign. Just the place to triumph over a case of diver's block. The dive operation, while highly professional, is friendly and casual. The resort is also a crackerjack place to relax. David Birch created the coral rock-and-pine complex 30 years ago and, together with his family, has been running the isolated property with an eye to stress-destroying basics ever since.

Good fellowship is integral to the Small Hope Bay experience. Other than being met pleasantly, shown to a room and informed of meal times, directives are minimal. New arrivals learn the ropes by questioning members of the ubiquitous Birch family, by checking the green chalkboards in the dining room for dive times and scheduled activities, or by asking other guests. Query tablemates during whatever-you-want breakfasts and buffet lunches of lasagna or curried chicken, plus offerings from the copious salad bar and a selection of frosted cakes. At dinner, when batik cloths replace map-of-the-Bahamas placemats, take a place at six- or eight-seat tables after helping yourself to savory soup and a varied array of salad bar staples. The entree choice—piquant and tender conch curry or thinly sliced roast beef one night, lobster tails or lightly-sauced spare ribs the next—is served.

"This," said the psychiatrist, with a sweeping gesture that included the outdoor bar and tables, the sea grape and palms at the water's edge and the dive shack set out over the bay on pilings, "is the champagne of diving." Why were the bubbles that floated up from the diver's oxygen tanks sweeter at Small Hope Bay than elsewhere? I wondered. Five experienced divers tripped over each other to tell me. "Visibility over 100 feet." "The dive sites, no more than a 1/2 an hour away, are tremendously varied." "Solicitous divemasters." "The resort keeps its section of the Bahamas reef pristine."

This 20-room colony beside a widely curving bay lined with feathery Causerina trees is an excellent place for a beginner, though the 2-acre resort also attracts experienced divers from all over North America. But not all the 40 guests were divers. Mary, a secretary from Seattle, enjoyed herself immensely alone, discovering plenty of non-diving diversions. Explore Andros' one road on fat-tired blue and pink bikes. Ride 30 minutes to Fresh Creek village to shop for seconds of the colorful batik clothing made at Androsia, the batik factory run by Birch's son Jeff. Birders take to the marshes. Others comb the backlands with Dr. Bob, an octogenarian well-versed in the medicinal values of local plants. ("Doan touch that leaf unless you be wantin' five children.")

Books, more books than I have ever seen at a Caribbean resort, fill shelves in the ping pong room and spill into the lounge. Inside my stuccoed coral-rock quarters, the cheerful Androsia curtains billowed in the cooling trades. Some rooms are fashioned of reddish Andros pine, others of stone, but all have louvered glass windows facing the sea, and each simply furnished rectangle is enlivened by vivid batiks.

Nothing jars at Small Hope Bay. The hand-fashioned (and old-fashioned) property becomes its 30 years. Peeled branches serve as closet rods, a wooden spindle holds the toilet paper. Each room comes with a couple of rush mats for sunning, a citronella candle and a flit gun filled with insect repellent. Outside, rope hammocks sag beneath the weight of napping guests. The rates, which include the resort course, but not regular dives, are eminently fair. Just what one would expect from Small Hope Bay, a pleasantly unaffected resort with old line sensibilities.

SMALL HOPE BAY LODGE, Fresh Creek, Andros, Bahamas (809) 368-2014; reservations: (800) 327-0787. The 6-night dive package includes all meals, bar and beach activities. Rates are slightly lower for non-divers and for rooms without bath or with shared bath. Moderate.

LA POSADA DEL SOL and BAYMAN BAY CLUB
Guanaja, Bay Islands

The DC-3 braked beside a thatched hut on the mountainous island of Guanaja off the coast of Honduras. Fifteen minutes from the port of La Ceiba and the banana groves on the Honduras mainland, I found myself on a roadless tropical island set in the crystalline shallows of the world's second longest barrier reef.

The Bay Islands, which include Roatan and the smaller Guanaja, anchor this reef stretching from the tip of the Yucatan Peninsula to Honduras. Isolated Guanaha (Gwah-NAH-ha), may be the last of the-way-the-Caribbean-used-to-be islands; the ultimate getaway for the adventurous diver who has had the foresight to tote insect spray as well as a bathing suit to the plane.

Thus fortified against no-show luggage and no seeums, the diver has two compelling resorts to choose from, La Posada del Sol and the Bayman Bay Club.

The Spanish-hacienda-style "Inn of the Sun" (La Posada Del Sol) incorporates an elevated deck on which the hotel's public areas, pool, and 12 of its 23 bedrooms rest. From this enormous platform wedged into the base of Mount Stanley, guests look straight through the crowns of palms into the Caribbean. The fully-seasoned 5-year-old dive resort, lodged in the former estate of a Canadian industrialist, is professionally run but just a tad unpredictable.

My wake-up call came about 7:30 am when half-a-dozen parrots in the mango trees outside my door started whistling and cackling "Hullo, hullo, hullo." Dive boats leave promptly at 8:30 am, and in the dining room, guests stocked up on just about anything they wanted, served swiftly by gracious Bay Islanders. By the time Posada's impressive, 42-foot dive boats (captained by roundly praised divemasters) returned around noon, the trim rooms were clean, and tasty lunches, such as a *tipica* repast of spicy picadilla on floury Honduran tortillas, were ready and waiting.

Maybe divers have more fun. I've never experienced such camaraderie at a Caribbean resort. Undoubtedly a sense of shared adventure had something to do with it. Guests pushed tables together to share homey meals: a puree of black bean soup, an assertive wine and mushroom gravy on filet of beef, outstanding batter-fried grouper with fresh coconut coating. Everyone seemed to agree with the Denver psychologist who proclaimed, "In 15 years of diving, this is the most attractive place I've found."

About the diving there was less unanimity. Some raved. Some said it didn't compare with the Caymans (Those who complained about the hour-long trip to dive sites on Guanaja's leeward side will be glad to know that a recently-completed canal cuts the traveling time in half.) Divers and non-divers alike played games in the bar, swigged Honduran beer at umbrella-shaded tables, and tripped around Guanaja on a 36-foot boat.

All the shrimp we could peel and crusty fried chicken provisioned a hearty picnic followed by snorkeling. Those with boots or sneakers hiked the rugged, orchid-lined trail up Big Gulley to admire the waterfall and staggering view. Others traveled to Bonacca town, Guanaja's astonishing "capitol," an entire cay standing on stilts. There's also a night-lit tennis court and anglers can stalk the elusive bonefish.

The sturdy terra-cotta-and-stucco Posada del Sol insulates guests somewhat from Guanaja's tropical wilderness; at the tree-house-inspired Bayman Bay Club, they are in the scenery.

Banana fronds, spiky bamboo and breadfruit leaves obscure the 14 pine cabins and open-slat Bayman Bay Club house on approaching from the water. In 19 years, ex-Green Beret Tom Fouke has created a Caribbean resort adapted to its jungly, hillside perch. Connected by a network of board-walks and stairs, the weathered buildings are *in* perfect harmony with their surroundings.

My screened and louvered one-room shack was distinguished more by its water view than by its simple wooden furniture. Generated electricity ran the fan, the bed lamp and the water heater for showers that rained through slats in the basic bath onto plants below. Navy blue sheets, a handwoven spread and a framed Panamanian Mola completed the scene, which lacked only a string hammock on the shaded deck; several cabins have them.

Bayman Bay is scuba-oriented and has recently inaugurated certification courses. From the 40-foot *Nimitz*, (which now shares a brand new dock with the 38-foot *Royal Sovereign*), I snorkeled over air bubbles as diver's plummeted from the shallows to sapphire depths at the Pinnacles and later, as they threaded the coral chasms to Paradise. Next evening, thanks to an in-house lab, photographers screened videos and slides of the dives. Diver-guests praised the abundance of soft corals and plant life found at numerous sites close to the Club.

There are plenty of attractions for non-divers between the scimitar-shaped beach and the Nursery Reef. I sighted an octopus, blowfish, and red Christmas worms among the undulating sea fans. A 300-book library, regulation pool table and board games accommodate guests below the world's most perfectly-placed hammock on the lodge's top floor.

A sophisticated bunch of seasoned divers in faded t-shirts from Belize, Bonaire and other scuba haunts set the tone at Bayman Bay. Tanned and glistening, the Big Chill crowd sat at dinner in deck chairs around tables for 8 or 12, exchanging reef tales over split pea soup with croutons and bacon. Entrées were well-seasoned and delicious: fresh grouper one night, a succulent snapper à l'orange zapped with hot pepper, the next. Top-notch desserts, especially coconut-topped banana pie, followed.

A somewhat cavalier attitude toward meal times has vanished since Helen Murphy was promoted to manager; originally the club's live-in horticulturist, she runs a taut but happy ship. Breakfasts of huevos rancheros, black beans and sautéed mortadella-and-onion mix arrive on schedule, as do savory lunches: tostadas topped with minced meet, grated cheese, hard boiled egg, and hot sauce, as well as guacamole and Honduran tortillas.

On Guanaja guests boat to entertainment. Saturday night, by all accounts, the Bonacca disco really rips. Roatan's new jetport poses a threat to this splendidly off-beat island, but with luck, the ripple effect won't be felt for years.

POSADA DEL SOL, 1201 US Highway 1, Suite 220, North Palm Beach, FL 33408, (800) 642-3483. The 7-night dive

*package includes a 2-tank morning boat dive, 1-tank after-
noon dive and 1 night-dive a week. Non-divers pay slightly
lower rates. Moderate.*

*BAYMAN BAY CLUB, 11750 NW 19th St., Plantation, FL
33323, (800) 524-1823 or (305) 370-2120. The 7-night dive
package includes 2 boat dives per day plus unlimited shore
and night diving. Daily rates are also available. Moderate.*

VICTORIA HOUSE
Ambergris Cay, Belize

Ambergris Cay, sandwiched between bonefish flats and the
176-mile-long barrier reef, has lured divers and fishermen to
Belize for years. The rambling frame lodge and 10 *casitas*
comprising Victoria House, built a dozen years ago by a con-
sortium of Texas fishermen, blend right in with the low-key
island. Next to the lodge, neat white bungalows with
thatched roofs form an arc around a plot of brilliant grass.

Easy-going Victoria House is perfect for novice divers,
especially in late spring, when the visibility is over 100 feet.
Professional Association of Diving Instructors (PADI) certification and resort courses are held within sight of the still-
pristine reef. The divemaster also rents out Sunfish, Lasers,
and sailboards.

My *casita* facing the sea was Spartan but orderly, with
indigo print spreads, simple mahogany furniture, patterned
tile floors, and a shower for two. Come evening, when the
palms are deftly floodlit, these sensible digs take on a glamorous glow. Indeed, for all its pleasing plainness, Victoria
House is one of the snappiest fishing and diving resorts on
Ambergris.

Serve-yourself suppers in the bromeliad-hung dining
room starred seafood of extraordinary tenderness and flavor.
Famished fishermen and divers plundered heaps of spiny lobster tails from the buffet. The next evening, there were
mounds of tender shrimp. While dining isn't family-style at
the wooden tables set with cut oranges, brown sugar and
homemade iced tea, the mood's resolutely informal and I had
no trouble meeting other guests.

Southwesterners kept the Victoria bar jumping, but guests can also rattle the cratered road to San Pedro for Belikin beer and conch fritters at the Hut or under the colored Christmas lights at Fido's. Belizeans, an English-speaking population composed of Creoles, Garinagu, Mayans, Mexicans, and Ketchi Indians, are poised and straightforward. You won't find flash in unaffected San Pedro, where the floors of the balconied frame houses, as well as the sun-baked streets, are mostly sand.

VICTORIA HOUSE, PO Box 20785, Houston, TX 77225, (800) 247-5159 or (713) 662-8000. Rates are for lodging only; a stay in the casita costs more than in the lodge. Inexpensive to Moderate.

 ## *Other Voices* _____

SCUBA WORLD
Sand Dollar Package, Bonaire and Hyatt Regency Package, Grand Cayman Island

"About 2 weeks before a trip, I decided to learn to scuba dive. I thought scuba would be interesting and a good way to meet other people." Beth is a financial analyst, 29, at a brokerage house in New York. She took herself off to Scuba World, a New York dive store, and in the course of a year, booked two dive trips, one to Bonaire and another to Grand Cayman.

"Scuba World puts together lots of these trips. You don't have to bother about anything, and they're really friendly and helpful. You take a course with them beforehand, and then you only need a few open water dives to get certified. I then went down to the Caribbean, where it's easier to learn because you're not in a pool. You're in a restricted area in the ocean, and it's never dull.

"In my Bonaire group there were about 20, lots of singles. You fly down on a one-price deal, teaching included. I finished my certification. Basically, to get my time in, I spent from 9:00 am to 5:00 pm in the water, breaking for lunch. You can't go out on a boat until you're certified, so you're limited to shore dives, but shore dives are just fascinating, some of the most beautiful diving around. You keep practicing until your skills are perfect. Then Friday, we did a 1-day dive off the boat, which was fabulous.

"Scuba World put us up in the Sand Dollar Condominiums, a new complex, five people per condo. If you need your own room, you pay extra, otherwise they match you up. The dive shop is right next to the restaurant, which is right next to the bar. It's a real friendly atmosphere.

"Breakfast was included. You could buy food there, and most people made their own lunches. You're on your own for dinner....

"My next dive trip was to Grand Cayman and it was radically different. Much more luxurious, *really* nice. I stayed at the Hyatt, totally deluxe, with people following me around with towels all over the place, but the Cayman dive operation wasn't as cozy as the one on Bonaire; they don't get to know you because it's so big.

"The boats also are bigger, so there were others who weren't in our group on board. We used the Hyatt dive shop. A couple of nights our Scuba World group ate together, but everyone's on a different budget. In the Caymans you can easily spend what you'd spend in New York to eat. Pretty upscale traveling.

"Go to a resort alone and you run the risk of not meeting anyone you think is really fun. On a dive shop trip, everything is arranged and you all have fun together. There's bound to be someone you'll enjoy."

SCUBA WORLD, 167 West 72nd Street, New York, NY 10023, (800) 447-2822 or (212) 496-6983. The 7-night Sand Dollar package (Bonaire) includes 2 boat dives daily, unlimited shore diving and breakfast. Moderate. The 7-night Hyatt Regency package (Grand Cayman) doesn't include meals. Expensive.

TRIMARINE
British Virgin Islands

"The diving was fabulous. We even tried some night diving, which was worth the trip in itself," recalls John, age 28, a marketing manager for a national restaurant chain in Louisville. He dove the British Virgin Islands from the largest trimaran in the world, the 103-foot *Cuan Law* owned by Trimarine.

"I'm a certified diver, but this was my first time on a liveaboard. I was looking for a ship that provided comfort and spaciousness with plenty of opportunities to dive. I found it.

"We arrived on Sunday and left the following Saturday. There was a large dive school from Alabama and one from Georgia aboard.... The crew was great, very professional and very friendly. The food was outstanding, better than I eat at home. They just really went out of their way to make our stay wonderful.

"The briefings, every aspect of the dives, were well done. They didn't hold your hand, but they kept an eye on you. There were two divemaster/instructors who dove with us all the time, and they knew the areas we were diving very, very well. Occasionally the captain dove with us, too. Several people on board were finishing up their certification, so one of the divemasters would work just with them off to one side.

"It's perfect for anyone looking for a good dive vacation with all the amenities to make it a comfortable sailing vacation as well. Trimarine really focused on comfort and space. The *Cuan Law* will house 20. Most of the staterooms are doubles, although you can get a single. The cabins are built around a central lounge like a living room with a bar in the center, and all have private baths with showers. The huge top deck is basically for relaxing, sunning, leisure time. There was enough room that you could read or [have]...some privacy. Near the diving platform, where we took our meals, were some comfortable chairs and tables. They do motor some, but we were under sail quite a bit, too. I will definitely dive on the *Cuan Law* again."

TRIMARINE, PO Box 4065, St. Thomas, US Virgin Islands 00803, (809) 494-2490. Very Expensive.

COUSTEAU SOCIETY
Project Ocean Search, Fiji Islands

"Next year's trip location hasn't been chosen yet, but people are already applying. They just say, 'I'm going. It doesn't matter to me where.'" A lecturer for the Cousteau Society in Virginia, Pete, age 38, took the Society's Summer Field Course, known as Project Ocean Search, when it was given in the Fiji Islands. He describes the 2-week course and a selection process that should discourage the underwater dilettante.

"Admission is first-come-first-served after a lengthy application process involving a detailed physical and even an essay about the motivation involved. You have to want to go. We were 35 mostly-single Americans, from high school seniors to a 75-year-old retired architect.

"We stayed at a resort on one of the out islands, sleeping in open-sided, thatched huts called bures, four to a cottage, with full use of resort facilities such as canoes and Hobie Cats. It was very pretty and simple, though some Cousteau trips are strictly camping.

"Everyone congregated on the beach at 7:30 am, when three boats would leave for three different sites: one for the science group, one for the photographers and another for recreational divers. The dive sites were wonderful. Lunch back at the resort was followed by afternoon lectures.

"A lecture might be in a hut, on a boat or out on the beach somewhere. The focus of the science lectures included the human environment as well as marine biology, so we visited two villages and had local speakers on Fijian culture. There were also humanities classes dealing with literature of the sea. We'd motorboat over to a tiny island, explore a bit, then sit down to read and discuss, say, Moby Dick or some sea poetry. It was a wonderful counterpoint to the science.

"Evening lectures and films dealt with the activities of the Cousteau Society world-wide. Jean-Michaud Cousteau, Capt. Cousteau's son, shows up the second week of each of the two summer sessions to narrate films, lecture and dive with the students. After checking us out, the divemaster paired the inexperienced with the more experienced. After a few days, you were free to dive with whomever you wanted, so long as you dove with someone.

"There were several parties, and a no-talent show in the evenings, but most of the participants were so serious about improving their photographic and diving skills we didn't stay up late. It was hard work. The Cousteau trips aren't for people who like to sit around a pool and drink mai tais."

COUSTEAU SOCIETY, 930 West 21st Street, Norfolk, VA 23517, (804) 627-1144. The rates for the 2-week trip include round-trip air fare from Los Angeles to Fiji and all meals and program costs. Expensive.

 Other Scuba Choices ──────────────

The 7-vessel Aggressor Fleet is probably the world's largest liveaboard line. Beginning with the *Cayman Aggressor* in 1984, the Louisiana-based company converted 7 oil-rig supply boats to fully-equipped 16- to 20-passenger dive ships in 6 years. The *Truk Aggressor*, located in Micronesia, is the latest on line. Singles outnumber couples on the Bay Islands, Belize and Costa Rican boats according to the management, while pairs predominate on the Hawaiian and Cayman Island cruises.

AGGRESSOR FLEET, PO Drawer K, Morgan City, LA 70381, (800) 348-2628 or (504) 385-2416. Moderate.

Captain Don's Habitat, the scuba resort originally developed by the "Father of Bonaire Diving," Captain Don Stewart, has entered the villa/condominium age. Now 10 pseudo-Spanish villas and 16 new condo units fan out from the 11 older cottages and dive complex. Expansion hadn't interfered with the bonhomie at this renowned, five-star PADI hangout when I visited. Hearty Tex-Mex meals kept the divers fueled; the twin-engined flat top and two open launches left on schedule; divers shared underwater sightings in the thatched bar every night.

CAPTAIN DON'S HABITAT, PO Box 88, Kralendijk, Bonaire, Netherlands Antilles. For reservations: 1080 Port Boulevard, Suite 100, Miami, FL 33132, (800) 327-6709. Rates for the 7-night stay include breakfast, 1 boat dive per day and unlimited offshore diving. Moderate

Excursions to the Galapagos, the Sudan, Indonesia, and the Capricorn and Bunker Islands on the Great Barrier Reef were among the 12 dive voyages organized by Quark Expeditions—represented by Salen Lindblad Cruising—last year. Small, first-rate ships, remote and famous dive sites, and scuba experts like Australians Ron and Valerie Taylor are the among the features of these classy cruises.

SALEN LINDBLAD CRUISING, 333 Ludlow Street, Stamford CT. 06912-0076, (800) 223-5688 or (203) 967-2900.

"An informal poll of veteran scuba divers reveals a consensus that the diving off Little Cayman is the most spectacular in the Caribbean," wrote *Outside* magazine. I've stayed at the Southern Cross Club—built in the 1960s by anglers in pursuit of Little Cayman's bonefish and tarpon—and thoroughly enjoyed the sandy solitude of this unpretentious, old line refuge, now frequented by serious divers as well as fanatical fishermen. Twenty guests, who share meals at one long table in the lodge, sleep in 5, 2-bedroom duplexes right on the beach.

SOUTHERN CROSS CLUB, 1005 East Merchants Plaza, Indianapolis, IN 46204, (317) 636-9501. Rates cover lodging and three meals a day. Tanks, a diving guide and transportation to the dive site cost extra. Moderate.

 ## Scuba Diving Certification _____

PROFESSIONAL ASSOCIATION OF DIVING INSTRUCTORS (PADI), 1251 E. Warner Avenue, Santa Ana, CA 92705, (800) 729-7234 or (714) 540-7234. The largest of the several organizations providing scuba instruction.

NATIONAL ASSOCIATION OF UNDERWATER IN-
STRUCTORS (NAUI), PO Box 14650, Montclair, CA 91763,
(800) 553-6284 or (714) 621-5801. With a 35% share of the
business, this nonprofit organization is the second-largest
teaching group.

YOUNG MEN'S CHRISTIAN ASSOCIATION, 6083-A
Oakbrook Parkway, Norcross GA 30092, (404) 662-5172 (or
contact your local YMCA). Gives the names of local dive
shops and instructors. The smallest of the three teaching
organizations.

 Scuba Reservations Services _____

OCEAN CONNECTION, 16734 El Camino Real, Houston,
TX 77062, (800) 331-2458 or (713) 486-6993. Specializes in
Caribbean resorts but also books liveaboards.

SEA SAFARIS, 3770 Highland Avenue, Manhattan Beach, CA
90266, (800) 821-6670 or (213) 546-2464. Divides its business
between resorts and liveaboards.

SEE & SEA TRAVEL SERVICE, 50 Francisco Street, San
Francisco, CA 94133, (800) 348-9778 or (415) 434-3400. In the
liveaboard business for over 25 years.

TROPICAL ADVENTURES, 111 Second Avenue North,
Seattle, WA 98109, (800) 247-3483 or (206) 441-3483. Books
resorts and boats.

Bibliography

Undercurrents, Atcom Publishing, 2315 Broadway, New York, NY 10024, (800) 521-7004 or (212) 873-5900, $58 a year. Monthly newsletter chronicling trends and critiquing equipment, dive tour operators and resorts.

Best Dives of the Western Hemisphere by Jon Huber, Joyce Huber and Christopher Lofting, ($16.95, Hunter Publishing, Inc., 300 Raritan Center Parkway, Edison, NJ 08818, 1990). A commendable guide to dive sites in the Western Hemisphere.

Fly Fishing

"The fly fishing business has grown 25% a year over the last 3 years," reports an executive of Orvis' renowned fishing school. "There was a flurry of yuppies in the late 80s, but in fact fly fishing is egalitarian. People are interested for a variety of reasons, and while it's not generally realized, women excel."

Angling classes spawn bonhomie, but once past the lesson stage, anglers are likely to be one-on-one with nature, which can get expensive. At a number of the fancier fishing lodges, anglers pay the double rate for a single room and, if a partner can't be found, there's an extra charge for a guide and/or boat, unless wading without a guide is preferred. Consider camping trips for less expensive fishing forays, or put up at a local motel and fish from a tackle store located on a prime trout river.

Pre-arranged fishing jaunts are probably more companionable than finding a river and hiring a personal guide. Frontiers, the premier fishing and hunting agency in the US, keeps a list of singles willing to join an existing group.

Pricing Categories: *Daily expenses in this chapter are a combination of the fee for the fly-fishing instruction and/or guide and for accommodation at a nearby hotel or lodge (listed directly below the course information), unless a program includes both.*

Pricing Categories

Inexpensive	————	Under $75 a day
Moderate	————	$75 to $125 a day
Expensive	————	$126 to $200
Very Expensive	————	Over $200 a day

*Where they are separate, the pricing category is listed at the end
of the course information.*

THE COMPLETE FLY FISHER
Wise River, Montana

"They do everything for you but breathe at the Complete Fly
Fisher," explained a hand at the Montana fishing resort as we
sped south from Butte toward the Big Hole River in August.
"The guides are really the best," he continued, "patient,
knowledgeable, caring." Thank heavens. The Complete Neo-
phyte, I arrived sans rod, sans waders and sans any idea whatsoever about how to throw a line. "We specialize in beginners," Chris Decker, wife of owner/manager Dave, told me as I
watched the Big Hole, a classic, 127-mile-long fishing stream,
flow swiftly by the appealing modern lodge.

Chris had other words of comfort for novices. "August
is a good time to come. In June and July, when it's too hot to
fish at noon, the fishermen often start as early as 5:00 am and
set out again, after a siesta, until 10:00 or 11:00 pm. In
August, guests usually fish the day through."

Monday, I arrived too late to fish, and stalked the valley
beneath Montana's limitless sky. After a zesty meal accompanied by wisely-chosen wines and a tranquil sleep beneath
Hudson Bay blankets in my knotty pine cabin, I was ready for
my baptism the next morning at 9:00 am. The other anglers,
decked out in fly vests and polypropylene waders, headed for
the stretch of river their guides had selected to fish that day.
Happy to watch them disappear down the drive; I wanted no
witnesses. It was time to practice casting.

A half hour's flailing the cropped lawn with a flyless
leader earned me a place on the river. The Big Hole, with its
prolific stock of wild, trophy-sized rainbow and brown trout,
owes its fecundity to stringently-enforced no-bait and catch-
and-release policies. The Deckers and a host of feisty envi-
ronmentalists have fought hard to keep the river unspoiled.
Now it harbors "America's cleanest and strongest fighting
trout," according to one knowledgeable guest-fisherman.

Most of the guides have been with the Fly Fisher since
Dave took over six years ago as manager. This colorful ("Call

us eccentric") group of college-grads-turned-guides vies with the Big Hole River as the outfit's premier resource.

I was totally indebted to Wayne, my astute and able instructor, for my conversion from greenhorn to enthusiast. Wayne rowed, maneuvered and tutored as I drifted down a 3-mile stretch of river in the swivel seat of an inflated raft. For seven hours I cast. I tried to use the energy inherent in my nine-foot graphite rod: to keep the radius between the forward and back swing relatively small; to use my whole forearm. But what if the fish struck the hand-tied Royal Wulff? I couldn't hook the trout because at first, I couldn't see the fly. Every time I was about to give up, however, Wayne craftily changed the pace. We paused to savor the scenery, or to break for a tasty lunch.

Tabouleh, tarragon chicken salad sandwiches, home-baked cookies, tea and wine (upon request) were set out on a checked cloth atop the cooler. Other natty touches, like the cotton napkins in plexiglass rings, are commonplace at the Fly Fisher. The fixings are first-class but casual, no flash, which can also be said of the (mostly) well-heeled clientele.

Tuesday night, 12 khaki-clad diners exchanged views on fishing and logging policies around Dave's handmade oak table. In the glow of candles and backlit river grasses, fresh, marinated swordfish steaks and a succession of California chardonnays followed salads of home-grown lettuces. A foursome of Wyoming ranchers, a lawyer couple from Memphis, the bone fishing guide from Key West, a Darien, Connecticut investment counselor, and a Salt Lake City professor-and-radiologist couple managed to down bread pudding redolent with rum before heading past the towering cottonwoods to boxy new cabins, spaced well apart on an immaculate lawn.

After a blueberry pancake breakfast, it was time to take to the lawn again to cast for Dave and a gallery of kibitzing guides. Not even the mortification this caused could lessen the joy I experienced that gray Wednesday when I landed 6 rainbows (8 to 15 inches) and 2 brown trout (17 and 18 inches respectively). Here was a taste of what lay ahead, if I became an adequate fly fishermen. No matter that my third, and last, day was a bust. I was hooked.

Casting wass at once energizing and tranquilizing. Around us always was the gorgeous scenery and wildlife. A quartet of Golden Eagles whccled against the searing blue sky. Here, finally, was a sport much to my taste. And I had found an ideal place to practice it. There is an integrity to the Fly Fisher's carefully run operation that is deeply appealing. I made only one mistake: I didn't sign up for the full five days.

THE COMPLETE FLY FISHER, PO Box 105, Wise River, MT 59762, (406) 832-3175. Rates for the 5-day, 6-night fishing trip include all meals, drinks, airport transfers, and instruction. Fishing alone with a guide is extra. The Fly Fisher holds a "Ladies Only Week" in early September with fly fishing champions as instructors. Expensive.

 Other Voices _____

ORVIS FLY FISHING SCHOOL
Manchester, Vermont and

SILVER CREEK OUTFITTERS
Ketchum, Idaho

"Fly fishing seems to attract a very thoughtful, decent kind of person, usually a man, and I think that's really what a magazine I freelance for had in mind when they offered me a piece on fly fishing. They wanted to send me to where the boys were, but that's not what I found when I got there," recalls Kathryn, 42, the head of a Massachusetts art association and a freelance writer. If her mission was abortive from the "singles" point of view, it was a success otherwise. An utter novice, Kathryn began with a 2 1/2-day course at the Orvis Fly Fishing School in Manchester, Vermont. So enraptured was she that within weeks, Kathryn was floating down a famous trout steam with Silver Creek Outfitters in Idaho.

"You don't go to Orvis for romance. In the class I took there were no singles, male or female. At least half were already fishermen; there were these guys with their little boys, a fair number of young Manhattan stock broker types, and many older men who had brought their wives or companions to learn their passion, but it was completely comfortable being there alone.

"I didn't get enough experience at Orvis to fly fish with real adeptness; in fact the guide at Silver Creek later spent as much time teaching me as he did guiding, but you do not leave Orvis without catching a fish. Their pond is well stocked, and the instructors feed the fish with protein pellets, which send them into a feeding frenzy. It may seem like a pretty dishonest way to catch a fish, but it didn't diminish the excitement any.

"We stayed at a lovely, old Victorian inn called the Equinox House, a 3-minute walk from Orvis. The rooms don't measure up to the public areas or the exterior, but they're more than adequate. Everyone leaves class and returns to the hotel with the instructors for a buffet lunch. It's a nice mid-day break. Most of the people in my class fished on their own in the evening. Orvis taught me enough to get impassioned.

"After this I actually went to Idaho on a fishing trip, alone, and I really got into it. I stayed for a week at the Idaho Country Inn, a pretty, posh bed and breakfast in Ketchum, just outside Sun Valley. I hired a guide from Silver Creek Outfitters; I don't think they've ever had a woman come and do what I did, not alone.

"They use float tubes a lot there because it gives you access to places you can't get to by boat. They're basically inner tubes onto which a seat has been attached and a back rest, and you put flippers on. Getting into one is a hoot. When I started out I said I'd probably only be up to fishing a half day. By the end of the week I wanted to fish all day. The fishing is all catch-and-release, but I got unbelievably excited the couple of times I got fish. I felt like a true angler. I would have said 'You've got to be kidding' if you had told me this 6 months ago...."

ORVIS FLY FISHING SCHOOL, Historic Route 7A, Manchester, VT 05254, (800) 548-9548. Lodging and meals for 2 nights during the 2 1/2-day fly fishing course is at the Equinox. Expensive.

SILVER CREEK OUTFITTERS, PO Box 418, Ketchum, ID 83340, (208) 726-5282. The fee for a full day's fishing for 1 or 2 people includes lunch. Very Expensive.

IDAHO COUNTRY INN, 134 Latigo Lane, Ketchum, ID 83340, (208) 726-1019. Rates include full breakfast and afternoon tea.

FRONTIERS
Boca Paila, Mexico

"I went in March with friends, but you could go by yourself very, very easily. You go to fly fish the flats. You can spin fish, too." Tucker is talking about Boca Paila in the Yucatan, where for the past 2 years this intrepid fisherman, 47, who runs a salmon camp in Canada, has taken a busman's holiday. The trips were arranged by Frontiers, and it looks as if Tucker is becoming a regular.

"Boca Paila is about 100 miles south of Cancun, a 2-hour taxi ride, which is included in the package. The Boca Paila resort has about 12 thatched units, all incredibly comfortable, with little kitchenettes. There's a central eating area, living room and bar, where everybody gathers for cocktails before dinner.

"If you're down there to fly fish for salt water fish, you're going to have a marvelous time. You're fishing for bonefish, tarpon and permit. ...Permit is an incredibly difficult fish to catch. I've gotten little school permit, but I've never caught one of those big ones. I've had better luck with tarpon, which is an enormous herring, and with bonefish, which are hard to see and put up an enormous fight. We catch and release virtually everything.

"You go out after breakfast with your guide in a Boston whaler type boat. He spots the fish in maybe 3 or 4 feet of water and tells you where to cast.... You can either take your lunch with you or go back to the Inn to eat. ...The lodge is right on the Caribbean. You just put your bathing suit on and go swimming. You come back, have a nice fresh water shower, a few beverages and lunch. Then you go out a little later and fish some more. You can stay out all day if you want.

"Meals are at group tables. I found the mostly seafood, Mexican cooking delicious. We're not talking burritos...there were mangos, papaya, pineapple. It's really marvelous food.

"There were four us there, like me, without wives. The other guests included six couples, a couple of single men, two single ladies one year. Serious fishermen. Upper income bracket.

"The four of us are planning to go down again next April; two of the guys are also going dove shooting with Frontiers. In fact, Frontiers offers lots of other programs, basically shooting and fishing, which are suitable for single travelers."

FRONTIERS, PO Box 959, Wexford, PA 15090, (800) 245-1950 or (412) 935-1577. The Saturday-to-Saturday Boca Paila package costs more with a single guide rather than a shared guide. Very Expensive.

THE BIGHORN ANGLER
Fort Smith, Montana

"You show up with all your flies—your pride as a fisherman kind of demands you do—but as you start to fish, you use whatever Mike recommends because he knows the river. You're a newcomer." Peter is referring to Mike Craig, at whose tackle shop The Bighorn Angler on the Bighorn River, Peter fished out of for 3 days. The 35-year-old sportswriter from New York was enthusiastic about Craig and the Bighorn, with just one reservation.

"The river runs though the middle of a Crow Indian reservation, but it has started to get pretty crowded. There were a lot of drift boats, and it's close to Billings, so its easy for locals to get there and fish. If that kind of thing bothers you, you might want to try the Green River for the same experience.

"Anyway, I flew into Billings and drove over to Ft. Smith, which has two gas stations, a diner and a motel called the Bighorn Angler. The River begins nearby in Bighorn Lake. The rolling plains make it very scenic. When you dam a river to create a lake you've got very cold water from the bottom of the lake year round. That makes it a great cold-water fishery, and there's plenty of bug life to support the trout.

"We floated the river every day; nothing too strenuous, but some areas are pretty wild. The first day we hired Mike as our guide. These guys know the river so well, it's fascinating to go with them. As in all the really good rivers, this is primarily catch-and-release fishing. The people who fish with a real passion all do that; you have to if you care about the environment.

"We put in at the dam the first day and began to float, covering about 18 to 20 miles of the river. We stopped at various places and fished with what they call freshwater shrimp. It's a little piece of fluorescent pink yarn with a little bit of plastic wrapping to imitate a shell. I do these myself in advance, but when you book a guide for the day, he's pretty much responsible for all the flies.

"There are great mayfly hatches on the river, so you use those sometimes, too. I spent the day on the Bighorn, pulling out brown and rainbow trout and breaking for a shore lunch. At the end of the day, Mike has an assistant meet you, or he's already parked the truck at the takeout. You pull the boat out and drive the 15 miles or so back to Ft. Smith. The Bighorn Angler Motel—which Mike also owns—serves homecooked, Montana-style dinners to hungry anglers. Then you hit the pillow.

"You can just rent a boat, if you want, and go out yourself. That's what I did the next 2 days, figuring I knew the river well enough. That was a real adventure.... It's really wonderful fun."

THE BIGHORN ANGLER, PO Box 577, Ft. Smith, MT 59035, (406) 666-2233. Each day's fee covers a guide, inflatable boat and lunch. Expensive.

THE BIGHORN ANGLER MOTEL, 577 Parkdale Court, Ft. Smith, MT 59035, (406) 666-2233. Dinner is extra.

 ## Other Fly Fishing Choices: Outfitters ——

Lured by wild, as well as stocked, brook, brown and rainbow trout, no more than 3 fishermen to a 3/4-mile-long beat wade the prolific, 6 1/2 mile stretch of stream owned by Big

Moore's Run Lodge in rural, north central Pennsylvania.
Later, anglers drink up in the bar, eat heartily at big tables
and, in some cases, bunk 4-to-a-room, on the rustic, 5-bed-
room premises of the only Orvis-endorsed fly fishing lodge in
Pennsylvania.

*BIG MOORE'S RUN LODGE, RD 3, Box 204-A,
Coudersport, PA 16915, (814) 647-5300. The fee for a 4-night,
3-day package includes lodging, 3 meals, and guide.
Moderate.*

The Grand Traverse Resort offers just about everything
a spiffy, big resort should: a Jack Niklaus golf course, a John
Jacobs Golf School, a fitness and beauty spa, four restaurants,
sailing along Lake Michigan's "Golden Coast," tours of the
local wine country and in late spring and early summer, an
Orvis fly fishing school (one of approximately 30 located at
resorts throughout the US). The 2-day fly fishing course starts
with stream entomology, then proceeds to pond casting, followed by wading and the last day, casting from a boat.

*GRAND TRAVERSE RESORT, Streamside, 4400 Grand
Traverse Village, Williamsburg, MI 49690, (616) 938-5337.
The 2-day fly fishing course fee includes lunch. Moderate.*

The most popular fishing trip run by High Plains
Outfitters in Montana is the 5-day float down a 60-mile
stretch of the Smith River. Singles have their own roomy
tents, the campsites are chosen with care, and the homestyle
fare is delicious. Lisa and Mike Bay also offer extended fishing tours of the Blackfoot and Yellowstone Rivers plus day
trips on the Dearborn and Missouri, not far from their headquarters.

*HIGH PLAINS OUTFITTERS, 31 Division, Helena, MT
59601, (406) 442-9671. The Smith River trip is all inclusive, 2
fishermen to a boat. Very Expensive.*

Charlene Sassi, owner with her husband Ken of
Weatherby's, seats singles at her table until they get
acquainted with other habitués of this unpretentious, 16-

cabin fishing lodge in northeastern Maine close to the New Brunswick border. Book well in advance for May and June, when the salmon head upstream and the small mouth bass in the lake snap at flies, as well as lures. The L. L. Bean Fly Fishing School holds two 4-day Intermediate sessions at Weatherby's in July. "They're beautifully run," says Charlene, "and wonderful people come from all over the country to attend."

WEATHERBY'S, Grand Lake Stream, ME 04637, (207) 796-5558 (winter: PO Box 396, Stratton, ME 04637 (207) 246-7391). The rates for a cabin include 2 meals a day. Guide Service is extra. Moderate. See also the STEAMBOAT LODGE in INNS *for fishing on the North Umpqua River in Oregon.*

 ## *Other Fly Fishing Choices: Classes*————

The Joan & Lee Wulff Fishing School was created by a duo of formidable pros. Lee may have been the "Dean of American Fly Fishermen," but his wife, who has cast a fly 161 feet, is no slouch. Joan, with the assistance of five instructors, teaches weekend Trout Fishing classes from late April to July at the 100-acre spread bordering the Beaverkill River in the Catskill Mountains of New York. Most students elect to stay at the plush, Victorian Beaverkill Valley Inn where they plunder the Inn's buffet before attending evening classes 1/2 mile downstream at the Wulff's.

JOAN & LEE WULFF FISHING SCHOOL, Beaverkill Road, Lew Beach, NY 12753, (914) 439-4060. Expensive.

BEAVERKILL VALLEY INN, Lew Beach, NY 12753, (914) 439-4844. Rates include all meals.

The L. L. Bean Fly Fishing School's intermediate classes are currently held at Weatherby's (see above) but the 16, weekend "Introductory Fly Fishing" sessions take place at Fogg Farm, a farmhouse-and-casting-pond complex not far from company headquarters. The 20 to 30 people attending the Friday-morning-through-Sunday classes make their own arrangements for breakfast and dinner (Bean provides lunch) and lodging.

L. L. BEAN FLY FISHING SCHOOL, Casco Street, Freeport, ME 04033, (800) 341-4341. Accommodations are separate.

In 1967, Orvis opened the first US fly fishing school, in Manchester, Vermont; some 1,500 students have attended classes there every year since. Orientation begins in the classroom across the road from Orvis' headquarters store, after which students practice, without flies, in casting ponds. Sunday, casting is done with hooks (see Kathryn, above). Three other Orvis stores arrange classes.

ORVIS DISTRIBUTION CENTER, 1711 Blu Hills Drive, Roanoke, VA 24012, (703) 345-3635.

ORVIS, Route 7A, Manchester, VT 05254, (800) 548-9548.

ORVIS, 1423 Walnut Street, Philadelphia, PA 19102, (215) 567-6207.

ORVIS, 300 Grant Avenue, San Francisco, CA 94108, (415) 392-1600. Operates school at resorts in California and Oregon.

About 30 of Orvis' 400 clothing and tackle dealers from coast to coast conduct fly fishing schools based on Orvis techniques, and the schools aren't all that have been Orvis-branded. Orvis also endorses lodges, outfitters and guides. Call Alan DeNicola, (800) 548-9548 for information about Orvis-accredited facilities or write Orvis, Historic Route 7A, Manchester, VT 05254, (802) 362-3750.

 Fly Fishing Reservations ─────────────

FRONTIERS, PO Box 161, Pearce Mill Road, Wexford, PA 15090, (800) 245-1950 or (412) 935-1577. A highly-reputable organization that represents 80 quality light tackle outfitters throughout the world, 10 or 12 of them in the US.

TROUT UNLIMITED, 800 Follin Lane, Suite 250, Vienna, VA 22180, (703) 281-1100. Sponsors group trips in conjunction with Frontiers.

ORVIS also has a tour planning service. The latest information on Orvis-endorsed lodges, outfitters and guide is available from Regional Information Centers located in the Rocky Mountain Area, (307) 733-5407, at Orvis San Francisco, Orvis Houston, the Thornapple (Michigan) Orvis Shop, Orvis New York, Orvis Manchester, and Orvis Roanoke. A list of these facilities appears in the Orvis catalog (800) 548-9548.

OFF THE BEATEN PATH, 109 East Main, Bozeman, MT 59715, (800) 445-2995 or (406) 586-1311. Another source of fly-fishing guidance in the Rocky Mountain States.

Bibliography

Fly Fisherman, PO Box 8200, Harrisburg, PA 17105-8200, (717) 657-9555. Check the "On Stream" classified section in the back of the magazine for names of outfitters.

Western Fly-Fishing Vacations by Nanci & Kirk Reynolds, ($12.95, Chronicle Books, San Francisco, CA, 1988). Describes 80 lodges and ranches in nine western states.

Skiing Cross Country and Back Country

Long, narrow skis, tall poles, flexible boots and knickers define Nordic skiing. Rhythmic snow gliding is ages old. Cross country skiing is also grand exercise, and following trails deep into uncut woodlots is naturally satisfying.

Back country skiing, a synthesis of cross country and downhill skiing, is on the rise. Skiers trek the trailless flats to clamber uphill and schuss down on metal-edged skis. Both sports have solo-appeal. The lodges frequented by cross country skiers are often homier and more friendly than the downhill spots. Back country tours usually consist of a handful of people who overnight cozily in yurts, wall tents or spare wooden huts.

Pricing Categories

Inexpensive	Under $75 a day
Moderate	$75 to $125 a day
Expensive	$126 to $200
Very Expensive	Over $200 a day

BLUEBERRY HILL INN
Goshen, Vermont

The sound of laughter and a 13-year-old shepherd named Sniff welcomes guests to the low-ceilinged interior of the Blueberry Hill Inn. Arrive around 6:00 pm and the cocktail hour will be underway. In high season, a full house of 26 guests crowds into the cranberry-red parlor in the Green Mountain National Forest southeast of Middlebury, Vermont. The casually-dressed crowd's obvious enjoyment can be infectious, so after a quick "Here's the bar.... The coffee's next to the Toll House cookies," from owner Tony Clark, pour a glass of wine and join them.

Seventy-five kilometers of groomed and well-packed trails are the pride of the Inn and its partner, the Blueberry Hill Ski Touring Center, located just across the dirt road. Tony, a dedicated innkeeper as well as cross country enthusiast, established the duo in 1970, in the process creating what is now one of the oldest and highest Nordic ski complexes in Vermont. More often than not, there's plenty of packed powder. Even after a heavy rain, Moosalamoo Trail, at 1600 feet (the same elevation as the inn) and Romance at 2500 feet, a 45-minute climb, are usually skiable.

While the clapboard Blueberry Hill with crimson red doors and the shed-roofed ski lodge are postcard perfection when mantled in white, the inn's interior radiates a sensible charm that's as inviting in summer as in winter. Two parlors lead to the homey open kitchen, off which the combination greenhouse/corridor comes as a verdant, brick-lined surprise. Past the door of the pine-paneled room, guests peer through jade plants and hibiscus into the great white outdoors. Coffee-sipping early risers sit reading, feet propped on the pot bellied stove. By 8:30 am most guests have assembled to take seats beneath exposed beams in the windowed dining room.

Triumphant meals are a Blueberry Hill specialty. "Delicious," "Superb," and other encomiums float from two trestle tables as each beautifully conceived meal progresses. Spinach-stuffed ravioli of homemade artichoke and tomato pasta, and braised partridge sided by shitake mushrooms typify the winter menu. The famished skiers seem as content as Vermont's famous black-and-white cows, munching through dinner. There's freshly-baked bread, red or white wine and tumblers of ice water spiked with lemon or orange slices as a matter of course.

Saturday nights, guests from other lodges join the Blueberry Hill crowd. Solos may be placed at the head of the

table so as not to skew the pair-by-pair seating, but the
hostesses pride themselves on putting guests where they'll be
most content.

At breakfast, take any chair for raisin-and-walnut croissants, hot, blueberry-laden muffins, and other breakfast specialties, including a ravishing red flannel hash. Toward the
end of the breakfast, the ski center director appears in front of
the fire to outline the options for the day.

A paucity of snow needn't bother experienced skiers.
Pros in lustrous lurex take to the still-packed expert trails.
Novices take to the road. Ripton, a gem of a four-corners village where Robert Frost summered, has a stove-warmed general store that's exceedingly picturesque. Twenty minutes
away, down by Otter Creek in Middlebury, is a collection of
interesting shops. Frog Hollow, a state-sponsored outlet for
top-of-the-line crafts, and Black Hawk, which stocks arrest-
ing men and women's clothing, are worth a stop, as is
Woody's, a ship-shaped restaurant with a riverside purchase
and plenty of Parmesan in the Caesar salad.

Once the snow falls, anyone can ski. The ski center
director is free for lessons after the pros take off along
Blueberry Hill's carefully-numbered trails. By the time guests
return to the frame ski center, Clark has set out a steaming
soup pot. After rest and conversation by the crackling wood
stove, hit the trails again before turning sore muscles over to
a masseuse.

Most people depart Sunday afternoon. During the week,
Blueberry Hill runs at about half capacity. Those who remain
have gotten to know one another and are thoroughly at
home. It would be hard to be anything less than comfortable
at blessedly unselfconscious Blueberry Hill. Kudos are due
the calico-curtained rooms, some with elaborate oak or white
iron beds, and the cheerful and accommodating staff.

Booked to its flower-hung rafters with skiers in winter,
the inn overflows with hikers, backpackers, kite fliers, croquet players—active people of many stripes—during the rest
of the year, when Tony Clark hosts a panoply of sports-ori-
ented weekends for his gratified guests.

*BLUEBERRY HILL INN, Goshen, VT 05733, (800) 448-0707
or (802) 247-6735. Breakfast and dinner are included in the
rates, which change from December 26 to March 10.
Expensive.*

 Other Voices _____

JACKSON SKI TOURING FOUNDATION
Jackson, New Hampshire

Fifty two kilometers of scenic trails are maintained and carefully groomed by the Jackson Ski Touring Foundation in New
Hampshire. "There's a trail that's not even on the books,
called the 'Hot Chocolate Trail.' It just circles the village, and
you stop along the way to have hot chocolate at all the inns.
That's a nice way to introduce a new skier to the area." Paula
is talking about Jackson, New Hampshire, where ex-Olympic
skier Tom Perkins operates the Jackson Ski Touring
Foundation. Paula, 54 years old, is a long-time member of the
Mt. Washington ski patrol, lives in the area, and occasionally
skis Jackson, with members of the Maine Singles Network.

"Sometimes I'll just call Tom and say, 'There are 10
people coming down who've never skied before,' and he takes
over from there. He'll outfit them, arrange their lessons,
whatever. The Jackson cross country facility is probably the
best in the US. The trails are always groomed excellently. A
man who knows exactly what he's doing runs the place.

"You can join the Foundation for $50 a year and do all
kinds of things with them: on-snow workshops, waxing
demonstrations, socials, ski-skate workshops, carnivals, barbecues, races. There's so much. Very professional. Besides the
Jackson trails, there are nearly 100 miles in the White
Mountain National Forest monitored by ski patrols. These
trails aren't groomed, but they do use skidoos to make tracks.

"My favorite Jackson trails are Popple Mountain and the
East Pasture Loop, which is absolutely beautiful. The Ellis
River trail goes from the village up to Dana Place Inn for

beginners. You can ski up, have lunch, a glass of wine, spend the night, if you want. Skiers can also stay at the Appalachian Mountain Club in the notch beyond Jackson. It's the most family-style place, with huge, dormitory-style accommodations. That's near Tuckerman's Ravine, famous for spring skiing. In town, the Christmas Farm Inn on the Hot Chocolate Loop is a nice place to stay."

JACKSON SKI TOURING FOUNDATION, Jackson Village, NH 03846, (603) 383-9355. Open to the public.

THE CHRISTMAS FARM INN, Box CC, Jackson Village, NH 03846, (800) 443-5837. Rates include breakfast and dinner. Moderate.

WILDERNESS LODGE AT ROYAL GORGE CROSS-COUNTRY SKI RESORT
Soda Springs, California

"With 300 kilometers of trails, this is the largest cross country facility in the country. Night skiing there, with a moon, is just gorgeous," says Greg, 28, a computer designer in Costa Mesa, California, who has stayed in the Wilderness Lodge at Royal Gorge 7 years running.

"At Summit Station, California out of Reno, Nevada, the sleigh picks you up if you're going to Wilderness Lodge. The driver throws animal skins over you and pulls the sleigh behind a snow cat to the lodge, some 10 kilometers into the woods.

"When you arrive at the old lodge, which was recently expanded and renovated, there's cheese fondue, wine, a fire burning in the fireplace. Wilderness holds up to 80 people, and many are there alone. You're just bunked in small rooms, typically two or three to a room, men and women together, unless you request otherwise. Bathrooms are down the hall.

"They have 8 to 10 guides and lessons at four levels: Beginner, Intermediate, Advanced, and Suicide. In Suicide, the instructor will say, 'See that ridge 30 kilometers away? We're going there and back by dinner.' Then he picks the worst possible path to get there.

"Half the people ski at night.... The instructors take a well-defined trail, and everybody stays between the front and rear guides. It's safe.

"The lodge hot tub has a family hour, suits only, and a women-only hour. Otherwise it's come-as-you-like. A few wear suits, not many. You run out of the tub and jump in a snow bank, then jump back in the hot tub.

"The area is called Royal Gorge because of the geological site, but we call it that because of what you do all weekend. You ski all morning, and you're hungry. Breakfast is just a bunch of food on the table, help yourself. Lunch is a smorgasbord, and their soups are amazing. You'd be hard-pressed to find food quality like this in many restaurants.

"Dinner is a sit-down meal, served by the guides, country-style, at group tables. They always play some classical music...and out march the guides with the pre-filled plates. It's wonderful. Everything's served on stuff you'd find in a school cafeteria, but they have four full-time chefs!"

WILDERNESS LODGE AT ROYAL GORGE CROSS COUNTRY SKI RESORT, PO Box 1100, Soda Springs, CA 95728, (916) 426-3871. The Sunday-to-Friday ski week is all-inclusive. Moderate.

LONE MOUNTAIN RANCH
Big Sky, Montana

"What appeals to me is that the rates are inclusive—your log cabin, your 21 meals are covered—and the trails are right there. The Lone Mountain Ranch picks you up at the Bozeman, Montana airport and takes you back. If I want to downhill, I can take a bus to Big Sky. Everything is taken care of. All I have to do is ski." Lonnie, 40, who works at the State Department in Washington, DC, went to Lone Mountain for a week's cross country skiing. Three times.

"The ranch accommodates 50 to 55 people with a staff of 56. I called in October to reserve for February, as a birthday present to myself. What I didn't know was that they made a note of my birthday. So 4 months later...the staff came out carrying this little pastry and singing 'Happy Birthday.' It was so sweet.

"Lone Mountain is basically a cross country resort in winter, though some of the Big Sky downhill skiers stay there, about 6 miles from the slopes. They've got 75 miles of groomed, tracked trails, and outsiders are limited so the guests can enjoy the solitude.

"Last year I had a cabin to myself, and they offered me the same cabin for this year. You have a whole pile of wood for your fireplace or woodstove. You eat in a gorgeous, new, million-dollar dining room, which seats 90. It's booked solid every night. Day skiers can eat there, if there's room, but you're never mixed with the public. Guests eat all together, family-style.

"The food is amazing. There's a choice between three of four entrees, including buffalo fillets. I felt perfectly comfortable as a single woman everywhere. The guests have their own bar, no public allowed, and I never once felt uncomfortable there, like you do sometimes at those downhill resort bars.

"When I first came, they'd place me at a table with other people for dinner, so I didn't have that awkward moment choosing where to sit or introducing myself to strangers. I met people the first year that I saw the second year, and we've made arrangements to meet during my third visit in February. I can't imagine vacationing anywhere else now, and going alone is the best way."

LONE MOUNTAIN RANCH, Box 69, Big Sky, MT 59716, (406) 995-4644. Accommodations for the 7-night, all-inclusive package are 1-room cabins. Expensive.

BARK EATER
Keene Valley, New York

"The food is as good as the skiing—superb," insists Larry, who's had at least his share of both at the Bark Eater, a country inn and ski center in Keene Valley, New York. A lawyer, 46, in Binghamton, New York, Larry is something of a regular at the inn, where he stays while using the extensive trails in the area.

"The Bark Eater's a pretty, former farmhouse, set on a back road in the Adirondacks and surrounded by fields, with big trees out front. There's a ski shop there, so you can rent if you want. The rooms are nicely decorated, but by no means luxurious; some are small and share baths. There's a main lodge and a log cabin about a 5-minute walk away, where I've stayed, too. Very nice.

"At any one time I'd guess there are about 30 people there. The dining room has one main table and a smaller one in the corner that accommodates about seven or eight. Everyone comes in from skiing and enjoys wine and cheese in front of the fire before sitting down and eating together. There are always people there by themselves because Joe Pete Wilson, the owner, makes it such a friendly, comfortable place. Wilson, by the way, was an Olympic skier before he became a skiing coach.

"Bark Eater grooms and maintains about 20 kilometers of trail. You can also take the Jack Rabbit trail from the Bark Eater to Saranac Lake. Then there is about 100 kilometers of track at Mt. Van Hoevenberg, the site of the 1980 Winter Olympics."

BARK EATER, Alstead Mill Road, Keene, NY 12942, (518) 576-2221. Rates for a room with bath include breakfast. Moderate.

 ## *Other Cross Country Choices* _____

Canyoneers manage both the North Rim Nordic Center and the adjoining Kaibab Lodge on the Kaibab Plateau 18 miles from the Grand Canyon. Cross country, as well as back country, enthusiasts, transfer to the Canyoneers' snow van at Jacob Lake for the 26-mile journey to the Lodge, located at 9,000 feet. From there, ski to the North Rim, read, set tracks in the meadows, soak in the communal hot tub.

CANYONEERS, PO Box 2997, Flagstaff, AZ 86003, (800) 525-0924 or (602) 526-0924. The rate for a room in the lodge goes down after a 2-night stay; cheaper bunks in a yurt are also available. Meals and transportation are extra. Inexpensive.

A clutch of small, homey inns in north central Vermont beckon the Nordic skier. The Long Run Lodge, the Chipman Inn and Churchill House Inn, all connected by the Catamount Trail, have banded together to provide self-guided, inn-to-inn trips. Participants in the 2-, 3- and 4-night "Country Inns Along the Trail" programs ski 5 to 10 miles between each point.

COUNTRY INNS ALONG THE TRAIL, c/o Churchill House Inn, RR 3, Box 3115, Brandon, VT 05733, (802) 247-3300. The 4-night trip is all-inclusive. Moderate.

Guests in from skiing the 53 kilometers of trails Maplelap maintains in western Minnesota are pampered by saunas, massages and an enormous hot tub inside the huge, stained glass lodge. Coffee and homemade cookies are available between family-style meals served from the open kitchen. A dance follows the talent show held on Saturday night; guests who'd rather read or play board games do so in the library upstairs, before rolling out the sleeping bags they've brought in cabins or twin-bedded rooms.

MAPLELAP, Route 1, Callaway, MN 56521, (218) 375-4466. A 2-night, weekend stay is all-inclusive. Inexpensive.

Moose Mountain Lodge is that rarity: a small, 12-room lodge with a live-in cross country skiing guide. Guided moonlight, as well as daytime, tours are included in the rates, as are informal ski lessons and highly-praised homecooked dinners. There's rental equipment on-premises and the 350 trail-laced acres are available only to Moose Mountain clients, a mostly over-50-year-old group of serious skiers.

MOOSE MOUNTAIN LODGE, PO Box 272, Etna, NH 03750, (603) 643-3529. All meals are included. Moderate.

An Olympic Gold Medalist laid out Norden Hem's 30 miles of trails in the late 40s and it was here, 3 miles from Gaylord, Michigan, that America's Cross Country Ski Team trained for many years. Now, to the original log lodge built in 1945, 42 rooms have been added (many with jacuzzis) in a variety of new buildings. Guests can ski the State Forest trails nearby as well as the private Norden Hem tracks. Weekends, skiers gather in the ski hut to dine on free chili and hot dogs before hitting trails lit for night skiing.

NORDEN HEM, PO Box 1367, Gaylord, MI, 49735, (517) 732-6794. Continental breakfast is included. Moderate to Expensive.

Resuscitated and embellished, the network of huts used to train the 10th Mountain Division of the US Army during World War II now comprises the 10th Mountain Trail Hut System. Twenty-two huts dot the 350 miles of trail, which today connect Vail with Aspen. Paragon Guides is the largest and oldest of the several outfits that conduct scheduled tours of the system. The guides do the cooking; food, sleeping bags and other necessities are provisioned. Ah, wilderness! The backcountry skier packs only his or her personal gear.

PARAGON GUIDES, PO Box 130, Vail, CO 81658, (303) 94-4272 Trip rates are all-inclusive. Expensive.

Yurts or wall tents provide shelter for the backcountry skiers traversing Idaho's Sawtooth Mountains with Sun Valley Trekking. No permanent structures are allowed in the Sawtooths or in the Boulder Mountains where Sun Valley also guides yurt-to-yurt. On a standard or "participating" 3- or 4-day tour participants help haul and cook; a chef skis along with the "catered" trips and the sherpas (or guides) carry most of the gear.

SUN VALLEY TREKKING, PO Box 220, Sun Valley, ID 83353, (208) 788-9585. Moderate.

Bibliography _____

Cross Country Skier (319 Barry Avenue S., Wyzata, MN 55391, (612) 476-2200). The October travel issue carries the most destination pieces and ads.

The Best of Cross Country Skiing ($8.95 postpaid, The Cross Country Ski Areas Association, 259 Bolton Road, Winchester, NH 03470, (603) 239-4341, 1990). Lists more than 500 cross country ski areas in the US and parts of Canada.

Skiing Downhill

Skiing is one sport where solo participants have absolutely no trouble finding a group. Few other solo endeavors have spawned 1,300 clubs, and that number is nowhere near all-inclusive, according to an industry source who hazards total ski club membership at around 750,000 people. "About two-thirds of all ski club members are single," says the founder of the National Ski Club Newsletter, who states that "Ski clubs, most of which sponsor all kinds of non-ski events and meet year-round, are the prime hunting grounds for 30-year-olds in half the cities in the United States." "Ski Club" appears to be a generic term for a social group. Club members hit the slopes in winter, and they bowl, play tennis, kayak, party, and travel together all year long. There are also ski clubs just for singles, nonprofit city clubs, company clubs, and church clubs, among others. [See "Ski Clubs" section at the end of this chapter for listings.]

Obviously, one needn't be a joiner to travel happily to the slopes. Homey inns, lodges, and dorms provide comfortable accommodations in ski villages throughout the United States.

Pricing Categories

Inexpensive	Under $75 a day
Moderate	$75 to $125 a day
Expensive	$126 to $200
Very Expensive	Over $200 a day

ALTA LODGE
Alta, Utah

The temperature outside averages 26 degrees, but inside the snow-covered Alta Lodge the atmosphere is warm and inviting. A pleasant young staff welcomes arrivals sincerely. The dining room hostess smiles as she seats guests beside amiable fellow skiers. The owner's wife pours après-ski tea.

The 53-year-old lodge gets five stars for hospitality. Alta Lodge is owned by Jim Levitt, the Mayor of Alta (population 400), and run by his daughter, three sons and his wife. The family spirit is catching. Sure, William Buckley and Milton Friedman meet at the wood-and-glass lodge facing the chiseled Wasatch Mountains. So does the Pasadena Hunt Club. Ten silver-haired members of the New York Stock Exchange's ski club stopped by for lunch. Still, the Lodge, where most of the guests are repeaters, is more an extended family than an exclusive club. The common denominator at this pleasant but totally unpretentious inn is its gung ho cadre of middle-aged skiers.

Alta recently celebrated its 50th anniversary with pride but little brouhaha. Aficionados claim that Alta offers the deepest base (60 inches early in December), the lightest powder—in fact the best snow in the United States. Lift tickets and lessons at the 95-instructor Elf Engen Ski School, cost about half the rate at other prime areas. That, and Alta's no-nonsense approach, attracts the no-frills skier. Party-goers and the pink-spandex set head for the upscale shops and lively après-ski scene at Deer Valley and Park City nearby.

One of the lures of Utah skiing is its accessibility: an hour by shuttle bus from the Salt Lake City airport. If coming from the lowlands, leave some time for altitude adjustment. Novices should be prepared to commute to Alta's ski-school-practice-slope axis via an arm-wrenching transfer tow. Most guests at Alta Lodge are pros. Experts swoop out of the locker room down to the Wildcat and Collins lifts in about 20 seconds. Of Alta's eight chair lifts (there are also two learning rope tows) only Albion is suitable for beginners.

Skiing is rigorous. Alta Lodgers are surrounded by practical comforts to ease the strain. Around 4:00 pm, they thump down the cork paneled halls to the two whirlpool baths—one hot, the other hotter—from which they can watch intrepid skiers take their last run down rugged High Rustler. Fruit breads and shortcake accompany English Breakfast and herbal teas three afternoons a week. Help-yourself coffee, tea and hot chocolate are available anytime.

Fires flicker in the lobby and upstairs in the cozy Sitzmark Lounge. Along with Mexican salsa, guacamole, and tortilla chips, the lounge offers a view of the sun setting over the Ocher Range at the end of Little Cottonwood Canyon. Snowy peaks are visible from most of the Lodge's 56 functional rooms, which run the gamut from the original wooden cubicles to demi-suites with sitting areas and fireplaces.

I had a mid-priced room with an Uccello print on one white cement block wall, floors carpeted to match two rust-red chairs, a homespun Indian cotton spread, and a stunning valley view. Acoustic tiles failed to deaden the voices next door, but it didn't much matter. Everyone was asleep by 10:00.

Appealing meals are an Alta Lodge forte. Call the style "gourmet homecooking." Flowers, wine glasses and white cloths covered tables where groups of 4, 8, and 10 devoured the subtle cream soups that precede filet mignon or fresh poached salmon. Guests informally dressed in cotton turtlenecks, jeans, or slacks choose between three entrées nightly. Crisp salads, and small portions of chocolate decadence, scoops of rich ice cream and first-rate coffee intersperse the conversations. Alta Lodge regulars are good talkers, but not into the wee hours. Skiing is job one.

Shortly after the dining room opens at 8:00 am, the majority of the guests, having polished off homemade granola, cream of wheat and ham and eggs, zip into their powder suits for another assault on the mountain.

ALTA LODGE, Alta, Utah 84092, (801) 742-3500. Shared dorms and single-occupancy standard rooms are available; rates include full breakfast and dinner. Inexpensive and Expensive.

HOTEL ST. BERNARD
Taos Ski Valley, New Mexico

A country music trio adds verve to the already pulsating dinner scene 9,207 feet up in New Mexico's Sangre de Cristo
Mountains. Concho-belted locals get up to dance at the Hotel
St. Bernard in the Taos Ski Valley as diehards scrape the last
crumb of Tarte Tartin from their plates. Dessert over, the
band begins to play in earnest and hotel guests of all ages
headed for the dance floor.

Earlier, the ebullient diners had been momentarily
stilled as Jean Mayer, the St. Bernard's puckish owner and ski
instructor extraordinaire, described the menu of sauteed
quail, rare roast beef with horseradish cream, baked potato,
and vegetable melange. Smiling beneficently as usual, Mayer
returned afterward with dessert. Every evening, and at lunchtime, too, Jean Mayer circles the low, beamed dining room
depositing help-yourself platters at each table. At breakfast
the ubiquitous host is behind the buffet extolling the virtues
of the daily specials in Gallic-accented English.

Mayer's wattage hasn't dimmed since he arrived at Taos
in 1958 as an 18-year-old ski instructor at the invitation of
Ernie Blake, the legendary creator of the Taos Ski Valley. He
continues to teach master ski classes while choreographing
imaginative meals for his lodgers.

The vibrant bar/dining room at 30-year-old Hotel St.
Bernard is endowed with a Franco-New Mexican patina.
Thousands of pairs of ski pants have left a buttery finish on
the leather chairs; wear has turned golden pine paneling a
russet brown. Leaded glass panels and copper utensils, most
notably the funnel-shaped chimney suspended above the
round stone fireplace in the dining room, add luster to the
scene enlivened by day skiers. Later, when St. Bernard guests
are soaking sore muscles in the hot tub, the lodge is jammed
with beer-drinking Southwesterners fresh from the slopes. At
7:00 pm, the hotel regulars reappear: contented Texans,
Californians, New Yorkers, Georgians, and Floridians who
book their reservations for the next year on the day they
check out.

The Taos Ski Valley is renowned for its demanding trails—51% of the 71 trails are graded expert, 25% intermediate; 24% beginner—and for the fact that everyone, even hotdoggers, take lessons every day. Guests at the Hotel St. Bernard have their tryouts Saturday and are assigned, according to ability, to the yellow-jacketed instructor with whom they'll ski for the duration of their stay. Even though lessons weren't de rigueur, novices would probably want a teacher to assay even the green, or easy, trails.

Mastering the Taos skiing technique—weight centered on the arch of the foot and edging hard into a turn—is demanding. The patient, but unrelenting, teachers can often be heard shouting. "Face downhill and edge that ski."

Relatively effortless skiing is the result if the technique is carefully learned. Long runs and short lift lines help. Add the ebullient lodge scene to these pluses and the Ski Valley is even more appealing.

The fact that most rooms at St. Bernard open directly onto the slopes is another plus. Guests can store skis and boots (rented, if necessary, at the little support village a few slippery yards away) outside their doors. From there it's 30 seconds to either the beginners slope or the four-chair intermediate lift. Only the drone of the snow-packing machinery at night detracts from the foot-of-the-slopes location.

With neither phone nor TV, the accommodations are pleasant enough, especially when one considers the age of the hotel. Guests are seldom in their quarters in any case. The full house of sixty, mostly 35- to 65-year-old professionals, is either on the slopes or schmoozing around tables for four, six or eight in the lodge. Singles are assigned a table upon arrival and, if the match takes, remain there throughout their stay.

Just a taste of this low-key but masterfully-managed ski valley could provoke even a novice to commit to a week a year for life.

HOTEL ST. BERNARD, Taos Ski Valley, NM 87525, (505) 776-2251. The 6-night ski package includes lift tickets, ski instruction, lodging, and meals. Expensive.

Other Voices _____

DAMAN-NELSON TRAVEL
Singles Week at Sun Valley, Idaho

"It's the land version of a cruise ship, the most integrated, all-inclusive package of non-stop fun and things to do I've ever seen." This is why Ralph, a Silicon Valley executive, 44, has gone to the Singles Week run by Daman-Nelson Travel at Sun Valley in Idaho for 15 years running.

"The scenery is gorgeous, the closest to Switzerland you'll get in the States, and the skiing conditions are always at least fair to excellent on a good array of well-groomed trails. The Sun Valley Lodge is so elegant, with tea and crumpets in the afternoon, and the service wonderful.

"Singles' Week [usually the second week in January] draws about 1,000 people each year. You fly in to Twin Falls, Idaho, and take a chartered bus to the Sun Valley Lodge, where the price, based on double occupancy, covers the 7-day week, air fare, the bus, a 5-day lift ticket, several parties, and local transportation. It's extra for a single room. Accommodations at the Sun Valley Inn across the street are cheaper.

"I go out to dinner at any of the fine restaurants in the area the first night, usually with a small group, then start skiing the next day. If you're a good skier, a bus whips you off to Baldy Mountain. Beginners are whisked off to Dollar Mountain.

"Sun Valley Lodge has the largest hot tub facility in the world. It will hold 150 to 300 people, outdoors, with cocktail service by bow-tied waiters. People come back from the slopes all achy and tired, peel off their clothes and sip a few hot buttered rums in the hot tub. You make your dinner plans there.

"Sunday night there's a welcoming party at the Lodge meeting room. Most of these parties are sponsored by liquor companies, and the crowd is about 50% single and 50% otherwise involved. There are parties with live music, dancing, free booze, and snacks Tuesday and Thursday nights. One night you get toured around in horse-drawn sleighs.

"There's always something exciting going on every minute. If you want to head into town, there's everything from high-stepping music to meat-market bars. Of course, you could sit in your room and read a book, but no one does."

DAMAN-NELSON TRAVEL (headquarters), 501 Howard Street, San Francisco, CA 94105, (800) 782-4554 or (415) 982-9860. Rates for the Sun Valley Singles Week at the Inn or the Lodge are all-inclusive. The agency arranges shared accommodations at the Inn. Moderate and Expensive.

SUGARLOAF/USA WOMEN'S WEEK
Carrabassett Valley, Maine

"There's a slope up there called Chicken Pitch, which made me panic every time I encountered it. My goal was to ski this trail with no fear, and I made my goal on the third day." The slope was at Sugarloaf in Maine, where Bev, 38, a Maine housewife, participated in the Monday to Friday Women's Week.

"There were about 50 to 55 women at Sugarloaf for the week, with all female instructors. That was key. We had little jokes that women ski differently than men because they're built differently. What I liked especially was that everybody helped each other.

"We were grouped by ability, and there were five in my group. It wasn't frustrating because we all moved at about the same pace. We learned a lot about each other, talking on chair lifts.

"You had no time off. You were on the slopes at 8:00 am, and you'd ski all day. At night you'd have dinner, lectures, wine and cheese parties, speakers, a fashion show. There were aerobics and weight-lifting facilities. When you got to bed, you were really ready. I stayed in the family condo, but for a special rate you could stay and eat at the Sugarloaf Inn.

"The week was geared to make you feel good about yourself. How to deal with our own fears—we heard about that every day, through the instructors on the slopes and in lectures.

"...You just didn't want it to end, it was so exhilarating and liberating.... Now, it's the highlight of my year."

SUGARLOAF/USA, Carrabassett Valley, ME 04947, (800) 843-5623. The 5-day Women's Ski Week includes instruction and lodging (no meals). Single rooms are on a space-available basis. Expensive.

PURGATORY-DURANGO SKI RESORT
Durango, Colorado

"They separate men and women in the classes so the women can have women instructors. It was probably better for the men, too. You just ski as well as you can without worrying about how good you look," figures Bob, 52, from Phoenix, Arizona, whose early retirement from his job as a technician leaves him time to ski. He has skied at the Purgatory-Durango Ski Resort in Colorado, 7 or 8 times.

"In the morning they took us to the top of the mountain with a bunch of instructors, 15 men and 15 women, and watched us ski down the hill. Then they divided us, according to ability, into men's and women's groups. We were lucky there were relatively few people there, because we wound up with only three or four to an instructor. That was great.

"We all met again for lunch, and they'd show videos of us skiing, critique them and give us some pointers. One night we had a wine and cheese party and talked about how skis are made and what to look for when you buy skis or boots.

"I'd always wanted to try Nastar, but I never felt comfortable enough to try it with people standing around watching. It's a standard race course which they have at every ski slope. There are about 30 flags, and you jump out of a gate. You get points depending on how fast you run the course. Well, they set up a course for us and practically forced us to go through it at least once. I ran it 4 or 5 times in 2 days, until I felt I could just get in line anytime and run the course for a dollar without feeling intimated.

"You can stay anywhere in Durango and drive, or take the shuttle bus, the 25 miles up to Purgatory. There are also several hotels between Durango and the resort, plus there's a new base lodge right at the mountain. If you're by yourself you can get a room right on the mountain and just ski out your door to meet people or have dinner at one of the three restaurants there."

PURGATORY-DURANGO SKI RESORT, PO Box 666, Durango, CO 81302, (303) 247-9000. The Men's (or Women's) 3-Day Workshop includes lift tickets and lunch. Rates for the Purgatory Village Hotel do not include meals. Expensive.

THE SKI CLUB of WASHINGTON, DC
Arlington, Virginia

"Every night we'd all meet at 5:00 pm to go to the hot tub," recalls Claire, an occupational therapist, age 26, from Silver Springs, Maryland. The clubby tubs were in a condo complex, The Phoenix, a portion of which the Ski Club of Washington, DC had rented for a week in Steamboat Springs, Colorado. "The temperature was just right, not too hot after the cold slopes.

"As a woman, I look for things I can do safely alone. This was an organized group trip, with a nice mix of different age ranges, couples, some singles, about 30 to 40 people in all. Non-members could come for a special fee. You felt very relaxed because the focus wasn't on meeting somebody.

"We all stayed in the same complex, eight to a condo, which were like townhouses. You shared a bedroom with one other person. I didn't know my roommate, but we got along fine. There were fireplaces and beautiful kitchens, where you could fix a light breakfast. Besides the hot tub, the complex had a heated swimming pool, a reception area, and a party room, where the club had a little wine and cheese party the first night so you could get your lift ticket and meet everyone else.

"We were about a block from the gondola at the base of the mountain, but I rented a locker at the slope for $3.50 a night to avoid dragging my rented boots, skis, and poles around.

"The group leader was pretty diligent about keeping track of what was going on and letting you know that 'tonight we're going to...and if you want to join us, you're welcome to come.' Planned activities took up 2 evenings out of 6: one night, a sleigh ride was followed by a steak dinner; another, we took pot luck in one of the condos. Each unit contributed part of the meal.

"If you didn't feel like joining the group, the Steamboat restaurants were very comfortable. The town has a casual, camp-like atmosphere. Everyone in the service industries was friendly—at the hotels, in the ski rental place—the whole town."

THE SKI CLUB OF WASHINGTON, DC, Lee Highway, Arlington, VA 22207, (703) 532-7776. The rate for the week in Steamboat Springs includes lift tickets, skiing, accommodations for 7 days and air fare. Moderate.

SUGAR HILL INN
Franconia, New Hampshire

"Cannon Mountain can be real challenging. They call it a lumberjack mountain because there's nothing elegant about it," says Bill, a film critic, 30, from Florida. He vacations at Sugar Hill, New Hampshire, staying at the Sugar Hill Inn. Bill explains his ski vacation strategy.

"I work my way up to Cannon Mountain.... Cannon is a mean mountain with it's own personality. Remember, it's state-owned. If they run out of money for snow-making in late February (which they often do) snow-making stops. Very Yankee. There's little grooming, and more often than not, the terrain's all ice.

"The locals love Cannon, so you see the high school kids from the area having macho contests on the slopes, plus a lot of expert skiers and people who want to say they skied it once....

"The Sugar Hill Inn is the best lodging in the area, and I often go by myself. When I want to be alone, I can be, and I sit at my favorite table, where I can see the bear who comes to pick at the garbage cans behind the restaurant (when it's warm enough for bears). Last visit, I was alone and a whole group of women invited me to join them for dinner. After that, we ate all our meals together. It's a very social place. The food is excellent, not gourmet elegant, but hearty elegant. You won't find Oyster Wonton here, but you will have the best Swiss Eggs for breakfast you've ever had.

"The trademark of Sugar Hill is the hand stencilling along the walls and wainscoting. Beautifully done. I love how the floors in the original wing slope and creak when you walk on them. You can go out and test your masculinity on Cannon Mountain, and then come in at night and be cossetted."

SUGAR HILL INN, Route 117, Franconia, NH 03580, (603) 823-5621. Breakfast and dinner are included. Moderate.

HEATHERBED MOUNTAIN LODGE
Aspen, Colorado

"I stayed at the Heatherbed Mountain Lodge in Aspen just across the street from the Aspen Highlands Ski Resort," recalls Marilyn, a scientist from North Carolina. "There are horseback riding and hunting day-trips from the lodge in summer, but I went in winter to ski."

"This B&B is quieter than the typical ski resort, and it's quite personal, because the owners are in residence. There are only about 20, very nice but sparingly furnished, rooms. Heatherbed is on the road to Maroon Bells, the most photographed spot in Colorado. The lovely living room overlooks the river and the hills; they also have a sauna and a pool. Excellent continental breakfasts and apres ski cheese gave me a chance to talk to the other guests.

"I just walked across the road to ski. Aspen Highlands is one of the oldest ski areas, and a little more advanced than many mountains. The classes there tend to be fairly small and are another good way to meet people. I didn't need a car because free buses take you to any of the ski areas in Aspen, as well as into town.

"The Heatherbed's owners encourage a sense of camaraderie, although they don't serve dinner. Lunch you usually
get on the slopes. You can go into town to eat. Christmas Eve
I went to a dinner theater, the only one there alone, but they
had tables set up for four and placed me with a couple. We
chatted. It was a very pleasant evening."

*THE HEATHERBED MOUNTAIN LODGE, 1679 Maroon
Creek Road, Aspen, CO 81612, (303) 925-7077. Moderate to
Expensive.*

 ## *Other Downhill Choices* _____

Club Med isn't just beaches. Twenty-two villages around the
world cater to skiers. In the US the Club Med Copper
Mountain facility is located near all the lifts at the base of
Union Peak. Helicopter skiing, guided out-of-bounds ski
tours, snow-cat ski tours and other adventures cost extra, but
lessons from 40 Club Med instructors are included in the
rates.

*CLUB MED COPPER MOUNTAIN, 50 Beeler Place, Copper
Mountain, CO 80443, (800) 258-2633. The weekly rate
includes all but air fare. Expensive.*

Demanding ski weeks have been a feature of Gray
Rocks for over 25 years. When not taking twice-daily classes
at the Snow Eagle Ski School, skiers work out at Le Spa, or
join solo classmates at a group table for dinner at Le Chateau.
Accommodations vary; so do options. Weekend packages and
Nordic ski weeks are available, as is the chance to ski Mt.
Tremblant 5 miles distant.

*GRAY ROCKS, PO Box 1000, St. Jovite, Quebec, Canada
JOT 2H0, (819) 425-2771. The 6-night ski school package is
all-inclusive. Expensive.*

Lodging options for the famed Tahoe North ski region
are as varied as Squaw Valley, Northstar-at-Tahoe, Alpine

Meadows, and Sugar Bowl, among other local slopes. Skiers can stay at Harrah's in Reno, the Hyatt at Incline Village, Caesar's at Stateline and any number of motels, or can opt for a smaller, more intimate property like the 21-room River Ranch Lodge, located on the Truckee River near Alpine Meadows, and well-regarded for its food.

RIVER RANCH LODGE, PO Box 197, Tahoe City, CA 96145, (916) 583-4264. Full breakfast is included. Inexpensive to Moderate.

At Squaw Valley proper, two new lodges recently opened right on the slopes. Bring sheets to the 95-bed Squaw Valley Hostel or pay extra for linens for a dorm stay. A triple lift carries skiers to the 405-room Resort at Squaw Creek, which is adjacent to the 4,000-acre Squaw ski complex with 32 lifts.

SQUAW VALLEY, PO Box 2007, Olympic Valley, CA 96145, Central Reservations: (800) 545-4350. Inexpensive and Very Expensive.

For those who yearn for skiing's pioneering days, and for the lean of purse, there is the Skylight Ski Lodge 4 miles from Bromley and 13 miles from both Stratton Mountain and Magic Mountain in Vermont. Come nightfall, skiers at this 25-year-old hostelry chat in front of the fire before sitting down to family style dinners that begin with homemade soups. Then it's upstairs to sleep in a same-sex dorm room outfitted with single beds and double decker bunks.

SKYLIGHT SKI LODGE, RR 1, Box 2000, Manchester Center, VT 05255, (802) 362-2566. The rate for a dorm room bed includes full breakfast and dinner. Inexpensive.

Van round-trip from Denver's Stapleton Airport to Winter Park where 19 lifts connect skiers to 106 trails on 3 mountains. Choose between condos or a score of small, rustic-looking but up-to-date inns for lodging. Timber House and Woodspur are among those featuring buffet dinners, big, shared tables, and hot tubs. A Winter Park reservationist helps skiers pick a congenial lodge when they sign up for a Winter Park package.

WINTER PARK, PO Box 36, Winter Park, CO 80482, (800) 453-2525. A 4-night, 3-day "One-for-Fun," package and a 4-night, 3-day Women's Workshop both include lift tickets, lodging and 2 meals a day. Moderate.

 Other Choices _____

Best Solo Ski Resorts

Respondents to *Ski* magazine's 1990 survey selected Vail, Colorado; Whistler/Blackcomb, British Columbia; Jackson Hole, Wyoming; Deer Valley, Utah; and Aspen Mountain, Colorado (in that order) as the five best resorts for singles. We in turn asked the reservations service at each resort which accommodations they thought most appropriate for the solo skier, and they chose the following:

VAIL, CO, (800) 525-2257 or (800) 445-8245. "Anywhere in the Vail Village area." Peppy's Gasthof Gramshammer, (303) 476-5626; the European Style Christiania; or the upscale Sonnenalp, with rates that include a full breakfast. Expensive to Very Expensive.

WHISTLER/BLACKCOMB, BC, CANADA, (800) 634-9622. "Any of the pensions, for example the 7-room Durlacher Hof," which includes breakfast with the room. For a standard hotel, try the top-flight Chateau Whistler, in Little Whistler Village. Inexpensive and Very Expensive.

JACKSON HOLE, WY (800) 223-4059 or (307) 733-7893. The Sundance Inn, a downtown B&B, includes breakfast and after-ski treats; the Inn at Jackson Hole is a full service hotel at

Teton Village; and the Spring Creek Resort has fireplace rooms. Inexpensive; Moderate; Expensive.

DEER VALLEY/PARK CITY, UTAH, (800) 424-3337, (800) 453-1360 or (800) 545-7669. The elegant, Victorian-style Snowed Inn costs more on weekends; the modern, lodge-style Resort Center condos have studios available; and then there's the much-acclaimed Stein Ericksen Lodge. All Very Expensive.

ASPEN, Colorado, (800) 262-7736, or (800) 421-7145. The St. Moritz has a swimming pool, hot tub and dorm rooms and rates that include breakfast; also recommended are the small, family-owned Uller Lodge, and the lovely Aspen Club Lodge, 1/2 block from the Silver Queen gondola. Inexpensive; Moderate; Very Expensive.

 Ski Clubs _____

SKI CLUB FINDERS, (516) 536-2130. This outfit has a list of close to 900 ski clubs throughout the country and, by matching zip codes, will provide the names of 4 nearby clubs to individuals free of charge.

SKI CLUB OF WASHINGTON, DC, Lee Highway, Arlington, Virginia 22207, (703) 532-7776. The largest club, with 7,000 members.

ATLANTA SKI CLUB, 6306 Barfield Road, Atlanta, GA 30328. With 5,000 members, this group takes second place.

NATIONAL BROTHERHOOD OF SKIERS, PO Box 49490, Chicago, IL 60649. This black membership group has 12,000 members and 70 chapters.

APRÈS SKI CLUB, (San Francisco Peninsula), PO Box 1027, Mountain View, CA 94042-1027. Social activities as well as skiing attract members to this Silicon Valley Club.

SINGLE SKI CLUB OF ALBANY, PO Box 1821, Albany, NY 12201. An old, well-regarded club.

SINGLE SKI CLUB OF LOS ANGELES, PO Box 2684, Culver City, CA 90231-2684. This active club has members throughout the Los Angeles area.

SINGLES FOR SKIING, PO Box 1043, Manhasset, NY 11030.

 ## *Reservation Services* _____

Call a ski area's 800 reservations number for a particular mountain. If looking for information, try the ski tour operators and services listed below.

ADVENTURES ON SKIS, 815 North Road, Westfield, MA 01085, (800) 628-9655. Represents some 300 first class and deluxe hotels in the Alps, the Rockies and Quebec.

ALPHORN SKI TOURS, 5788 Route 202, Lahaska, PA 18931, (215) 794-5651. Favors the European resorts, especially St. Anton, for solos.

CAVALCADE TOURS, SKI DIVISION, 204 East 11th Street, New York, NY 10003, (800) 822-6754 or (212) 673-9200. Skiers man the phone lines, booking budget-minded singles into shared accommodations at Aspen and Snowbird, for example, as well as arranging trips to most ski destinations.

D-FW, 7616 LBJ Freeway, Dallas, TX 75251, (800) 527-2589. Wholesales packages to Chile, Canada, Colorado, Utah, and the Sierras, but also books for individuals.

DAMAN NELSON TRAVEL, (800) 782-4554. With offices in Los Angeles, Orange County, Sacramento, San Diego, and San Francisco, this is the largest ski tour operator in the west. They offer three single's trips: Sun Valley, Idaho (see "Other Voices" above), Park City, Utah, and Snowmass at Aspen, Colorado.

SUN AND SKI ADVENTURES, 635 Chicago Avenue, Evanston, IL 60202, (800) 735-0461. Reserves ski vacations for groups and individuals around the world.

VIC VAC, 2100 Central Avenue, Boulder, CO 80301, (800) 800-8888. Computerized to match the right ski package to the individual.

Bibliography

Ski, 2 Park Avenue, New York, NY 10016, (212) 779-5000. The October and November issues feature the latest ski developments and destinations.

Great Ski Inns and Hotels of America by Miles Jaffe and Julie Robinson ($14.95, Ski The Best, Inc., New York, NY, 1988). A descriptive, well-photographed guide.

A Skier's Guide to North America by Brent K. Pickard ($11.95, Wise Guide Publishing, Box 610, Miami, FL 33137, 1988). A 235-page description of slopes, facilities and accommodations.

Skiing America 1992 by Charles Leocha ($14.95, World-Leisure Corp., PO Box 160, Hampstead, NH 03841, 1991). A 431-page compendium similar to the Skier's Guide, with detailed maps instead of black and white pictures.

Appendix

Solo Travel Specialists _____

How do you beat the single supplement? That's the question most single travel organizations address, either directly or indirectly. Whatever form these groups take—travel agency, tour operator, club—arranging shared accommodations is one of their primary functions. With good reason. Single occupancy on a cruise ship costs between 50% and 100% more than the per person, double occupancy rate. Touring solos commonly pay 50% or more for a room of their own. Solo specialists also have another role, however.

Several single travel groups cater to those who want to vacation with other solitaries. There are also companies and clubs to help solos find travel companions, although for many members, saving money is as important as finding romance or a new friend.

Besides agencies, tour operators, and matchmakers, there are services especially for traveling solitaries. Listed below are a couple of newsletters, a network of gourmet clubs and special associations for older vacationers and for women.

Singles-Only Tour Operators _____

GALLIVANTING, 515 East 79th Street, New York, NY 10021, (800) 933-9699 or (212) 988-0617. This two-year-old agency offers a dozen up-market itineraries for singles 28 to 48 years old. Roommates are matched by sex and smoking habits after a phone interview. Tour participants (about 10 to 15 per trip) automatically become members in the Club for Adventure. The $50 membership fee is refunded when participants sign on for Gallivanting trip.

MARION SMITH SINGLES, a sibling of Marion Smith Travel, 611 Prescott Place, North Woodmere, NY 11581, (516) 791-4852 or (212) 944-2112. Special Marion Smith Singles trips for the 27- to 47-year-old set to various Club Meds and to skiing, tennis, sailing, and holiday destinations have been offered since 1976. Traditionally, more women than men participate.

SINGLEWORLD, 401 Theodore Fremd Avenue, Rye, NY 10580, (800) 223-6490 or (914) 967-3334. Founded in 1957, Singleworld specializes in cruises for two groups of solos: the "Under-35" set, and passengers of "All Ages." The membership group also sponsors several escorted tours annually. On cruises, Singleworld arranges same-sex shares in double, triple and quad accommodations. Currently, 10,000 people — women outnumber men two to one—are paid up members ($25 annual fee).

SOLO FLIGHTS, 127 South Compo Road, Westport, CT 06880, (203) 226-9993. Since 1973, this travel agency for solitaries has booked solos on singles tours and cruises. If no packaged singles' trips are available, they suggest the best alternative.

TRAVLIN' SINGLES, PO Box 1343, Bellflower, CA 90706, (213) 920-9009. A dozen or so vacation trips a year are run by this group for its 1,000, 30- to 60-year-old members. The club, founded in 1980, charges an annual $15 membership fee and, surprise, fewer men than women enroll for the trips.

Special Solo Trips _____

AMERICAN JEWISH CONGRESS, 15 East 84th Street, New York, NY 10028, (800) 221-4694 or (212) 879-4588. The AJC's International Travel Program, established in 1957, includes 10 or more departures for solos. More women than men sign on for "Under 40," "30 to 50" and "Over 50" singles tours to Israel, Latin America, Western and Eastern Europe and the Soviet Union.

AMERICAN WILDERNESS EXPERIENCE, PO Box 1486, Boulder, CO 80306, (800) 444-0099 or (303) 494-2992. Among this 20-year-old agency's many western adventures are several for solos only: a llama trek into Colorado's Zirkle Wilderness, a horseback/camping ride in the Sierras, a couple of singles' weeks at a ranch in Colorado.

BACKROADS BICYCLE TOURING, 1516 5th Street, Berkeley, CA 94710-1713, (800) 245-3874 or (415) 527-1555. This well-regarded outfit, founded in 1979, runs a dozen or more inn-to-inn or camping bike trips for 26 singles at a time. An equal number of women and men, aged 25 to 65 participate in the 3- to 14-day tours.

BICYCLE ADVENTURES, PO Box 7875, Olympia, WA 998507, (206) 786-0989. Singles-only bike trips (some include sea kayaking), to Puget Sound and the San Juan Islands, are offered by this 8-year-old company. A maximum of 22 peddlers, average age 30, participate in the week-long jaunts.

ESCAPES UNLIMITED, 269 North Glassel, Orange, CA 92666, (800) 243-7227 or (714) 771-3154. This offshoot of the Good Earth Travel Agency has, for the past 6 years, included a couple of singles departures among the "soft adventures" it organizes to exotic destinations.

LES ROUTES DES ETOILES, David B. Mitchell & Co., 200 Madison Avenue, New York, NY 10016, (800) 422-1323 or

(212) 696-1323. New in 1992 are several deluxe itineraries through France planned by Mitchell & Co. for singles (and a few for single parents and "their well-behaved children"). In escorted groups of six to eight, voyagers see the most vaunted sights, are put up in chateaux and dine in stellar restaurants.

Tours with Many Single 18- to 38-Year-Olds __

CONTIKI, 1432 E. Katella Avenue, Anaheim, CA 92805, (800) 626-0611 or (714) 937-0611. Founded in 1961, Contiki sponsors world-wide tours for an international clientele. Get their 130-page catalog, select a tour and then book through a travel agent. More than half the participants are single, about 55% are women, 45% men, and the average age is 20 to 24. Contiki keeps a "rooming list" and pairs people on a same-sex, smoking-preference basis.

TREK AMERICA, PO Box 1338, Gardena, CA 90249, (800) 221-0596 or (213) 321-0734. Since the firm was founded in Britain in 1972, it has specialized in participatory camping tours for 18- to 38-year-olds. A maximum of 13 campers per trip (about 10% Americans, 80% single, 60% women) travel to destinations in North and Central America in specially-designed vans for periods of 10 days to 9 weeks. Tent shares arranged.

Tours with a High Proportion of Singles Over 50 _____

GRAND CIRCLE TRAVEL, 347 Congress Street, Boston, MA 02210, (800) 321-2835 or (617) 350-7500. Some 20,000, over-50-year-olds a year reserve the 100-odd vacation tours sponsored by this direct market travel agency founded in 1958.

The company takes no profit on single supplements and, in Europe, books supplement-free rooms when possible. Three programs are offered Grand Circle travelers, some 34% of them single, 50% of them men: extended "Live Abroad" vacations, "Countryside Tours," which focus on three areas for one week each, and traditional, escorted tours.

Grand Circle also inserts the "Pen Pals" column, a get-acquainted service for mature travelers, in a number of their brochures gratis.

SAGA INTERNATIONAL HOLIDAYS, 120 Boylston Street, Boston, MA 02116, (800) 343-0273 or (617) 451-6808. Saga operates a branch in Boston, but is in fact a 60,000-member worldwide organization founded in Britain in 1950 for travelers over 60. The direct market agency offers a few solos-only departures, tries to find single rooms for solo travelers and, if unsuccessful, pairs roommates, with "a 95% success rate." Supplementless singles options still include rooms in university dorms, but the Odyssey Tours offered in conjunction with the Smithsonian are an indication that Saga is going upscale.

To help clients connect, Saga publishes and distributes a newsletter called "Pen Friends and Partnerships" free of charge.

Partnership Clubs

GOLDEN COMPANIONS, PO Box 754, Pullman, WA 99163, (509) 334-9351. A relative newcomer to the roster of companion exchanges, this 700-member association founded in 1987 for travelers over 45, publishes brief, personal descriptions in a directory circulated to seniors who pay $85 for an annual membership.

THE ODYSSEY NETWORK, a subsidiary of Charles River Travel, 118 Cedar Street, Wellesley, MA 02181, (617) 237-2400. This group, started in 1988, pairs up partners for trips offered by Charles River Travel by means of phone interviews and detailed questionnaires. Members pay $50 a year for the matching service and for a quarterly newsletter describing upcoming trips.

PARTNERS IN TRAVEL, PO Box 491145, Los Angeles, CA 90049, (213) 476-4869. The highly personal, bi-monthly newsletter is crammed with travel facts for the mature solo traveler and includes would-be partner listings. Approximately 500 people (20% under 50, 80% over 50) pay annual $40 dues to belong to the 11-year-old group. Other services include "Cruise Mates," a shipboard matching service, and information about singles-only packages.

TRAVEL COMPANION EXCHANGE, PO Box 833, Amityville, NY 11701, (516) 454-0880. Founded by Jens Jurgen in 1980, the Exchange is 8,000, 25- to 75-year-old members strong. To publish a blurb about yourself in *Travel Companions*, the bi-monthly newsletter, and to receive listings for travel companions of the same sex, costs $36 for 6 months; listings for the opposite sex cost $66 for 6 months. Addresses are not published. After surveying the short descriptions, members request a profile: the detailed questionnaire filled out upon joining the Exchange. Membership entitles you to a profile a month. Extra profiles cost $2.00 each.

TRAVEL IN TWOS, a subsidiary of ATC Travel, 239 North Broadway, Suite 3, North Tarrytown, NY 10591, (914) 631-8409. Begun in 1988, this association offers its 250-or-so members two services: travel-mate matching, which costs $10, and a quarterly newsletter ($20 a year) noting trips sponsored by Travel in Twos as well as other singles agencies and clubs.

For Women Only

RAINBOW ADVENTURES, INC, 1308 Sherman Avenue, Evanston, IL 60201, (708) 864-4570. The brainchild of a former Peace Corps volunteer, Rainbow designs adventure trips for women over 30 who tend to be married or single professionals. African safaris, New Zealand walkabouts, Irish horse treks, and Salmon River rafting trips are among the 17 adventures the firm, founded in 1981, offers.

SHARED ADVENTURES, Fairview Plaza, 420 W. 75th Street, Downers Grove, IL 60516, (708) 852-5533. If one of the 200 women now on Shared Adventures' roster is looking for a companion (for example, Nancy J. wants to share a trip to Hawaii in June) then this free service sends out a "Network Alert" (a postcard) advising any interested enrollees to get in touch with Nancy.

WOMANTREK, PO Box 20643, Seattle, WA 98102, (206) 325-4772. Founded by a former Outward Bound instructor in 1983, WomanTrek now offers as many as 30 soft-adventure departures a year. Usually 25- to 70-year-old, but not necessarily single, women book these tours; the median age is around 30.

WOODSWOMEN, 25 West Diamond Lake Road, Minneapolis, MN 55419, (612) 822-3809. Founded in 1977, the Woodswomen call themselves the grandmothers of adventure travel for women. About 900 women pay $20 a year to receive a quarterly newsletter, a list of members and to take part in campouts. They also receive one free planning session about the 70 biking, canoeing, climbing, rafting, trekking, skiing, and scuba diving activities Woodswomen plans each year.

Dining Solo ━━━━━━━━━━━━━━━━━━━━━━━

SINGLE GOURMET, 133 East 58th Street, New York 10022, (212) 980-8788. This is just one of 21 single gourmet chapters currently in operation throughout the United States and Canada. Membership in one chapter (in New York, $75 for the first year, $40 a year thereafter) guarantees reciprocal privileges with the other branches. Members not only dine together in local restaurants but vacation together on cruises and in good-eating cities around the world.

Newsletters for Solos ━━━━━━━━━━━━━━━━

Going Solo, PO Box 1035, Cambridge, MA 02238. Subtitled "The Newsletter for People Traveling Alone," *Going Solo* is the zesty and informative 8-page creation of food writer Jane Doerfer. The articles, which appear eight times a year neatly typeset, are germane, well-written and carefully researched. A subscription costs $36 a year; separate issues are $5 plus $1 postage.

Travel Companions, PO Box 833, Amityville, NY 11701, (516) 454-0880. The bi-monthly newsletter that comes with membership in the Travel Companionship Exchange, can also be subscribed to outright for $36 a year. Cruise-going singles will be pleased with Editor Jens Jurgen's close attention to bargain fares and cruise deals. Others will find the many facts and tips concerning solo travel useful.

INDEX